Astrology of the Seers:

A Guide to Vedic /Hindu Astrology

David Frawley
(Vamadeva Shastri)

Editor: Kenneth Johnson Illustrations: Jane Adams

Cover & Page Design/Layout: Linda Khristal

Author Photo: Mira Foung

Reprint: 2020

First Edition: June 2000

Printed in the United States of America

Library of Congress Cataloging-in-Publication Data

Astrology of the Seers, A Guide to Vedic/Hindu Astrology

includes bibliographical references.

ISBN 978-0-9149-5589-4

Library of Congress Catalogue Control Number 99-96595

Published by:

Lotus Press, P.O. Box 325, Twin Lakes Wisconsin 53181 U.S.A.

800-824-6396

e-mail: lotuspress@lotuspress.com

website: www.lotuspress.com

Dedication

I would like to dedicate the new edition of the book to Dr. Raman, who recently passed away at the age of 86 at his home in Bangalore, India. His passing marks the end of an era.

May we have the insight and the dedication to continue the task of reviving Vedic astrology in the modern world that he guided throughout most of this century!

By the wisdom and grace of such great teachers may Vedic astrology truly flourish and may all people come to benefit from its many blessings!

David Frawley (*Vamadeva Shastri*)
Santa Fe, New Mexico
Jan. 16, 1999

Table of Contents

Foreword

by *Gayatari Vasudev*

It is with a sense of great responsibility that I write the following lines as a foreword to Dr. David Frawley's latest edition of the *Astrology of the Seers*, which is a welcome and comprehensive addition to the existing literature on Jyotisha from western authors. Dr. Frawley is one of those few scholars who, though coming from the West, is imbued with the spirit of the East, especially India. His immersion in the spirit of the land of Jyotisha provides him a major advantage in portraying Jyotisha as it should be, free of adulteration at the level of the spirit of the science.

Hindu Astrology or *Jyotisha*, which is the subject matter of this volume, is one of India's greatest gifts to mankind. Although at least 7000 years old and an integral and inalienable part of Indian culture and life, it was relatively unknown in the West until the 1950's.

It was in the 1890's that my great grandfather Prof. Suryanarain Rao brought Jyotisha to the English-knowing public through the *Astrological Magazine*, which he started, and through his books on the subject. Unfortunately the *Astrological Magazine* was discontinued shortly thereafter and it was only in 1936 that my father Dr. B. V. Raman restarted it and was able to take it to readers all around the globe.

Dr. Raman made the *Astrological Magazine* the only magazine of its kind, the most authentic and informative journal on Jyotisha in the world. His solo editorship of the magazine for over 62 years set a record unsurpassed so far by any other journal editor in the world. Through the pages of the *Astrological Magazine* he introduced astrology into a wide range of subjects emphasizing its relevance to modern times, thereby catching the interest of the western world.

Interest in Jyotisha has since then grown by leaps and bounds and has also created a crop of highly learned scholars in the subject of whom Dr. David Frawley is easily one of the most outstanding. Known more in India for his historical work refuting the Aryan invasion theory proposed by colonial-period Orientalists and historians, Dr. Frawley is better known in the western world for his expertise in Jyotisha and Ayurveda. He has had the opportunity to meet and interact with Dr. Raman several times and discuss with him Hindu astrology and Indian culture and has dedicated the new edition of his book to him.

As a scholar in the Rig Veda and its related astronomy, Dr. Frawley has also made a deep study of its sister-science of astrology. Astrology or Jyotisha is more than a discipline in its own right; it is an integral part of Indian culture and life intricately interwoven into the warp and woof of one's daily activities - mundane, spiritual, financial, mental, and filial and every other aspect that goes into creating life for an individual in the society to which he belongs. Dr. Frawley succeeds in presenting the spirit of astrology to his readers in this volume. His *Astrology of the Seers* is a journey into the spirit of astrology. Especially for one born in a land with a culture totally different from Indian culture and thought, the volume opens up a whole new realm of thinking that encompasses not only the celestials moving around the skies but also human experience on earth in the waking state.

Frawley sees astrology as "a means of converting all the universe into a symbol, a language for the development of the soul." In this perspective, he proceeds with amazing clarity to expound how to use Jyotisha to grow in reverence for the Self and to move gradually towards Self-realization in one's journey on the earth.

Whether Hindu astrology is about a cause and effect relationship between man and the planets or a correlation between the two, or whether it is the language of the stars as a holy script embodying the all pervasive, all destructive Time — the past, present and future — is a question that will continue to baffle and engage the attention of all thinkers. But there can be little doubt about its delivering the goods in helping us to achieve the fourfold objectives of life identified by the great Rishis of India. These are *Dharma* (obligations between man and man and man and society), *Artha* (earning money), *Kama* (satiation, through legitimate channels, of the physical urges) and *Moksha* (liberation). All activity of the human being is directed towards attaining one or more of these goals and astrology enables one to move towards these goals in an organized manner.

The biggest casualty of modern civilization, where the emphasis is on Artha and Kama at the cost of Dharma and Moksha, has been mental peace and humaneness. An understanding of Jyotisha contributes to harmony and a more compassionate approach to our fellow humans, forgiving others for their lapses. This is because it sees these lapses towards us being only the consequence of our own past deeds (*Karma*) and therefore to be laid at our own doors. This karmic accountability can act as a deterrent against wrong action and be the catalyst of right action. And this accountability is obvious in one's birth chart to a good Vedic astrologer.

With the philosophy that has come down through the ages from the Rishis (*seers*) of ancient India, Frawley takes up a discussion of Jyotisha starting from the basic step of calculating the chart to the more interesting part of understanding the chart — the planets, their qualities, characteristics, the signs and their descriptions, *Nakshatras*, houses, *Yogas* which are a unique feature of Indian Astrology, Divisional charts, *Dasas* and *Bhuktis*. From this point, consistent with his specialization in oriental medicine that includes Ayurveda, Dr. Frawley goes on to medical astrology — humors, diseases, constitution and psychology.

Astrology is a Vedanga and cannot be conceived of without its spiritual angle. A *sadhaka* (spiritual aspirant) of many years, Dr. Frawley is indeed at his best as he looks at the spiritual factors in the chart. He also includes remedial measures of gems, colors, mantras and propitiation of the planetary energies and deities. Finally he analyzes 18 charts to illustrate the main principles of astrology.

The expertise and ease with which he wields his pen on astrology, presenting the important aspects of the science without, at any stage, making it appear dreary and technical, easily enable him to take the Western mind and intellect on this inner journey into the celestial connections that man has with his cosmic environment. Not only is the *Astrology of the Seers* a good introduction to Hindu Jyotisha but it is also a mine of information on the subject.

Gayatri Devi Vasudev
Raman Publications
The Astrological Magazine
"Sri Rajeswari", 28, (Nagappa Street),
Nehru Circle, Seshadripuram,
Bangalore 560 020 INDIA

Preface to the New Edition

Revising an old title is a rewarding experience. First it enables one to correct the errors in the previous edition ("Did I really say that?" one sometimes thinks). Second, it allows one to improve the style. Third, and perhaps most importantly, it enables one to update the material, which in a rapidly developing field can be considerable.

Vedic astrology has come a long way in the ten years since I first wrote this book. At that time there was only one other title on the subject in print in the West (James Braha's *Ancient Hindu Astrology for the Modern Western Astrologer*) and very little available by way of Vedic astrology computer programs. In writing the book I wasn't even sure whom I was writing for. There was as yet no real audience of Vedic astrologers in the West. The book was written in an attempt to find or to perhaps create an audience for the subject, and from there I was uncertain. I looked to two potential audiences, first from Western astrologers interested in another system of astrology and second from followers of Indian gurus and their teachings who might be interested in the astrological side of the tradition. Both audiences took to the book but perhaps more the second group.

The book, now as then, is intended as a general but comprehensive introduction to the subject. It is not simply inspirational in nature but contains some technical data. On the other hand, it is not a purely technical book for advanced astrologers but tries to provide an access for a reader that may have no significant background in the subject.

For the second edition the book has been rewritten and corrected, with hopefully greater clarity given and with a few more topics covered. The book is devised as a textbook of Vedic astrology on a beginner to intermediate level, as a means of leading people into deeper study of this vast system.

I began my study of Vedic astrology in 1973. It was a few years earlier, on first discovering a book of Sri Aurobindo on the *Vedas*, that I became what could be called a Vedic person, seeing in the *Vedas* the highest wisdom. I also studied Western astrology, but my Vedic background and my use of telescopes as a child caused me to prefer a zodiac that was based upon the fixed stars and made Vedic astrology the preferable way to go. I began fitfully practicing the system starting in 1975, gradually shifting from Western astrology to the Vedic.

In the late seventies and early eighties I did a series of studies of the *Vedas* and *Upanishads*, the spiritual background of Vedic disciplines, which were published in India with the help of M.P. Pandit, the then secretary of the Sri Aurobindo Ashram. In 1984, when I was teaching along with Dr. Vasant Lad at his Ayurveda program, I started my first Vedic astrology class, mainly for the Ayurvedic students. Though the students were all at a basic level (and probably the teacher too) it was at least a beginning. This encouraged me to write a correspondence course on the subject that I introduced in 1986. The course provided the basis for this book which first came out at the end of 1990, and in turn I expanded and developed the course further.

It was not until 1992 that a Vedic astrology community began to emerge in the West. This was aided greatly by the first Vedic astrology symposium in the United States that I helped arrange along with Dennis Harness and Stephen Quong. No less a figure than Dr. B.V. Raman, by most accounts India's greatest astrologer of this century, attended and blessed our new endeavor and, with his entire family, has remained a staunch supporter ever since.

In 1993 this led to the founding of the ACVA (American Council of Vedic Astrology) at the second symposium, which has since blossomed into an organization of nearly four hundred people and represents perhaps the majority of Vedic astrologers in the United States. This is quite an achievement when one considers that in related fields like Ayurveda such an organization has not yet come into being. The ACVA is affiliated with the ICAS (Indian Council of Astrological Sciences), the largest such organization in India, led by Dr. Raman.

Over the same ten-year period I have been very active traveling to India, which has included contacting various astrologers. Vedic astrology is not only alive in India but undergoing a renaissance. Though there are many charlatans, there are many serious astrologers producing good books and good research.

In the meantime, aided by the forum created by the ACVA symposiums, many Vedic astrologers have come here from India and begun teaching in this country. Several have written books on Vedic astrology specifically for Western or English language audiences. The available English titles from India has greatly increased both in quantity and quality.

Today there is a community of Vedic astrologers in the West that is rapidly growing. The level of expertise in the subject that they have achieved is becoming to Vedic astrologers in India. All these factors point to a renaissance in Vedic astrology and its spread worldwide. I am most happy that this has occurred and no doubt it will continue to expand in coming years.

I would like to thank Dr. B.V. Raman and Chakrapani Ullal for their inspiration and guidance in my astrological work. I would like to give a special thanks to Dennis Harness who has been the energy behind the ACVA, without whom this community of Vedic astrologers in the West would not have been formed.

I would like to thank Ken Johnson for editing the manuscript, a job that he has done for several important Vedic astrology texts, Jane Adams of England for her excellent original drawings of the planetary deities, and Robben Hixson of Passage Press, who brought out the first edition of this book ten years ago.

Part I

The Vedic Vision

Sun

Standing on a lotus, with the luster of a red lotus, who has two arms, with a lotus in his hand, the creator of the day, the teacher of the world, whose vehicle is a horse with seven heads, with a ruby crest jewel on his head, making the gesture that grants boons — may the Divine Sun ever grant us his grace.

Hymn to the Planets

by *Vyasa*

1. *I worship the Sun, who has the luster of a red hibiscus flower, who has the power of perception, of great effulgence, the dispeller of darkness, who destroys all sins, the maker of the day.*

2. *I worship the Moon, who has the color of yogurt, seashell or snow, who arose from the ocean of milk, whom Shiva wears as a crest jewel on his head.*

3. *I worship Mars, born from the womb of the Earth, who has the beautiful brilliance of lightning, the Divine youth who carries a spear in his hand.*

4. *I worship Mercury, dark like the priyangu flower, who has an unequalled form, the intelligent son of the Moon, endowed with a gentle nature.*

5. *I worship Jupiter, the teacher of the Gods and the seers, who has the luster of gold, endowed with wisdom, the ruler of the three worlds*

6. *I worship Venus, with the beautiful luster of a snowy mountain, who is the supreme teacher of the demons, who explains all the scriptures.*

7. *I worship Saturn, dark blue in color, who is born before the God of death, the son of the Sun and shadow.*

8. *I worship Rahu, with only half a body, great in valor, who oppresses the Sun and Moon, who was born from the womb of a lion.*

9. *I worship Ketu, whose head is the stars and planets, who has the dark luster of a palasha flower, who is fierce and terrible in nature.*

1

A New Vision of Astrology

Astrology is the original science or system of knowledge devised by human beings. Astrology was the basis for the first cosmologies through which the ancients comprehended the structure and movement of the universe. It was the science of fate or destiny, used for understanding events on earth, which were seen as originating in the heavens. Astrology was not only the original and foremost of the outer sciences, it was also the most important of the inner or spiritual sciences.

Astrology shows the cosmic source and background for the forces working in any field of endeavor. In this way an astrological view precedes that of the other sciences. As it shows the language of cosmic energy, it can help us understand all spheres of life. For example, ancient systems of medicine like Ayurveda in India or classical Greek medicine gave close consideration to the astrological influences. The practice of yoga is based upon balancing the solar and lunar forces within the body.

The spiritual cultures of antiquity — Egypt, Babylonia, India, China and Mexico — were founded on the cornerstone of astrology. Their social systems derived from it, as exemplified in the rule of sun and moon kings. Astrology was the original physical, psychological and healing discipline. The astrology of a culture, therefore, is a good key to its development and its connection with the greater universe.

Without astrology, that is, without understanding the significance of the movements of the heavens relative to our lives, there can be no true or integral knowledge. Our connection with the universe cannot be grasped, and it will not be possible to ward off the negative effects of cosmic forces or to draw in those that are beneficial. Our relationship with the stars mirrors our relationship with the cosmos and shows the secrets of our psyche and our inner Self. Where astrology does not flourish, the culture must be lacking in higher knowledge and without any real communication with the universe itself.

In this regard, modern culture is evidently deficient. Though our astronomical knowledge is more extensive than that of any previous civilization, without astrology it is like a body without a soul. We have turned the sacred powers of the cosmos into mere numbers and chemical reactions. Such an attitude does not show any real sensitivity to life. It is like reducing a human being to measurements of height and weight, or looking at a great painting according to the chemistry of its pigments. We cannot understand who we really are or what the world truly is through such a limited form of knowledge.

We are proud of modern science for the energy it has provided for us through technology, but it has not yet come close to the Divine presence in all things. The ancients, with their own sciences such as astrology, were ahead of us in understanding the soul, and we must return to their approach if we are truly to go forward in our development. Today we even refuse to regard astrology as a science because it sees the spirit in things, not just the form. Yet if the universe has a dimension of consciousness, as many physicists have come to suspect, then science must recognize the spirit. Then astrology must be acknowledged as one of the legitimate sciences of consciousness — and without consciousness, how can we really speak of science or truth anyway?

For a new spiritual age to dawn, it is essential to bring astrology back into the mainstream of human knowledge. There can be no higher age for humanity if we do not connect with our greater cosmic being through the stars. This requires applying astrology on a deeper level than the one upon which it is usually understood. Our rejection of astrology has caused astrology to become superficial. It has not been given the attention and examination that it requires. The endeavor to renovate astrology is one of the most important works of our time, should we have enough awareness to attempt it. I hope that individuals of both intellect and intuition (for such work requires both) will be called to this task.

THE SCIENCE OF TIME (*Kala Vidya*)

Time is the original power that rules the universe; all things originate through time. The world is time, and the creation and destruction of the entire universe is present in every moment. The laws of time structure all things. Therefore, to be in awe of time is no mere superstition. We all wonder at birth and fear death. This too is a kind of reverence for or worship of time. We all value and count our moments. We want to live forever. Time is the field in which we live. The rhythm of time is the basis for all our actions, though the days, seasons, months and years.

Time is the great God who rules the cosmos. Great Time, Mahakala, is the great God Mahadeva, Shiva the transcendent Lord. The force of time, Mahakali, is the great Goddess, his consort Mahashakti, the supreme Power.

Time is the Divine breath that creates, sustains and destroys the cosmic life and form. Time is the dance of the great God, and it projects the beauty and the terror of the great Goddess.

The gods are, first of all, personifications of time. The first gods of time are the Sun, Moon and planets that direct the movement of time through this solar system. The gods of the planets are the gods of time. The planets reflect the powers of the cosmic intelligence that rules all things through the force of time.

According to modern science, time is not a mere empty continuum. It is a force field determined by the gravity of the objects within it, the foremost of which, for us, are the Sun and planets. The planets possess large magnetic fields. They are points of light in a vast energy network connected by subtle lines of force, linking the solar system into a single organism. Though the planets appear in the distant sky, their energy fields are present on Earth, responsible for the formations of the earth life and our own bodies and minds.

According to the ancient seers, time possesses a rhythm and is not a uniform line. Time is the river of life that is modulated according to the music of the spheres. It projects the plan of manifestation that externalizes as space. Time gives birth to, sustains and destroys all things, which are but waves in its flow as it overflows eternity.

Each planet in its orbit both gathers in and gives out forces, transmitting a particular wavelength of energy necessary for the order of the solar system. The planets are perpetually flashing forth with different patterns of energy, weaving the web of life and creation.

The movement of the planets determines the nature of the different phases in which we live. It sustains the forces that direct the play of our lives. The Earth, by its movement on its axis, determines the day. The Moon, by its orbit around the Earth, unfolds the month. The Sun, by the Earth's orbit around it, creates the year. The movement of Saturn determines the cosmic month or thirty years.

Great time cycles, yugas of many thousands of years, follow special planetary conjunctions. They reflect the orbiting of the sun around other stars or its movement around the galactic center. There are cycles within cycles, ad infinitum in the great spiral of creation. The whole universe is just a day in the life of the Lord of Creation, who must sleep a night in the bosom of the Uncreated.

Each moment of time possesses a certain quality. A certain karma, destiny or synchronicity exists relative to the forces operating during any specific time period. Everything that happens at a particular moment shares the nature of that moment. In the moment of our birth, therefore, we can read the pattern of our lives, just as the nature of a tree can be discovered in the seed from which it springs.

Similarly, the moment that we establish any endeavor, like the time of marriage, shows how it will develop. The entire universe speaks to us at every moment and shows us, through the simultaneity of the events of our lives with the cosmic life, the pattern of what we must be. In this regard, life is always an open book. But in order for the book to be of value, we must learn to read it. The book of life is the book of time, which is the book of the stars.

As the lords of time, the planets are lords of *karma* or destiny. They show the cosmic energies that we are developing and the level on which that development is taking place. They show us which forces we are susceptible to and may cause us harm. We are living in an ocean of cosmic influences transmitted by the planets. Yet, lacking true knowledge, we move blindly among them, not recognizing them at all; therefore we can be struck down by them unnecessarily. We experience such negative encounters with cosmic energies as the traumas of life: disease, conflict and death. On a collective level they occur as wars, plagues and cataclysms. Most of these are avoidable if our inner eye is open. Astrology helps us open this inner vision so that we can navigate safely across the swirling sea of life.

Astrology indicates more than the events of our current lives. The planets show past and future life conditions as well. They reveal the trends of time. All time follows a similar rhythm of birth and death. There is nothing alive, including the universe itself, that has not gone through many cycles of birth and death. What is born must die. What has died must be reborn. In seeing things as they are today, we are also seeing yesterday and tomorrow, the beings and worlds that have been and are to be; what we have been and what we are to become.

The planets, as the energies of time, flow into eternity. The planets not only show our bondage to time but also indicate the way of liberation from it, how we can move from the transient to the eternal. When we become conscious of the cosmic forces working through the planets, we pass beyond their outer rule. We integrate their powers within ourselves. We put the creation back together within our own hearts. We reintegrate the cosmic man who is our inmost Self. We gain mastery over the entire creation. The universe becomes a tapestry of thought in which we can play, rather than a net of desires in which we are caught. The planetary rays that rule us in our ignorance become aspects of our own eternity and immortality.

Astrology is a symbol of spiritual development or the evolution of consciousness. We can meditate upon its forms and find within them the archetypes for our own inner growth. We can use the language of astrology as a symbolic tool, even without any consideration for its calculations or particular forms. In the end we must understand all the forces symbolized by the planets and become all beings. We should not become attached to the pattern of our particular destiny but use it as a door on to the cosmic life.

PLANETS AND GODS

The ancients revered the planets as gods. In this they were expressing their reverence for the cosmos, their regard for the sacred order of existence. They recognized in the stars and planets the primal powers of cosmic intelligence. They worshiped these same cosmic powers within themselves as the powers of the soul.

The gods of the ancients are not relics of naive nature worship, as we may tend to view them through the bias of the modern mind. They are not products of fear, superstition or a lack of scientific knowledge about the outer world. They are expressions of a cosmic intuition, and they reflect a cosmic metaphor. The unconscious uses the language of symbols. Yet this unconscious, as we know from Jungian psychology, is not merely our repressed desires or instinctual patterns; it contains the deeper levels of our soul and the cosmic mind.

The most primary symbols or archetypes of the psyche are those of time. Our primary issues in life are birth and death and the meaning of our transient existence. As our myths and symbols are naturally of time, they are also of the planets. They reflect the dialogue between our souls and the cosmic energies or life-archetypes transmitted through the planets. The language of symbols — that language of the deeper unconscious which also contains our higher consciousness hidden within it — is essentially the language of astrology.

The gods are the powers of cosmic intelligence at the heart of our own deeper consciousness. They represent its structuring influences and the workings of its laws. In the stories of the gods — whether embodied in collective myths or in our dreams, which constitute our own private mythology — is the language of the stars. The stars are not only the stuff out of which our physical bodies are made; they provide the essential elements of the psyche as well. As such, they continue to operate within our minds and determine its workings — whether we acknowledge them or not.

Outwardly, the planets represent the seven rays that determine the play of creation. These seven forces exist in the world of nature as the elements and energies at work on all levels. They are the rhythm of time as well as the densities of matter. They form the seven levels of the cosmos, the seven planes of existence from gross matter to pure being. Life is a tapestry of seven times seven. Inwardly these seven rays create the rational and emotional sides of the mind along with the five senses.

In ancient religions the Sun is the symbol of the One God, the unitary cosmic intelligence, the force of spiritual evolution behind the workings of life and nature. The Sun is the cosmic lord and creator, the immanent Divine being, the Divine Son who is the father of the worlds. The Moon is the essential power of nature, the Divine field of manifestation, the mother of life. She is the great Goddess.

The cosmic creative rays come from the spiritual planes. As they descend, they take upon themselves greater density and differentiation and begin to clash. On all levels, it is these same basic forces which continue to interact in different combinations and disguises.

On a lower level, the planets represent the lesser deities, the astral powers that govern, sometimes capriciously, the destinies of men. This is the level of the Greek gods meddling in the affairs of men. Mars, for example, is the vital energy principle which, acting on its own, creates violence and conflict. The old myths and legends merely illustrate these cosmic energies and their inherent conflict and limitation on the lower levels. The corruption of the gods is the corruption of these forces in their outer workings. It is the fragmentation of the energies of life that must occur when we are not conscious of what we really are. The chaos of our unconscious merely reflects our lack of true awareness, our bondage to the ego.

At the next higher level, the planets represent the gods of the mind and intellect: our ideals of art, truth, justice, and outer religion. As mere forces of the mind, they have no real power of transformation. They disguise a more primal ignorance, for the same mechanism of egoism and desire lurks behind the workings of the mind, however noble the causes to which it aspires. The moral failure of the Greek gods mirrors the spiritual failure of an intellectual culture. It shows that behind the gods of the mind are the gods or powers of the vital realm, the great passions of anger, desire, and greed.

At the lowest level, the planets become the demons, the asuras or negative entities that obstruct our spiritual growth. Lucifer is traditionally the fallen star (Venus in its lower energy). These powers of falsehood work through illusion, hypnosis, deception, and arrogance. They are the gods of the lower vital realm who have separated themselves from any higher mental or spiritual connections. Yet ultimately they are only the higher rays inverted upon a lower field of manifestation. They appeal to our inner needs, but in a perverted way, causing us to seek a fulfillment from the outer world that can only come from an inner awareness and connection to the Divine.

The planets, therefore, are not only the gods that raise us up, but also the demons or Titans that pull us down. It all depends on how we understand them and use their energies. In our ignorance of the cosmic Self, we create both gods and demons. We project our divine and cosmic power outside ourselves and become enslaved to it. The gods and demons show the duality of energy in which we are trapped by our dualistic minds. Without an awareness of the inner Self we become victims of the outer world and fall under its bondage.

As the powers that rule this world of ignorance, the planets are perhaps primarily demonic in their effect. The Sanskrit word for planet, *graha*, also means a demon or something which possesses a person. On a lower level, the planets weave a veil of hypnosis in which we project their energy as if it were our own. The wars between peoples or nations mirror the disharmony between the planets. Disease reflects an excess of negative planetary rays. In our ignorance we are controlled by the planets and fulfill their will as if it were our own.

For this reason the ancients looked upon the planets with fear. They were aware of the awesome, terrible and often unpredictable universe in which they lived. While we may think that we are free of such feelings, they come back to us again whenever we face a catastrophe such as an earthquake or flood. Certain planetary combinations put us under the possession of negative cosmic energies, both individually and collectively. While in our deeper Selves we can control these forces, in our egos we remain their victims.

The planetary rays form and structure our mind, emotions and senses. They organize the systems of our physical body. The circulation of the blood, for example, mirrors the revolution of the Sun and Moon in the heavens. The intelligence of the planets lives within our bodies and minds, responsible for their marvelous functioning.

On the deepest level the planets represent our spiritual potential. The Sun is our inner Self, our Divine being. Venus is our sense of Divine love, beauty and grace (we will explore these meanings in our discussion of the planets). We must raise the influences of the planets from the lower to a higher level. To save ourselves, we must redeem the planets; we must reintegrate the cosmic rays. To use an ancient metaphor, enlightenment is resurrecting the Sun out of darkness. We must redeem the portion of the cosmos that we are, not for our own special salvation but to further the evolution of the cosmos. To do this is to cause the Sun of truth to arise in our own hearts.

ASTROLOGY AS A SPIRITUAL SCIENCE

Astrology should be a spiritual science. Our birth chart is a mirror of our soul and its particular incarnation. In our stars we see the growth and evolution of our inner being from life to life. This does not mean that we can find truth or liberation merely through reading astrological charts. It means that astrology gives us the keys to the unfoldment of the spirit and can be used as a key to inner unfoldment.

The stars and planets are not just outer entities; they exist within our own minds as our guiding lights. One could say that our own inner lights take shape outwardly as the stars and planets to guide the world's evolution. The outer comes from the inner and not vice versa, though the outer can affect the inner. The same rays of creation function outwardly in the heavens and inwardly in the heaven of our own higher mind. The stars determine our field of activity in life. They reflect the energies that we, as souls, project into this life. As we are a reflection of them, so they are a reflection of us. The stars form the cosmic man just as we, as human beings, form a solar system within ourselves.

Our own soul is itself a star, a sun, a point of cosmic light. Our own soul — often called the "causal being" because it is the causative power behind our life and thought — contains the power to create the entire universe. The light of our soul connects directly to the cosmic light, to the one Divine light that is in the Sun and all the stars.

Reflecting the universe itself, astrology can be used to examine all domains of life. From it we can learn about our health, wealth, career and relationships; our material, mental and spiritual manifestations. It shows the entire structure of energies through which we must act in life. As such, it is the most comprehensive science we have. Yet on its highest level, astrology should be part of yoga, the science of the spirit. Its purpose is to guide us beyond the net of these outer forces to their source. This source in not in the heavens, whether of this physical world or of one more subtle. It is not some mysterious or alien force, but what we really are when our minds are free of the bias of the separate self.

The planets show the energies that we need to master in order to calm our minds. Anger, a typical lower energy of the planet Mars, for example, is the power of truth to manifest what is right and not deviate from it. It appears as anger when we identify truth with some egoistic opinion or emotion. All the lower indications of the planets are simply the higher powers struggling in a state of limitation. They are different facets of the jewel of the enlightened mind, and they require reintegration rather than suppression.

The essential principle of a spiritual science is *self-knowledge*. As great sages have said repeatedly, "Self-knowledge is the basis of all knowledge." Yet self-knowledge is something far more than psychological analysis. It is not the knowledge of our outer personality or conditioned self but of our inner consciousness and unconditioned being. The analysis of memory confines us to a superficial aspect of our being. Self-knowledge is also something more than knowledge of past lives. This is only a more extensive memory, still caught in the veil of form and the limitation of time.

Self-knowledge is the knowledge of who we really are, of our true being, which is the light of awareness. This is the Self, of which all our incarnations are but masks. It is not found by knowing who we were or why we became this or that; it is found by negating all separative identity and reintegrating the world within our own hearts. This requires seeing all lives within us. Such seeing is a recognition of the Divine presence everywhere.

Astrology properly employed shows us the world within ourselves. It is a tool for moving our consciousness from its physical limitation in the human brain through the rays of creation to encompass the entire universe. It is a tool for meditation in which the planets represent the qualities that we must realize within ourselves. The planets are the limbs of the cosmic person that we must put back together to return to the original state of grace. Understanding astrology, our consciousness can soar through the planets and the stars to the central Sun of Truth in the inner heart of all.

All worlds, planets, stars, galaxies and whatever else lies beyond them are a manifestation of the seven rays of creation. These same rays of creation are the lights of our own soul. All nature is nothing but various combinations of these causal lights on different levels. Our solar system is designed to manifest these creative energies, in their dual power as the Sun and Moon and in their fivefold diversification as the five major planets of Mars, Mercury, Jupiter, Venus and Saturn.

Each planet is a teaching. It represents an integral aspect of the cosmic being in its self-manifestation. Each planet shows us a line of approach to the cosmic being. Through integrating within ourselves the energies represented by the planets, we regain our true wholeness as cosmic beings. Each planet therefore represents a door to liberation. If we do not understand the energy of a planet within us, it will bind and lead us into sorrow and conflict. If we take too much or too little of the energy of any planet, we will cause imbalance and disorder in and around us, both physically and psychologically. If we take the energy of a planet divisively or superficially, it will lead us into disintegration. If we take that energy as a part of our deeper self, it will lead us to a greater and higher unfoldment.

The planets are awesome forces. Yet we ourselves are part of this mysterious universe and have its tremendous power within us. A great power exists within our soul to deal with the incredible energies of life. Our ego must break or turn away. Through inner inquiry and surrender, this power to master the planets and the stars can come forth. Through it, the nebula of our own mind coalesces, concentrates, and finally becomes enkindled as a Sun of direct perception.

Each planet represents a particular kind of yoga, a certain way of the unfoldment of consciousness. Following a planet's characteristic ray back to its origin, we will arrive at the light of truth through its higher and subtler potential. The planets are different gifts of light to guide us back to our spiritual home. Their angle of approach varies, but their goal is one. In this return route their energies gradually come together.

Different souls fall under different rays belonging to the different planets. They belong to different planetary families. They are working for the development of the creative ray belonging to that planet, moving it forward in its evolutionary development, some at lower, some at higher levels. The evolution of the soul and that of the universe are thus the same. Each soul is a guiding force in cosmic evolution and in its liberation it will liberate a certain facet of the world being and further the evolution of all.

Different countries, races and religions also fall under different planetary rays. We are all part of the play of the gods, which is the play of the planets. Yet we are not just the puppets in the play, although we often accept this cosmic servitude while we are in ignorance of our greater inner potential. Inwardly we are the masters of this play, its guiding intelligence. All the intelligence inherent in the stars, produced by eons of cosmic evolution, is present within us as our own natural intuition and spontaneous insight.

Some families of ancient seers were said to belong to families of the planet Jupiter, while others were said to belong to Venus, the two planets of the Brahmins or priestly class. Ancient Egypt and America followed a calendar centered on the planet Venus. Ancient India and China followed one based upon the planet Jupiter. Their cultures were based upon these planets and their creative ray as their guiding inspiration.

The ancient rishis were identified with different constellations, particularly the stars of the Big Dipper, which were called the seven sages, and the Pleiades, which were said to be their wives. This again was because of the cosmic light they brought down to Earth through the power of their awareness. The stars are our parents. The beings of other worlds, other solar systems, and other Suns have seeded this one. So, too, we are seeding other worlds by the power of our actions. It does not require actually travelling to other worlds; we are constantly sending our thoughts into the cosmic mind where they must have affects beyond this particular world. When we awaken to truth we find a creative sun dwelling within us. In our inner or Divine Sun we can give birth to entire worlds, not through the blindness of karma but through the natural effusion of our souls.

Some souls incarnate into bodies. Other souls incarnate as stars or planets to guide the evolutionary process. Some souls become worlds; others become beings within the worlds. It is not necessarily a sign of higher evolution for a soul to become a planet or a star. Some of these world beings are archetypal beings and have no evolutionary potential, though powerful and exalted cosmic forces are moving through them. Such an existence may be a karmic reward or evolutionary interlude rather than a manifestation of liberation. Such souls become the demiurges of the worlds, their indwelling spirits.

On material worlds like the Earth, the greatest challenge and the greatest inner growth can occur. Where limitation and ignorance are greatest, the truth can reveal its most powerful force by way of contrast. That is why for a human being to find truth is the greatest wonder and the most exalted achievement, which even the gods cannot equal, and which the lesser gods, out of pride, must strive to prevent.

At death the soul returns along the planetary rays and the elements they represent. We merge into one of these rays, usually through the Moon or the Sun. Depending upon our state of evolution, we may retain consciousness during this journey — it all depends upon the point or orifice from which we leave the body. The lower orifices take us to the lower worlds, the higher orifices to the higher. Through the planets we can find a gateway to the planets of other solar systems or other Suns, even to the great galactic Sun.

The Moon is typically the gateway to the astral worlds, the worlds of the subtle or dream plane. These include the heavens and hells of ordinary religious beliefs in the lower astral plane, as well as the worlds of art or religious mysticism on the higher. From such worlds, rebirth into the physical is inevitable.

The Sun, which we reach through the top of the head or crown chakra, is the gateway to the causal worlds, the worlds of pure intelligence. These are not worlds in the ordinary sense because they are formless and made of thought alone. The causal is the realm of cosmic law. There is the true home of our individual soul, where it holds its karmic residue and from which it can envision the materials for another birth.

This merging into the planetary rays is a merging into light. We may experience it as a particular light center or as the experience of a particular world. For undeveloped souls, little may be experienced after death but a long sleep. Some souls, however, return immediately into the physical world as part of a spiritual work on Earth and may also have little after-death experience in the subtle planes.

The planets are alive for us on an astral level, even though they are dead for us on a material level. We go to their domains in sleep as well. The souls of human beings have been traveling to different worlds and solar systems on an astral level since the beginning of time, and largely unconsciously, every night.

Our culture is proud of the technology that has allowed us to land a man on the Moon. Yet we fail to understand that we go to the Moon regularly, though on an astral rather than a physical level. Most of us seldom get beyond it, because on its lower level the Moon is our memory, our past or karmic storehouse. The past impressions of the Earth life are stored in the Moon. Our experiences in life feed the Moon and help it to evolve. The lunar realm is the conditioned sphere in which our minds are trapped. In the sphere of the Moon reside the worlds created by our collective karmic fixations, like our heavens and hells. The wonder is not that we are going to the Moon by space ship. The wonder is that so few of us have ever gotten beyond it inwardly.

At night when we sleep, our mind expands into an astral or dream body that encompasses the entire field of our waking experience. Then, in deep sleep, we return into the causal body that encompasses both waking and dream experiences. The waking state is like the Earth. The dream state is like moving through the atmosphere to the planetary spheres. Deep sleep is like returning to the stars in heaven. In this process of waking and sleep we gather all the stars within us, taking inside ourselves the light and consciousness of the entire universe.

This same expansion of awareness occurs in a more permanent way at death. Were it not for our attachment to physical form, we would experience death as a natural return to cosmic consciousness and liberation. True rest is only possible in deep sleep when our minds are temporarily resolved into their light source, the inner Sun of the soul.

The astral body, when fully developed, contains the entire physical universe. It can go anywhere within it, though it cannot interfere with its natural workings. Similarly, the causal body contains both the physical and the astral universes. We absorb and emit the light of the stars daily. They are nothing mysterious or foreign to our being; rather, they are its creative lights through which we move back and forth naturally and spontaneously in the soul's dance between the finite and the infinite.

In our ignorance, however, our consciousness remains bound to our body and senses. We become food for the Moon, as it were. We get caught in our own reflected light in the outer world and lose our true solar capacity for independent awareness. We are caught in time and matter and our awareness is dissipated. Instead of transforming the world, our fragmented energy feeds the negative forces in the world. This sustains the lower workings of cosmic energy and keeps us bound to primal powers of the earlier evolutionary stages. Our energy is trapped in the lower lunar circle, the realm of desire.

Our main problem in life is our own ego, through which we identify ourselves with the external world. We arrogate a certain portion of nature to ourselves as "I am this" or "this is mine." But there is only one nature, one law in the natural world, and one working out of cosmic energies. When I am angry, it is not that "I" am really angry. Anger is just one aspect of the energy of cosmic fire. To take it as our own is to misunderstand it and make it into a force of destruction. The problem is that we do not understand the cosmic implications of that particular energy, and hence try to use it in a limited way. Whatever is used for some self-centered end in a limited way becomes destructive in that limitation, as limitation is itself destruction.

The planets merely cast energy. We make that energy positive or negative by our use of it. What makes it negative is the ego, which is an arrogation of the energy. For example, if there were no ego to become attached to the energy coming from Mars, that planet's energy would manifest as fire, not as anger. This fire would increase our vitality and our perception. It would allow us act decisively but it would not make our action destructive.

To make of astrology a spiritual science, as it was intended to be, we must understand the spiritual meaning of the planets. We must learn which portions of cosmic energy they represent. We must know their place and function in the scheme of creation. In their harmonization and integration, we will then be able to liberate their energy within us.

Our *astral body*, the light of which we can see in the aura, is formed of stellar and planetary influences. Our birth chart is something like a photograph of our astral body. Our physical body is a grosser replica, an outer form of its astral counterpart. Astrology is naturally the astral science, the science of the astral body. This astral body is the mind, including memory, imagination, intellect and reason. Astrology allows us to read the wider scope of the mind, both instinctual and intuitive, including past life influences.

Just as we can read the state of the physical body through certain factors in the chart, so we can read the state of the causal body as well, though with greater difficulty. It relates more specifically to the Sun. Astrology can be elevated by higher perception into a causal science. On that level we can explore the movement of our soul from life to life and our true purpose as a soul, what we have inwardly set out to accomplish in this incarnation. However, our true being transcends all bodies as pure awareness. Astrology, like anything from the realm of creation, can only point back to or intimate that truth.

Actually, there is no real outer world at all. The outer world is just a combination of the sensory potentials of our own mind. The light of consciousness diffracted by the lens of the mind becomes the objects of the senses. Once we realize this, we become free of desire and discover our true Self in all beings. This is also the ultimate goal of astrology — not the acceptance of stars and planets as influences which we must blindly follow. Astrology shows us the manner in which these influences dwell within us, so that through the we may gain mastery over the entire universe.

Some may say that astrology, however true it may be, is not a spiritual science, that it is not a way of liberation but merely an occult science. It shows us our karma, but we are not bound to our karma. Only the ignorant are entirely subject to their birth chart, many have said; the wise are not concerned about it. Certainly astrology as it is commonly practiced is not spiritual. It is caught in the glamour of worldliness, ego and personality. Yet a higher form of astrology exists that reflects our higher Self that is not only divine but also universal, reflected in the entire cosmos.The Vedic vision of a spiritual astrology derives from this.

For establishing a true spiritual culture, this restructuring of astrology is a deep necessity. It is essential for our understanding of the language of life and for reclaiming our higher human heritage from our ancient spiritual progenitors.

VEDIC SCIENCE

Vedic astrology, like the science of yoga, arose from the vision of the ancient seers of India, the Vedic rishis. The rishis were great beings of spiritual realization and occult perception that lived in the legendary ages of light and truth. Their knowledge was passed down through the millennia by way of oral tradition. Much of it has been lost, but the core still remains. It is accessible on the deeper levels of the mind as the heritage of the spiritual humanity, a heritage from which we have fallen away. If we look to the presence of the rishis as our inner spiritual progenitors, their knowledge can again return to us.

From the meditations of the rishis arose the great system of Vedic science, an integral spiritual science comprehending all domains of existence. The rishis discovered the universal science of creative intelligence. They cast this in the language of mantra, the human replica of the cosmic sound vibrations at the origin of creation.

Mantras are seed sounds, the foremost of which is the seed-syllable Om, which contain the laws and the archetypes behind the workings of the universe. Applying this mantric knowledge on different levels, any domain of existence can be comprehended in its inner truth. Through mantra the rishis became adept in all fields of knowledge, including yoga, philosophy, astrology, geomancy, medicine, poetry, art and music. The root knowledge of mantra is an instrument on which all knowledge can be revealed by a shifting of scales. The *Maitriyani Upanishad* (VI.1) states:

> *The Self carries himself twofold, as the life-force (prana) and as the Sun. Two are his paths within and without by which he revolves by day and by night.*
>
> *The Sun is the outer Self; the life-force is the inner Self. By the movement of the outer Self, the movement of the inner Self is measured.*
>
> *But according to the Knower, who is free of sin, whose eye is turned within, it is by the movement of the inner Self that the movement of the outer Self is measured.*

The ancient seers used the movements of the Sun to understand the movement of the life-force in the body. This became the basis for the practice of yoga. Yet by meditating on the life-force they also came to understand the movement of the Sun in the heavens. In this way we can read the mysteries of the universe in our own body when our vision is open.

As Vedic science is a spiritual science, its central knowledge, in which all Vedic disciplines converge, is the knowledge of the Self, called in Sanskrit *Atma Vidya*. Vedic science is the science of Self-knowing. The Self is the one thing through knowing which everything is known. True knowledge is not a matter of facts and information but of what reveals to us the essence in things. This essence alone liberates the mind and fulfills the heart, bestowing bliss and immortality.

From this central Self-knowledge derives the mantra, the essence of cosmic sound and energy, which is embodied in the *Rig Veda*, the oldest of the *Vedas*. The *Rig Veda* is the record of the ancient rishis in their own language. Through it they transmitted the secret code of all knowledge. Vedic mantras form an intuitive and symbolic language that holds all the laws of the cosmos. Vedic astrology also looks back to the *Rig Veda* as its origin, and its great mantras to the planetary deities derive from that original source.

Vedic mantras have, as their primary meaning, spiritual knowledge and the practice of yoga. In the secondary sense, they relate to knowledge of the creation. This in turn relates primarily to occult knowledge, the knowledge of the subtle laws behind the workings of the physical universe. The foremost of these occult sciences is astrology. Vedic mantras also provide knowledge of the physical body, as in Ayurveda, the Vedic medical system. They contain the secret of the whole of human evolution and of the whole of cosmic evolution, from the original explosion of chaos to the ultimate perfection of the cosmos.

Perhaps the greatest of the ancient Vedic seers was the rishi Vasishta. He is the most famous sage of the *Rig Veda* and Vedic literature, and is found in Puranic and Tantric lore as well. It is to his grandson, Parashara Shakti, who himself is the seer of some of the most esoteric hymns in the *Rig Veda*, that the origins of Vedic astrology are traced. The work of his school, the *Brihat Parashara Hora Shastra*, though weathered by time and containing various accretions, is still the main book, the source book or scripture, in the field today.

Self-knowledge transcends time, space and person. It is the knowledge of the consciousness that precedes and underlies all manifestation. Therefore Self-knowledge is not limited to anything and is not the possession of any teacher, organization, or religion. The central principle of Vedic astrology is the primacy of inner knowing. Vedic astrology is meant to help us to our own direct knowing, not to impose an external authority or belief upon us. In the practice of Vedic astrology, the first principle is reverence for the Self in all beings, that entity who controls even the planets and for whom all the universe is but a shadow.

The purpose of Vedic astrology is not to make us feel subject to external forces but to help us use our lives for greater Self-unfoldment. For this we must first understand ourselves. Without some degree of self-knowledge the astrologer, even if he can perceive subtle planetary influences, will merely impose his own judgments upon his clients. He will only serve as another obstacle to the flowering of that individual soul. Such astrology will be centered in the ego and will not be of any lasting benefit.

VEDIC ASTROLOGY

Vedic astrology is the traditional astrology of India and its cultural sphere, going back to the ancient Vedic culture in times which we (at least) regard as prehistoric (before 3000 BCE). It is based on the *Vedas*, the original scriptures of India and perhaps all the Indo-European peoples.

Hindus, Buddhists, Jains, and Sikhs have all used Vedic astrology. It was practiced in the whole of India and in parts of present-day Persia, Afghanistan and Russian Central Asia. It still is used in Tibet, Sri Lanka and Burma. It followed Hindu and Buddhist influence into Indochina and Indonesia. Its influence spread to China and the Middle East, even to ancient Babylonia and Egypt in very early times. If the astronomical references in the *Vedas* are accurate, it may be the original form of astrology from which all the others emerged. It may best represent the astrology of the earlier spiritual ages, the mythical ages of light which were said to have preceded all those ancient cultures of which we presently have knowledge.

In the *Vedas* we find equinoctial positions of great antiquity, such as the many references in later Vedic literature to the vernal equinox in the Pleiades (Krittika), or the end of Taurus, indicating a date of 2500 BCE. References in the *Rig Veda* go back to the Gemini-Orion era (Mrigashiras, 4000 BCE), the Cancer era (Punarvasu, 6000 BCE) and even earlier.

The *Rig Veda* contains a system of astronomical calculations including twelve signs and a 360 degree circle. It has a lunar calendar using intercalary months. Its metaphor of the Sun as conveyed by seven horses implies knowledge of the seven main planets. It mentions the lunar constellations or *nakshatras*. The Vedic gods have many astronomical and temporal correspondences. The constellations were named according to the gods that rule them, all of whom are found in the most ancient stratum of Vedic literature.

The *Rig Veda* contains a mathematical and astrological symbolism that shows a profound but hidden cosmic knowledge. One hymn states:

> *Four are his horns, three are his feet, two are his heads and seven are his hands. Bound triply, the bull roars; Almighty God has entered into mortals.*
>
> Rig Veda IV.58.2

This suggests the later astronomical yuga era of 4,320,000,000 years, with the seven hands as the seven zeros.

Vedic culture was based upon an elaborate ritual attuned to the cycle of time, following the cycles of the day, month and year as revealed by the movements of the Sun, Moon and planets. The ancients looked to the heavens as their clock, meditated upon its influences and came to discover higher consciousness behind it.

Vedic astrology is also called "Hindu astrology" from the culture and religion that developed along with it. Like Hinduism, it is a pluralistic and adaptable system emphasizing many paths and taking on ever new incarnations. Therefore, it is certainly useful and adaptable in the West today, along with the yoga and meditation systems that have already come to us from India and from which so many people have derived benefit.

Another name for Vedic astrology is *Jyotish*, which means "the science of light." Jyotish means astronomy, astrology and meteorology. As a limb of the *Vedas*, the very eye of the Vedas, it was called *Vedanga Jyotish*, "Jyotish or astrology, the limb of the *Vedas*," which is how it is referred to in traditional texts.

THE FOUR AIMS OF LIFE

Vedic science recognizes four aims or goals of human life: *kama, artha, dharma* and *moksha*. Kama means desire and refers to our need for emotional and sensory fulfillment in life. As such, we could call it enjoyment. All that we do in life should be a source of happiness and not cause pain to any creature.

Artha means achievement of goals, but relates specifically to the acquisition of valuable objects and so could be rendered as wealth. Each one of us should have the necessary articles of wealth to allow us to fulfill our potential in life.

Dharma means principle or law and refers to our need for honor or recognition. We could call it vocation, as this is how our culture interprets this need. Each of us needs to be acknowledged for what we can do so that we can contribute to society without compromising who we really are.

Moksha means liberation or freedom and relates to our need for spiritual growth, including transcendence of the three lower values. We all must seek to go beyond who we are until we become one with all. All four goals are called dharmas, as dharma also means fundamental principle. Moksha or liberation is the highest dharma.

Vedic astrology recognizes the validity of all four aims of life and is oriented to facilitate us in the attainment of each of them. Yet the first three, enjoyment, wealth and career, are made subordinate to the last, spiritual liberation. Liberation is the primary and essential goal for all human beings, for all life. Without it the other goals have no real meaning. The others are useful as a means to an end but not as an end in themselves. Once we understand this, we will not get caught in them but only use them to further spiritual growth.

As a foundation for the four aims of life, astrology addresses the need of health or freedom from disease. This is the basis for all the aims of life, for without health, what else can be accomplished? Yet health is not just physical, it is also mental. So astrology must consider both physical health and psychological well-being as the means of approaching all the goals of life. Therefore medical and psychological astrology are, after spiritual astrology, perhaps its most important branches.

These four aims are a pyramid with liberation at the top. Each is meant to aid the others. We need to be happy in order to function at all. We need the resources to enable us to have leisure and peace of mind. We need the acknowledgement or recognition of others in order to realize our vocation or calling. Yet most of us are caught in the lower goals and do not appreciate the higher goal. Even our pursuit of the higher often remains a pursuit of the lower in disguise. In the name of God we may still seek pleasure, power or fame. Astrology is often made hostage to these lower goals. For astrology to reclaim its spiritual integrity, it must recognize the right orientation of the goals of life.

2

Astrology East and West

Astrology has existed all over the world since the earliest period. It was prevalent in ancient cultures like Egypt and Babylonia. The medieval Christian and Islamic cultures continued to use astrology, which they adapted, but it became a secondary pursuit that was often considered heretical. The religion of the One God would not admit the powers of the gods, which are mainly planetary in nature. Modern culture, with its scientific bent, continued the denigration of the astrological art as something imaginary and not verifiable.

However, India maintained its civilization from the most ancient times. It continued to worship the gods as well as to seek the Divine Self or pure consciousness beyond even the Creator. It retained freedom in the realm of spirituality and religion. There was no control of the culture by the forces of an exclusive monotheism or by an intolerant church. An older and more complete form of astrology survived in there. A ritual calendar based upon the stars and the worship of the planets as gods continues in India today, much as it did in Babylonia and Egypt thousands of years ago. Modern Hindus still perform prayers to the planets today, as did their counterparts in ancient Europe and the Middle East long ago.

Astrology has undergone a revival in the West over the past century. A new, modern, psychological approach has broadened the vista of astrology and released it from the shackles of the medieval mind. Astrology has survived the onslaught of the materialistic age, being so compelling to the soul that the intellect could not dismiss it. Once the symbol of the past, many now view it as the way of the future as we move into the age of space travel. Astrology is therefore a good point of dialogue between East and West, the ancient and the modern.

TWO VIEWS OF THE ZODIAC

Most of us are under the impression that there is only one zodiac, that of the fixed stars or constellations. We think that when an ephemeris, an astrological table of planetary positions, locates a planet in a particular sign, for example Jupiter in Sagittarius, we would see the planet located there if we were to look up into the sky to the stars of that constellation. This, however, is usually not the case. The zodiac used by most Western astrologers today, what is called the *tropical zodiac*, is no longer based on the stars. It does not correspond to observable positions. Our astrological Jupiter in Sagittarius would likely be found astronomically among the stars of Scorpio.

The signs of the tropical zodiac, over the millennia, have come to correspond to completely different constellations of fixed stars. Today, the tropical sign of Aries corresponds to the fixed stars of Pisces. Soon it will correspond to Aquarius, thus signaling the beginning of the Age of Aquarius. In ten thousand years, tropical Aries will correspond to the fixed stars of Libra, its opposite. The signs of the tropical zodiac are based upon the equinoxes, not upon the fixed stars. The beginning of the tropical zodiac, its first degree of Aries, is identical with the vernal equinox, the place of the Sun on the first day of spring, not with any specific stars. The orientation of the equinoxes to the stars changes over time according to the precession of the Earth on its axis. This phenomenon, a change in the tilt of the Earth, causes the point of the Earth relative to the fixed stars to move backwards in the zodiac. Over of a period of around 25,000 years the orientation of Earth relative to the fixed stars makes a full circuit of the zodiac.

The zodiac that corresponds to the actual constellations or the fixed stars is called the *sidereal zodiac*. Vedic astrology uses this, as does Western sidereal astrology, which took its orientation from the Indian model. Around two thousand years ago, when Western astrology was in its formative stages, the two zodiacs coincided. Since then, along with the precession, the two zodiacs have been slowly moving apart. The tropical zodiac shows the actual astronomical positions of some two thousand years ago.

The tropical zodiac is not based upon the stars but on the orientation of the Earth to the Sun. The Tropics of Cancer and Capricorn denote the places of the Sun at the summer and winter solstices. The tropical zodiac begins with the Sun's place at the vernal equinox, which it designates as the beginning of the sign Aries. Its regards the position at the summer solstice as the first degree of Cancer, at the autumnal equinox as the first degree of Libra, and at the winter solstice as the first degree of Capricorn. The seasons mark the cardinal points of the tropical zodiac. Yet as the precession continues, the fixed stars marking these seasonal points slowly change.

The tropical zodiac remains identical with the seasonal points and does not consider the precession. The sidereal zodiac, on the other hand, calculates the precession into its positions. Its signs are identical with the fixed stars.

Today most tropical astrologers realize that their signs no longer correspond to the fixed stars. They claim that it is valid for other reasons. Some say it is based upon the seasons; others say it is a temporal rather than a spatial symbolism, with the tropical signs being a division of time rather than of space.

Yet tropical astrology does consider the precession. It does so relative to world ages, with its recognition of the Age of Aquarius as the vernal equinox moves back into the fixed stars of the constellation Aquarius. Tropical astrology recognizes the sidereal zodiac and considers it to be of value for longer collective time periods, but not of direct relevance to the individual chart.

Vedic astrology, similarly, considers the position of the planets relative to the points of the equinoxes and solstices. Yet this is used as a point for determining planetary strengths and weaknesses, not as a major factor in chart interpretation.

We see, therefore, that two different methods of determining the signs of the zodiac exist. Each is based on a different kind of calculation. Neither is necessarily right or wrong. Both are using different measurements, though they employ the same language to speak of them.

When a tropical astrologer says that the Sun is in Aquarius, he does not mean that the Sun is in the fixed stars of the constellation Aquarius. He usually knows that it is probably in the fixed stars of Capricorn. He means that it is in the eleventh of a twelvefold division of the zodiac based upon the position of the Sun at the vernal equinox. Similarly, when a sidereal astrologer says that the Sun is in Capricorn, he means the fixed stars, not the tropical division, which he knows is probably Aquarius. Though both astrologers use the same terms, they refer them to different portions of the sky based upon two different ways of dividing the heavens.

Some people today try to relate the signs to the actual stars only, rather than to a thirty degree division in which they are located. They would see Aries as equivalent only to the stars of that small constellation, not the greater band around it. Vedic astrology does not agree with this. It sees the twelvefold division of the zodiac as a harmonic division of the light coming from the center of the galaxy. This harmonic division is the key factor, not the individual stars within it, though these have their significance as well.

As two different zodiacal systems exist, a controversy naturally arises between them. Some astrologers may consider one to be the true zodiac and the other to be in error. Some may consider both to be valid, though in different ways. The debate between them is bound to continue with various opinions abounding. Yet the usefulness of Vedic astrology is becoming apparent, even though it requires a different view of the zodiac to appreciate.

As Vedic astrology is sidereal in calculations, the positions of the planets in zodiacal signs will usually be different in the Vedic chart than they are in the tropical chart. A Taurus Sun sign person may find his Sun in Aries in the Vedic system. This shift of positions naturally causes some consternation, particularly for those who are familiar with their chart in the tropical system. An Aquarius Sun sign person may not be happy to become Capricorn in the Vedic system. On the other hand, a Capricorn Sun in the Western system may feel happier as a Sagittarius Sun in the Eastern. Therefore it is crucial that we understand the two zodiacs and their differences so that we don't confuse one system with the other.

Historically, the sidereal zodiac is probably the original one, as it is the observable zodiac. The tropical, which is an abstract zodiac, must have derived from it. The zodiac was invented long before the time when the vernal equinox was at the first point of Aries. It must have originally been based upon observation of the stars. When the Egyptian and the Babylonians spoke of the sign Taurus, it must have meant the fixed stars. Yet in their time Taurus marked the vernal equinox, not Aries. It is hard to imagine that in 2000 BCE, when the Moon was located in the stars of Taurus, that the ancients would have placed it in the tropical sign of Aries (which would have been the case if they had used the tropical zodiac). An abstract or symbolic zodiac would not have made sense in cultures that marked their calendar on observable planetary positions. If astrology came originally from India, then the sidereal zodiac would definitely come first, because India's astrology has remained sidereal throughout its long history.

An advantage of the sidereal zodiac, therefore, is that it is probably the original zodiac astronomically and historically. The complaint of astronomers that astrology cannot be valid because its signs no longer correspond to the stars cannot be lodged against sidereal astrology

Vedic astrology has existed for over many thousands of years. A number of changes of equinoctial positions, similar to our Age of Aquarius, as well as other shifts in the calendar, have been recorded in it. The Vedic system and its zodiac are based upon a continuity of culture that goes back to the age of the gods, when human beings still had communication with the intelligence of the cosmos. It may, therefore, provide us with keys to the working of that cosmic intelligence and our future as a planet. That we have discovered it again as we move into a new millennium shows its enduring value.

ORIENTATION OF THE SIDEREAL ZODIAC

Vedic astrology, according to my interpretation, orients the zodiac to the galactic center, the central galactic Sun whose influence comes to us through the fixed stars of the constellation Sagittarius. The galactic center is called *Brahma*, the creative force, or *Vishnunabhi*, the navel of Vishnu. From the galactic Sun emanates the light that determines life and intelligence on Earth. It directs the play of the seven rays of creation and the distribution of karma. It is the central point for determining the meaning of the signs, which reflect the twelvefold division of its light relative to our solar system.

In terms of the sidereal zodiac, the galactic center is located in the early portion of Sagittarius. In the Vedic system there is a lunar constellation (*nakshatra*) called Mula, meaning "the root" or "the source," suggesting that it is the first of the series of these nakshatras on a cosmic level. It marks the first 13° 20' of Sagittarius, in the middle of which is located the galactic center. The previous nakshatra is called Jyeshta, meaning "the eldest," which marks the end of Scorpio. This shows that the ancients knew of the galactic center and named their constellations in such a way as to acknowledge it as the beginning. There are three main points of orientation for the sidereal zodiac that form a triangle:

- *Aries*, as cardinal or creative fire, is the field into which the cosmic light is projected.
- *Leo*, as fixed fire, is the field into which it is sustained.
- *Sagittarius*, as mutable fire, is the field in which it is completed or transformed.

This orientation is fixed according to the Sun's relationship to the galactic center. The galactic light comes through Jupiter and early Sagittarius and triangulates itself through Aries and Leo (located in trines or 120° angles from it).

The sidereal zodiac maintains a consistent relationship with the galactic center. The tropical zodiac is based upon a consistent Earth-Sun relationship via the equinoxes. The sidereal zodiac measures the relationship between the solar system and the galactic Sun. It reflects the influences that emanate from the center of the galaxy, as mediated and transmitted by the planets of our solar system.

The energy of the galactic center is transmitted mainly by the planet Jupiter, called *Guru*, the teacher, in the Vedic system, and by Sagittarius, its positive sign. Jupiter is said to be the teacher of the gods, the cosmic powers of light. In this respect he is even the teacher of the Sun, who is the guide of the world. Jupiter represents and directs the light of the galactic Sun into our solar system. In this manner we can divide the zodiac into three groups of four constellations:

Aries — Taurus — Gemini — Cancer
Leo — Virgo — Libra — Scorpio
Sagittarius — Capricorn — Aquarius — Pisces

The first division of the zodiac is directed by Mars, which, through Aries, cardinal fire, initiates the zodiacal emanation of energy. This is the cardinal or creative (*rajasic*) quadrant of signs. It consists of Aries and Cancer, two cardinal signs, Taurus, a fixed sign, and Gemini, a mutable. The cardinal quadrant of signs is responsible for beginning movement, initiating activity, guiding and directing the manifestation, casting the seed forces.

The second division of the zodiac is directed by the Sun, which, through Leo, fixed fire, stabilizes the zodiacal emanation of energy. This is the fixed or stabilizing (*tamasic*) quadrant of signs. It consists of two fixed signs, Leo and Scorpio, one cardinal, Libra, and one mutable, Virgo. The fixed quadrant of signs is responsible for sustaining movement, stabilizing activity and bringing energy into form. It provides continuity to the forces at work in life.

The third division of the zodiac is directed by Jupiter, which, through Sagittarius, mutable fire, brings the zodiacal emanation of energy to completion and fruition. This is the mutable or balancing (*sattvic*) quadrant of signs. It consists of two mutable signs, Sagittarius and Pisces, one cardinal, Capricorn, and one fixed, Aquarius. The mutable quadrant of signs is responsible for completing movement, transforming energy, destabilizing form. It moves us away from energy and form into the domain of thought.

All three divisions begin with a fire sign and end with a water sign of the same quality. The first group has fire and water of a cardinal sign, the second group contains fire and water of a fixed sign, and the third contains fire and water of a mutable. These three groups of signs represent the movements of creation, preservation and destruction according to the galactic force transmitted through our solar system.

SOLAR AND COSMIC ASTROLOGIES

In summary, we could say that tropical astrology could best be called "solar astrology." Its signs may be more accurately called "solar houses" or "equinoctial signs." Its zodiac measures the Earth-Sun relationship but has no direct correlation with other fixed stars. As such, its concern is with psychology, the personality and character types, the solar side of our life. Its signs show how the planets distribute the solar force, but not how they distribute the energies of the stars and of the galaxy itself.

Sidereal astrology can be called "cosmic astrology." Its signs are the stellar constellations. Its zodiac measures the relationship between our solar system, the fixed stars and the galaxy. It possesses good predictive powers and is good for a spiritual astrology. For spiritual astrology we must consider the great galactic center and the position of the signs relative to it.

Both systems could be integrated. We see that both astrologies employ a system of houses. These are based upon the daily rotation of the Earth on its axis. The tropical zodiac reflects, in addition, the yearly rotation of the Earth around the Sun. The sidereal zodiac adds to this the millennial rotation of the solar system through the precessional cycle. In this way, one could measure all three of these factors and integrate Eastern and Western astrology. However, this becomes complex and cumbersome in actual prediction.

On the other hand, both systems can remain as alternatives, just as different healing systems exist. It could be argued that maintaining the differences between the two systems is good and allows for a broader development of astrological knowledge. Even if the two systems stay apart, aspects of one may still be helpful to add to the other. Many Vedic astrologers, particularly in the West, add Uranus, Neptune and Pluto to their system of interpretation. Divisional charts, which are becoming popular in tropical astrology today (like the duads), come originally from the Vedic system.

AYANAMSHA

The difference between the tropical and sidereal zodiacs is called the *ayanamsha*. In Sanskrit, *ayana* means "solstice" and *amsha* means "portion." The term refers to the difference between the point of the vernal equinox in the fixed stars and that of the first point of the constellation Aries.

The main controversy among sidereal astrologers is the exact degrees and minutes of the ayanamsha. Some Western astrologers consider that the vernal equinox is already in Aquarius. This would be an ayanamsha of over thirty degrees. Such a view is hard to validate astronomically, as the equinox is now still in early Pisces, far from the actual stars of Aquarius.

Western sidereal astrologers place the ayanamsha around 24° 02' as of 1950. Most Vedic astrologers place it between 21° 40' and 23° 10' for that same period. The latter correction is called the Lahiri ayanamsha, now used as a standard by the government of India but still not accepted by all. While it is easy to determine the exact point in the heavens to which the vernal equinox corresponds today, it is hard to measure what should actually be the first point of the constellation of Aries. The identity of the Vedic star Revati, said to mark this position, is a matter of dispute.

The main modern method is to use the star Chitra (Spica or Alpha Virgo, a first magnitude star) and place the beginning of the zodiac exactly opposite or 180 degrees from it. This is the basis for the Lahiri ayanamsha. Such an ayanamsha is called Chitrapaksha. Yet there is some dispute about the calculation of its position. Older Vedic astronomy employed a polar latitude for measuring the position of stars. Using this would make the Chitra ayanamsha forty minutes less than the Lahiri ayanamsha.

Common Ayanamshas for 1950

Lahiri	23° 10'
B.V. Raman	21° 42'
Sri Yukteswar	21° 46'
J.N. Bhasin	22° 03'
Fagan-Bradley	24° 02'

The rate of movement of the precession per year is also a matter of some difference of opinion and it varies slightly over time. Hence the date of coincidence for the two zodiacs is calculated differently. Vedic astrologers use dates between 200–550 AD for this event.

The system of Sri Yukteswar, the guru of Paramahansa Yogananda, explained in his book, *The Holy Science*, is noteworthy, as he was both an astrologer and a Self-realized soul. He begins the cycle at 499 AD and gives it a period of 24,000 years, divided according to the Vedic theory of the four yugas. Dr. B.V. Raman's calculations are close to his, diverging from it by only a few minutes, a negligible amount for calculations today, but Raman makes the cycle longer and the rate slower. Astronomy places the cycle at 25,800 years (and a rate of movement around 50.3") but admits fluctuations. Curiously, if we take 108 as the base number for the Yukteswar cycle rather than 100, we come to a total period of 25,920 years, close to the scientific value.

One can choose the ayanamsha one finds best. While most Vedic astrologers prefer the Lahiri ayanamsha, few have been able to match the accuracy of B.V. Raman for mundane predications based upon his ayanamsha. I followed the Raman-Yukteswar ayanamsha when I first wrote this book in 1989, but have since seen many brilliant readings using the Lahiri ayanamsha.

THE VEDIC CHART

The easiest way to calculate a Vedic chart is through a Vedic computer program. If you want to calculate the Vedic chart manually, it can be done the same way as one would calculate a tropical chart, only subtracting the ayanamsha from all positions. Any typical tropical chart can be turned into a Vedic chart through this procedure. For this reason, I will not go into the subject of chart calculation, discussions of which can be found in many common astrology books. While there is a special Indian way of calculating charts, it is too complicated to examine here.

Below is a sample chart in the south Indian style (the north Indian style uses a diamond pattern). The upper left-hand corner marks the sign Pisces, and the rest of the signs follow in clockwise order around it. All south Indian charts follow the same format of signs, so the signs are not usually marked within them. The exact degree positions of the planets and houses are usually listed separately, though for a simple reading they are not necessary.

PARAMAHANSA YOGANANDA, BIRTH CHART

Pis. Ju Ma	Aries Ra	Tau.	Gem.
Aqu.			Can.
Cap.			Leo Mo ASC
Sag. Su Me	Sco. Ve	Libra Ke	Virgo Sa

January 5, 1893, 8:38 pm LMT, 83E23 26N47

Ascendant 06° 31' Leo	Sun 23° 12' Sagittarius
Moon 03° 14' Leo	Mars 13° 18' Pisces
Mercury 00° 55' Sagittarius	Jupiter 23° 51' Pisces
Venus 24° 44' Scorpio	Saturn 20° 13' Virgo
Rahu 12° 40' Aries	Ketu 12° 40' Libra
Uranus 17° 41' Libra	Neptune 16° 37' Taurus Rx
Pluto 17° 21' Taurus Rx	

3

The Yugas or World Ages

Who knows now and who can declare the paths that lead to the God; only their lower habitations are visible, who dwell in regions of supreme mystery.

Rig Veda III.54.5

According to the Vedic seers, life on Earth is under the rule of vast cosmic forces that originate from the stars. All that happens locally on our planet is a result of forces coming from the distant regions of the universe. These are not just distant regions of the physical world, but also of the cosmic mind, the mysterious origin of things from which the underlying forces of creation arise. These forces determine the nature of the time in which we live. Usually we are so involved in the transient events of our personal lives that we miss these great powers altogether. Like fish, we fail to see the ocean.

Just as we resonate to the seasons of the year, so too are we individually and collectively under the rule of various time cycles. Each person, each nation, and each humanity has such a cycle, as does the planet itself. We exist at different stages in the processes of birth, growth, decay and death, not just in our bodies but also in our minds and souls. Yet this is not just a mechanical round that goes nowhere. Behind the cycle of time lies an ongoing evolution of consciousness. Just as a tree has annual cycles of growth and retreat but continues to grow year after year, so all things have an inner growth process in which consciousness continues to develop through life after life.

THE LESSER CYCLE OF WORLD AGES

The main time cycle governing the human race, the seasons of humanity, is the precessional cycle. This period of 25,000 years is about one year in the life of humanity. According to some Vedic astrologers, it reflects the period of revolution of the Sun around a dark companion. According to them, the Sun is a double star but its companion appears to be a dark dwarf possessing no real luminosity of its own. Modern astronomers have begun to suspect the existence of such a star and have postulated its existence to explain irregularities in the orbits of Neptune and Pluto, which suggest the gravitational influence of a more distant heavenly body within the solar system.

Besides the light from our own Sun, we also receive light from the center of the galaxy, the galactic Sun. Much of the light of this greater Sun, however, is not in visible frequencies. Some astronomers have suspected a central galactic light, like that of a quasar, whose light may be obscured by dust or nebulae in the region of the galactic center. According to Vedic astrology, the light from this galactic source has a special influence upon Earth. It nourishes and sustains intelligence in human beings. This is not the materialistic intellect but true intelligence, the capacity to perceive the real or divine spirit in things and act according to the Divine Will.

When the Sun is located on the side of its orbit where its dark companion comes between it and the galactic center, the reception of the cosmic light is reduced. At such times there is a dark or materialistic age on Earth. When the Sun is on the opposite side of its orbit and has an open reception to the light of the galactic Sun, there is a golden or spiritual age on Earth. Humanity then acts in harmony with cosmic intelligence and with Divine powers that are its functionaries and emissaries. The Sun's dark companion appears to possess a negative magnetic field that obstructs the cosmic light from the galactic center from reaching the Earth. Through this it creates cycles of advance and decline in human civilization.

Modern astronomy estimates this cycle at around 25,900 years. The rate of yearly precession does not appear fixed, so this duration is only approximate. Manu, the great Vedic lawgiver for the human race in the Golden Age, in his teaching the *Manu Samhita* (I. 68-71, also note *The Holy Science*, Sri Yukteswar, p. 11), places this cycle at 24,000 (100 x 240) years. Other Vedic astrologers have placed it at 25,920 years (108 x 240, with 108 being the occult or mystic form of the number 100). While the exact details are not known, the general affect of the cycle is certain.

Ancient astrology places humanity under the legendary four ages: the Golden, Silver, Bronze and Iron ages. We find this idea among the Greeks as well as the Hindus, but the time periods involved are not given. In Sanskrit these are called the *yugas* or world ages of *Satya* (which means truth, also called the fourth age), *Treta* (the third), *Dwapara* (the second) and *Kali* (the first). Manu fixed their duration at, respectively, 4000, 3000, 2000 and 1000 years, plus a transitional period of 1/10 of their respective length both before and after.

This makes a total of 4800 years for the Satya Yuga, 3600 for the Treta

Yuga Age, 2400 for Dwapara Yuga, and 1200 for Kali Yuga. The total for all four ages is 12,000 years. Two cycles of the four ages make up the 24,000-year precessional cycle.

Each precessional cycle is divided into two halves: an *ascending* half, in which the Sun is moving towards the point on its orbit closest to the galactic center, and a *descending* half, when it is moving towards the point on its orbit furthest from the galactic center. In the ascending half we move from Kali to Dwapara, Treta and Satya Yugas. In the descending half we move from Satya to Treta, Dwapara and Kali Yugas. This creates a cycle, ascending Kali, Dwapara, Treta and Satya Yugas, then descending Satya, Treta, Dwapara and Kali Yugas. In this system we do not move directly from Kali to Satya Yuga, as some other interpretations indicate, but must pass through all the intermediate ages.

The level of true intelligence on Earth diminishes one quarter for each world age. At the high point of Satya Yuga it is 100%, at the low point of Kali Yuga 25%. In Dwapara Yuga it is 50% and in Treta 75%. The bull of the dharma, who loses one leg during each of the declining yugas, symbolizes this.

According to some Vedic astrologers, the point of the Sun's orbit furthest from the galactic center occurred around 500 AD. This was when the point of the vernal equinox was at the first degree of Aries. This was the point of greatest darkness on Earth, since which there has been a gradual increase of light. Variant views would place this date sometime between 200–550 AD, as it is the same issue as that of the ayanamsha.

Therefore, while many Western astrologers already put us in the Age of Aquarius, Vedic astrologers would place its advent up to 500 years in the future (though by other measurements given here, some of them do agree that we are in a different world age this century). The historical dates that correspond to the four Vedic world ages (as given by Sri Yukteswar in his book *The Holy Science*, pp. 12-3) are as follows:

Descending Yugas

Satya	11,501 BCE – 6701 BCE
Treta	6701 BCE – 3101 BCE
Dwapara	3101 BCE – 701 BCE
Kali	701 BCE – 499 AD

Ascending Yugas

Kali	499 AD – 1699 AD
Dwapara	1699 AD – 4099 AD
Treta	4099 AD – 7699 AD
Satya	7699 AD – 12,499 AD

Considering the transitional periods, there is an intermediate age between Kali and Dwapara Yugas at 1599–1899 AD. By this we see that we are in the ascending Dwapara Yuga. This is the New Age into which we have just entered, as evidenced by the great advances in science and technology. It is no longer the dark Kali Yuga, as some continue to think, yet it is far from Satya Yuga as well. Moreover, Dwapara is still in its early stages and has not presented its complete form at this stage. This may not occur for a few centuries, perhaps not until the vernal equinox actually does enter into Aquarius. Until then, some difficulties in moving into this new era will occur, with wars, pollution, famine and possible cataclysms as indications of it. This system is approximate and may have to be modified, but its general features are quite useful in helping us understand the development of human history.

THE GREATER CYCLE OF WORLD AGES

According to the more common view of Hindu astrology, humanity is in a Kali Yuga, a dark or Iron Age of 432,000 years, said to have begun around 3102 BCE. We should note, however, that this view is a speculation of medieval thinkers and has several problems, not to mention how pessimistic it appears! Even from the standpoint of Vedic historical records, its accuracy is questionable. Ancient texts mention many kings and sages, not just of the preceding Dwapara Age, but also of the Satya and Treta yugas. If this longer yuga cycle is used, such people would have to have lived hundreds of thousands of years ago, if not millions!

For example, the avatar Rama is a figure of the end of Treta Yuga, the Silver Age. He is placed in Puranic king lists some thirty-five generations before Krishna. Yet if the Kali Yuga of 432,000 years began at 3100 BCE, Rama would have to have lived at least 868,000 years earlier in order to be in the Treta Yuga of this longer cycle. According to the precessional view of the yugas advocated by Sri Yukteswar, Rama would have to have lived somewhere not long before 3100 BCE in order to be in the Treta Yuga, and this is a much more likely date.

However, this issue is complicated because different cycles exist, both shorter and longer. Besides the 25,000 year precessional cycle, there must be other longer cycles of hundreds of thousands and millions of years, just as our ordinary lives encompass cycles within cycles of the day, the month and the year.

From the standpoint of such a greater cycle, we may indeed be in a Kali Yuga, perhaps one of 432,000 years (though I am not certain of the duration or point of beginning). Within that greater cycle of Kali Yuga, however, we do appear to be in a lesser cycle Bronze Age phase of 2400 years or so.

Humanity may appear to be in a greater dark age phase because, as evidenced in the *Vedas*, even in Satya and Treta Yugas the great majority of human beings were on a materialistic or vital plane level, concerned mainly with the ordinary goals of family, wealth and personal happiness. Only the higher portion of humanity, the cultural elite of a few percent, appears to experience the full benefits of the ages of light. This is the same as today, when the majority of human beings live on the same emotional level as always, and only a few really understand the secrets of science and technology, though all benefit from them. This greater Kali Yuga, however, may not have started in 3102 BCE. We may not have enough information yet to know exactly when it began or how far into it we are.

The confusion between the lesser and greater cycles has led to some errors in the occult view of history. H.P. Blavatsky and her followers exemplified such confusion, as they based their views on the Hindu texts that used the longer cycle and did not understand the precessional cycle. This caused Blavatsky to make the ages of ancient civilizations and earlier humanities many times longer than they probably were. On the other hand, modern historians, with their lack of sensitivity to spiritual knowledge, make ancient cultures many times shorter than they were. The truth appears to be that ancient civilizations like India go back at least ten thousand years in this cycle. A number of earlier cycles of civilization occurred tens of thousands of years before this one.

A civilization cannot apprehend the existence of any culture higher than itself in the cycle of world ages. Our current accounts of history go back only to the cultures of Dwapara Yuga that began around 3100 BCE, like ancient Egypt and Sumeria. Such cultures were typical of the entire world at the time. Earlier cultures of the Treta and Satya yugas existed as well. These we cannot find, because we do not understand the level on which they occurred. While highly spiritual, they were not advanced technologically. The existence of the cultures of the previous cycle of world ages before

12,000 BCE remains entirely unsuspected. The flood that followed the end of the Ice Age eliminated their traces.

It is not possible to say how many but civilizations such as we know of have been in existence for many tens of thousands of years. Nor is there any end to such cycles in sight. By some accounts, it may take up to a million years of evolution for the average soul to pass through the human domain. In this regard the human race may be quite young, even at an age of several hundred thousand years old.

Technology, particularly in its gross contemporary form with all its pollution, must be a rare and transient phase of human culture. It cannot exist very long, at most a century or two, without destroying the planet. If it existed in previous humanities, as it may well have done, it would have been passed through quickly and the damage it caused would have been cleaned up (which is why we find no traces of it). We must develop a cleaner and more natural form of technology, like solar energy, in order to survive in the long run as a species.

The majority of human cultures have always been religious and spiritual rather than materialistic in nature. All ancient and medieval cultures were of a religious bent, and those of the Orient have remained largely so into the modern age. Technology, particularly in its invasive form that disrupts the natural environment, does not characterize human culture. It is a temporary deviation from true human culture, which is that of the spirit.

Each precessional cycle marks a different age of humanity. Our present world age began with the end of the Ice Age over ten thousand years age. Its early beginnings, Satya and Treta yugas, are recorded in the hymns of the *Rig Veda*, the oldest scripture of India. Traces of this teaching are found in mythology all over the world and in the ancient worldwide solar religion. What archeologists see as the beginnings of agriculture and civilization in early ancient times was merely a shifting of culture brought on by many geological and climatic changes relative to the new age.

According to the Vedic view and the testimony of the ancients, the Earth goes through major changes of geography and climate. For example, a mere ten thousand years ago Chicago was under a permanent mass of ice, as was much of the northern hemisphere. Such global renovations are experienced by human beings as cataclysms, earthquakes, and floods. Many such dramatic changes are recorded in books like the Bible or the *Vedas*. While they are often dismissed as superstition, evidences of the ending of the Ice Age, great earthquakes and floods can be found in the ancient world.

Important rivers of Vedic times, like the Saraswati, have long since gone dry, though we can trace their dry river banks through aerial photographs. Such global cataclysms usually correspond with changes of world ages. Nature goes through constant changes and the Earth is periodically renovated a process which includes clearing out the influences of previous humanities.

It is difficult for humanities of one world age to see or appreciate those of a previous world age. Our present world age humanity originated with certain seed cultures in the Himalayas during the end of the Ice Age. The previous world age humanity was Atlantean. Only students of the occult accept the existence of previous world ages, with different opinions abounding. Some of these opinions are based on racial memories that may be subjective or confused. Yet the existence of such cultures long before the so-called beginnings of history is beyond doubt to those of deeper perception.

ASCENDING AND DESCENDING CYCLES

The two halves of the precessional cycle have their characteristic differences of mentality. In the descending side the spiritual energy is decreasing or retreating from a point of fullness, while in the ascending side it is increasing and expanding from a point of deficiency.

It is difficult for cultures in the ascending half of the world ages to understand those in the descending half. Descending cultures, like those of the Orient, are traditional, conservative and authoritarian. They are trying to preserve the light of truth from the past, the previous ages of light. Most ancient cultures were of this order. Ancient Egypt was a typical descending culture. It became so enmeshed in its cult of the past (which became a cult of death) that it eventually perished of its own inertia.

Ascending cultures, on the other hand, are non-traditional, liberal and revolutionary. They are moving towards the light of truth in the future, which has yet to be defined. Western culture is based upon Greco-Roman influences which go back only to 500 BCE and did not entirely surface until the Renaissance. Hence it cannot understand cultures that originate from earlier world views. America today is a more limited type of ascending culture, as its origins go back only a few centuries. It is basically an ascending Bronze or Dwapara Yuga culture. It is characterized by a certain seeking of light and truth but in a superficial and outward manner.

Not surprisingly, a natural misunderstanding exists between descending and ascending, traditional and non-traditional cultures, such as we observe in the world today. Descending cultures are based on a higher spiritual truth, but it has often become so rigid, traditionalized and stereotyped that they may misrepresent it, as with the caste system in India. Ascending cultures are more open and creative, with a freedom of thought and inquiry, but often in an arbitrary way that may be far from any real basis in truth. They appear immature, materialistic and sensate oriented.

We must combine both these cultural influences in a positive way. The freedom and humanitarianism of the ascending mind needs the balance of the reverence and spirituality of the descending mind. As we go forward in our cycle of development we will be able to see back further and achieve such an integration. This is one of the great challenges of the world today, and one that can only be met with great effort. The divisions of East and West, spiritual and material, ancient and modern — divisions which are so strong in our minds — show this problem.

Yet within all these cycles exists an ongoing human evolution, a spiral of growth. Even if it falls back for a time, it will arise again with new force. Though we have declined spiritually from ancient cultures, we may have gained something materially and intellectually that can enhance our ascent back to those heights. Ultimately, humanity is moving to the point where we can transcend all external influences and live in a perpetual Golden Age in which we can return to the inner Self which stands above the influences of time. No one can say when this great leap will occur. It is possible at any time; but so far it has been quite rare, even for individuals. We cannot expect it soon for the majority. Some of us can see the greater potentials of our world age. Fewer can see the potentials of more advanced world ages. Still fewer can discover the eternal that is our real home; but even one such soul becomes a beacon for all humanity and shakes the foundation of the ignorance that rules us.

HARMONIZATION WITH THE GALACTIC CENTER

An important cosmic event is occurring now. The winter solstice is now at a point of conjunction with the galactic center. There is some doubt as to the exact location of this point. I would place it at 06° 40' Sagittarius, or the middle of the nakshatra Mula. Depending upon the ayanamsha one uses, this conjunction may be occurring either right now or in the next few decades. The same event appears mirrored in the calendric calculations of the Maya, a culture that shared many practices with the Vedic people.

This indicates a harmonization of humanity with the Divine will as transmitted from the galactic center. The new spiritual thinking of today may be a result of this attunement process, which insists that we enter into a new ascending age of light and cast off the shadows of the dark ages of strife and dissension. Though some global shock and suffering must be endured, the outcome can only be ultimately for the good. We should have faith in the Divine will behind this process and not give in to the despair that the present state of the world must evoke in us. Though we may not be quickly ushered into an age of enlightenment, much positive growth will occur. A shift in history as significant as any to date will be experienced, with a movement from darkness to light and a new seeking of consciousness

By the accounts of ancient thinkers like Plato, the flood that destroyed Atlantis and ended the Ice Age occurred about 9300 BCE (9000 years before Plato). This was when the summer solstice was in conjunction with the galactic center, a point completely opposite the one today. Such new cataclysms are possible in the coming century, particularly as we continue to disrupt and destroy our ecosystem. More reverence for the cosmic powers would be a good thing for our culture. We live under cosmic laws, which, having violated, we must suffer for. It was not just superstition that caused the ancients to tremble before God and beg his mercy. It was such experiences of global retribution that we may yet also see. Unless we learn to respect our planet, nature, other creatures and spiritual teachings, we as a species may have to undergo a great purification that will not be pleasant for anyone.

THE STAR VEGA OR ABHIJIT

Vedic astrology regards the North Pole as the spiritual pole of the globe from which higher spiritual influences come into the planet. However, the North Pole star does not remain the same throughout the precessional cycle. At the opposite side of the precessional cycle, the point of greatest light, the bright star Vega (alpha Lyra) serves to mark the North Pole. Vega is part of a special constellation which is used in Vedic astrology and which is called Abhijit or "complete victory;" it is ruled by Brahma, the cosmic creative power.

Vedic astrology shows a connection between our sun and the star Vega. Vega may be a controlling star for our Sun, its guide; or perhaps our Sun may revolve around it or with it around some greater center. Vedic astrology looks back to a time some fifteen thousand years ago when Vega was the North Pole star. Apart from the galactic center, Vega may be another important point of light that governs life on Earth.

Part II

The Methodology of Vedic Astrology

Moon

Clothed in white, white in luster, whose ornaments are white, who has two arms, with a lotus in his hand, whose soul is immortal, who is a yogi, whose vehicle is a deer, with a pearl crest jewel on his head, making the gesture that grants boons — may the Divine Moon ever grant us his grace.

4.

The Planets

The Great Cosmic Significators, the planets, are relay stations for the reception and transmission of stellar energies. We should not view them just for what they do within our solar system; they are bringing to us the forces of the galaxy, of the universe itself.

The essence of astrology lies in understanding the meaning of the planets. The meanings of the signs, houses, aspects and other astrological factors are determined by the planets that rule and significate them. Astrology is nothing but the science of the planets, as the forces of the stars manifest through them.

As a basis for astrological study, we must first possess a firm grasp of the meaning of the planets, their various indications and their levels of correspondence. Astrological thinking is planetary thinking, using the planets as significators, encompassing all domains of life and the evolution of consciousness.

All of us are made up of different combinations and degrees of the energies of the planets. Each one of us is usually stamped by the rule of one planet as our planetary type. Most of the action that we perform in life follows the nature of the planet that dominates us. Most of our relationships are according to our planetary affinities. Once we have understood the meaning of the planets we can comprehend the entire field of possibilities of human life.

SEQUENCE OF THE PLANETS

In Vedic astrology the seven major or visible planets are normally listed in order of the days they rule:

Sun	Moon	Mars	Mercury	Jupiter	Venus	Saturn
Sunday	Monday	Tuesday	Wednesday	Thursday	Friday	Saturday

This shows an interweaving of two sequences. The days of the inner planets which lie between the orbit of the Earth and the Sun are positioned between the outer planets.

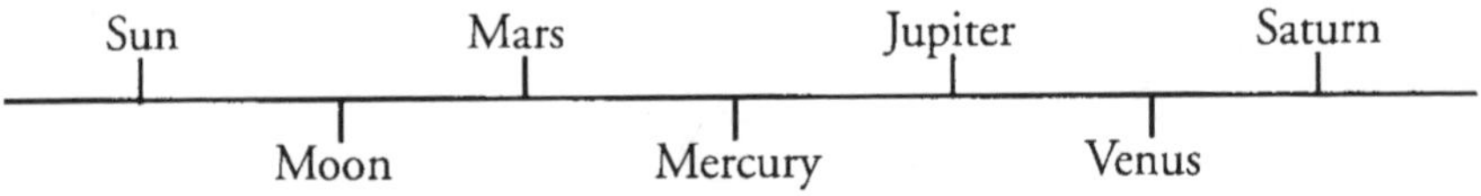

Each planet is given a certain number based upon this sequence:

1. Sun 2. Moon
3. Mars 4. Mercury 5. Jupiter 6. Venus 7. Saturn
8. Rahu 9. Ketu

These numbers correspond to the energies of the planets. The Sun is one, which is unity, the prime number from which all the others proceed. It is the origin, the guide, and the foundation. The Moon is two, the duality that is the basis for the workings of the mind and emotion. It is relationship, balance and interchange. Mars is three, the number of will and energy. It is power, penetration and decision. Mercury is four, the number of order, balance and reason. Jupiter is five, the number of law and intelligence in manifestation. Venus is six, the number of harmony, beauty and relationship. Saturn is seven, the number of control, limit and completion. Rahu is eight, the number of dispersion and new beginnings. Ketu is nine, the number of realization and liberation.

Planetary energy begins with the Sun and follows this sequence to Ketu at the end. Each planet represents a stage in the development and distribution of solar energy. Each planet can be understood through its respective number. Note, however, that other systems of planetary numerology exist within the Vedic system.

The Sun and the Moon, the two great luminaries, are the most important planets. Next in importance are Mars, Jupiter and Saturn as the major planets beyond the orbit of the Earth. Then come Venus and Mercury as the major planets within the orbit of the Earth and always close to the Sun.

The lunar nodes, north and south, called Rahu and Ketu, regarded as shadowy or secondary planets, are of tertiary importance. If we wish to use them, we can place the distant planets of Uranus, Neptune and Pluto after the nodes in significance.

PLANETS AND THE THREE GUNAS

From great Nature or Prakriti come the three primal qualities or *gunas* of *sattva*, *rajas* and *tamas*.

Sattva is the higher quality of the nature of light, lightness, clarity, harmony, balance and intelligence. It is the divine (devic) quality, and brings about the upward movement of the soul. It creates peace, love and faith and brings human beings into the spiritual life.

Rajas is the intermediate quality of the nature of energy, action, turbulence, disturbance, violence and passion. It is the demonic (asuric) quality, and keeps the soul in the middle worlds. It creates aggression and competition and causes the human being to seek worldly acquisition and achievement as the main goals in life.

Tamas is the lower or animal quality of the nature of inertia, darkness, dullness, obstruction, heaviness and lethargy. It is the animal quality that keeps the soul bound in the lower and unconscious realms. It brings about servitude, decay, domination and destruction and causes the human being to become harmful, useless, unproductive and unintelligent.

Each of these three qualities is necessary in nature. Tamas gives stability, as in the earth and the physical body. Rajas gives energy, as in the atmosphere and the vital body. Sattva gives light, as in the place of heaven and the mind.

Rajas and tamas, however, are out of place in the domain of the mind, which is the natural realm of sattva. Tamas becomes the ignorance and lack of attention that veil the mind. Rajas fuels the desire and fantasy that are projected through it. As astrology measures the mental quality or sattva of the person, tamasic and rajasic energies become negative in the chart.

All spiritual evolution consists of reducing rajas and tamas and increasing sattva. When sattva is pure, it allows for the perception of our true or Divine nature through which we go beyond the outer world of time and space to the eternal and the infinite.

A prevalence of sattvic planets in a chart gives ethical, religious and spiritual qualities and shows the ascent of the soul. A prevalence of rajasic planets gives worldly qualities and shows the soul in its state of attachment, seeking acquisition and achievement in the outer world. A prevalence of tamasic planets gives lower qualities and destructive tendencies, and shows the soul in its state of descent.

Planets and the Three Gunas

Sattva	Sun, Moon, Jupiter
Rajas	Mercury, Venus
Tamas	Mars, Saturn, Rahu, Ketu

The planets have secondary qualities as well. The Sun has some rajas, as it not only provides perception but gives energy. The Moon has some tamas or cloudiness to it. With their qualities of compassion and devotion, Mercury and Venus have some sattva. Mars and Ketu have some rajas, as they give energy and power of will. Rahu and Ketu are usually overpowered by the nature of the planets with which they associate.

The ultimate determination of the three gunas in a chart is complex. It is part of the ascertainment of the mental and spiritual nature of the person. It depends upon the nature of the soul as well. More evolved souls use the higher aspects of their planetary energies, while the less evolved gravitate toward the lower. Higher souls relate more to their sattvic planets, intermediate souls to their rajasic planets, and lower souls to tamasic influences. Hence some astrologers refuse to make any spiritual judgment of the person based upon the chart alone.

PLANETS AND THE FIVE ELEMENTS

From the three gunas arise the five elements. From sattva comes ether. From rajas come air and fire. From tamas come water and earth.

Elements and the Planets

Ether	Jupiter
Air	Saturn, Rahu
Fire	Sun, Mars, Ketu
Water	Moon, Venus
Earth	Mercury

The Sun represents fire and indicates the fire element in the chart in general. Yet as a dry planet, it contains some air as a secondary element. The Moon represents water and indicates the water element in the chart in general. Yet when weak in luminosity (close to the Sun), it tends to become airy or fiery depending upon its disposition.

Mars represents fire and indicates the fire element in the chart more specifically. Yet as a heavy planet it contains earth as its secondary element. Mercury is said by many to represent the element of earth in the chart, as it indicates basic earthly qualities of objective perception, commerce and communication. As a fast moving planet it is sometimes said to represent air. Yet as a changeable or mutable planet it takes upon itself the influence of the planets with which it is associated.

Jupiter, because of its spiritual nature, is said to represent ether. Yet as a heavy and liquid planet it can also represent water. Venus represents water and indicates more specifically the water element in the chart, as Mars does fire. Yet as a light and somewhat mobile planet it contains a secondary nature as air.

Saturn by its dry and nervous nature is said to represent air. But according to its attributes as dark, heavy, gross and coarse it may be said to rule over earth. Generally, when strong it gives earthly qualities, when weak or afflicted it creates air.

Rahu (the north lunar node) is said to be like Saturn and is more specifically airy, though like Saturn it can give the dark side of earth energy. Ketu (the south node) is said to be fiery like Mars but secondarily airy. As usual, we must judge the condition of the nodes through the planets that influence them because they are shadowy planets.

These elements refer to our nature in general: physical, mental and spiritual. None of them are necessarily good or bad, unlike the gunas, which imply a distinction of high and low. We can discriminate higher or lower types among each of the elements. A higher earth type, the sattvic type, would be a caretaker of the Earth, such as an environmentalist. A lower earth type, the tamasic type, would be a thief. But generally, too much of the lower elements, like earth, and earthly planets which are too strong, like Saturn, bring out the lower qualities of the soul, whereas a strong influence of the higher elements, like ether and air, and planets like Jupiter, raise the soul upwards.

KEY INDICATORS OF PLANETS

Each planet relates to various factors inwardly and outwardly. Their judgment depends upon how that planet is oriented in the chart. For example, the Sun is the significator of the father. If strong, one's father will usually be strong, healthy and successful. Naturally, each planet indicates many things. To be more specific, other factors, like various houses and their rulers, must be brought into consideration.

- SUN — father, ego, self, soul, individuality, rational mind, honor, status
- MOON — mother, emotions, personality, sociability, happiness, home, popularity
- MARS — brothers, friends, enemies, enmity, injury, energy, logic, science
- MERCURY — childhood, education, intellect, speech, commerce, vocation, adaptability

- JUPITER — husband (for women), guru, dharma, principle, wealth, fortune, grace, children, creativity, health
- VENUS — wife (for men), beloved, love, art, conveyances, beauty, comfort, charisma, charm
- SATURN — death, longevity, old age, disease, loss, sorrow, property, fate, limitation, obstruction, detachment
- RAHU — disease, psychic disturbances, collective trends, mass disturbances, epidemics
- KETU — injury, enmity, death, negation, knowledge, liberation, psychic or spiritual insight

PLANETS AS BENEFIC OR MALEFIC

Planets have long been classified as to whether their influence is benefic or malefic. This has been simplistically rendered as good or bad, according to a moralistic concept of good and evil. It has given rise to a stereotyped, judgmental or moralistic way of thinking, as if life were nothing but a school of reward and punishment, and it has spawned the misconception that the stars have no higher purpose than to administer justice to deviant mortals. Still, there is a truth behind these concepts that remains useful and important.

Benefic planets generally increase, promote, expand, or bring to fruition the affairs of the planets, signs, and houses that they influence. Malefic planets, on the other hand, generally decrease, obstruct, limit, or destroy the affairs of the planets, signs and houses that they affect. In a broad sense, one could say that malefic planets cause disease, difficulty, delay, conflict, separation, poverty and suffering. Benefic planets promote health, ease, comfort, peace, harmony, abundance and happiness. Yet in actual prediction, planetary influences combine in many different ways.

Malefic planets can function in a positive way by negating negative factors in the chart (like disease or poverty). Such instances of negative influences canceling each other in the chart represent great good fortune. Not only is good fortune gained but potential negative side effects are also neutralized. In the same way, benefic planets can function negatively. Too many benefic influences can render people weak and self-indulgent and make their life easy, superficial or without challenges.

In Vedic astrology, the nature of planets as benefic or malefic is not entirely fixed. There are two different ways of judging it. The first is what is called their natural status, Jupiter as benefic, Saturn as malefic, and so on.

This has been the main factor used in Western astrology. In Vedic astrology there is a second factor called temporal status, which is determined according to which sign governs the Ascendant in a particular chart. The nature of planets as positive or negative, benefic or malefic, creative or destructive, varies according to the particular houses those planets rule with respect to the Ascendant. For example, the ruler of the Ascendant, even if it is Saturn, becomes benefic in its temporal status (as for a Capricorn Ascendant). This will be discussed in detail in the section on the houses.

Moreover, planetary nature changes through association, through the aspects between planets, and through the nature of the signs and houses in which they are located. Friendship and enmity between planets also comes into consideration here. A preponderance of malefic influences and aspects can neutralize a benefic and vice versa.

Some astrologers have suggested that the terms benefic and malefic be done away with, as they sound moralistic. Such terms as expansive and contractive planets may be preferable, as these writers suggest, or planets that create or resolve difficulties. Yet the capacity of badly disposed planets to do harm should not be underestimated. Nor can the influences of such difficult planets be very easily neutralized. Similarly, the capacity of well-disposed planets to bring unexpected benefits should not be overlooked. Planets may not function in a simplistic way but they do reflect forces beyond our control that can raise us up or bring us down in ways we could never do of our own accord.

Which planets we consider to be benefic or malefic also depends upon what we want in life. Life has many domains, and what is good for one field of life may not be good for another. For example, what is good for wealth may not be good for spiritual development. For the spiritual life, which depends upon detachment, malefics like Saturn can be very positive in destroying our desires and aid in driving our consciousness inward.

A planet may give wealth or prestige but weaken one's health, furthering some of the outer goals of life but not all of them. We can observe this in regular human life, where overwork may be good for one's business but not for one's vitality. The planets must be as complex in their functioning as life itself.

Planets as Benefic and Malefic, Natural Disposition

Greater Benefic	Jupiter
Greater Malefics	Saturn, Rahu
Lesser Benefic	Venus
Lesser Malefics	Mars, Ketu
General Benefics	Moon, Mercury
General Malefic	Sun

The Moon is variable, being a strong benefic when away from the Sun and bright in nature. Yet it becomes malefic when close to the Sun. It is more benefic when waxing and more malefic than waning. Specifically, I consider the Moon to be benefic except when within 60 degrees of its conjunction with the Sun, and until it is at least 30 degrees past the Sun (some books count the Moon as malefic when it is within 72 degrees of the Sun). Yet even when close to the Sun, its benefic nature can still come out in a good sign and with good aspects. Mercury, like the Moon, is a general benefic, but, being mutable in nature, it takes on the nature of the planets with which it is associated, and so is sometimes regarded as neutral.

Some astrologers consider Mars to be more malefic than Saturn. This is because the malefic effects of Mars manifest more quickly, like its ability to cause accidents or injuries. However, the long term malefic effect of Saturn is greater.

The lunar nodes, Rahu and Ketu, are generally more malefic than their planetary counterparts, Saturn and Mars, but as shadowy planets they are more likely to take on the nature of planets with which they are associated. In this way they can sometimes function as benefics.

A planet's natural disposition as benefic or malefic can be overridden by other factors, yet we find that natural benefics always do some good, even when otherwise malefically disposed. Natural malefics, similarly, always do some harm, even when otherwise benefically disposed.

These dispositions of planets generally agree with those of traditional Western astrology. The most notable difference is the Sun, which Western astrology usually views as a benefic. In Vedic astrology it can sometimes be the most malefic of the planets. The Sun as a powerful and hot planet does have a destructive effect. It tends to limit the affairs of the house in which it is located. The Sun in the Fifth House tends to deny children or create difficulties with them. In the Seventh House it can give separation or delays in relationship. Western astrology also recognizes such effects. Planets too close to the Sun, or combust, usually do not give good results. The Moon loses its strength and becomes weak the closer it gets to the Sun.

However, the Sun in Vedic astrology is regarded as a sattvic or spiritual planet. This makes it different from the other malefics, which are regarded as tamasic or unspiritual in quality. In this sense of spiritual quality, the Sun is a good planet and gives high values like self-esteem, integrity and independence.

DISPOSITORSHIP

A planet is said to be the *dispositor* of planets that are located in the signs that it rules. Generally, it will rule over them and make them function according to its nature. If Saturn is in Sagittarius, for example, Jupiter will gain power over it and Saturn will be less malefic than usual. But Jupiter will also come to function a little like Saturn as well. If there are several strongly benefic or malefic planets in a sign, their nature can outweigh that of their ruler, who will come to function like them. When, for example, Saturn and Mars are located in Cancer, the sign of the Moon, the Moon may take on some of their negative nature. In order to determine whether a planet is benefic or malefic, we must also consider whether it is the dispositor of benefic or malefic planets.

By this principle of dispositorship, any planet can come to function like any other. Jupiter can function like malefic Saturn and Rahu, while Saturn can function like a benefic Venus. The planets are points of transmission and the energies that they transmit depend as much upon their associations as upon their given nature.

One planet may become the final dispositor of all the planets in the chart. This occurs if all planets are in signs ruled by one planet or in those of planets located in its signs. Such a planet usually becomes very strong and often marks the planetary type of the person.

5

Descriptions of the Planets

The Sun

I know that great being who has the effulgence of the Sun beyond darkness. Only knowing him can one go beyond death; there is no other path for the journey.

Shukla Yajur Veda 31.18

The Sun has yellow eyes which dispense honey, his body is square, he is pure, bilious (pitta) in constitution, intelligent, masculine and tends towards baldness.

Parashara 3.23

The ancient Vedic religion, like all the religions of the ancient world, was a religion of the Sun. The worship of the Sun was primary to all ancient cultures, including our ancient Indo-European ancestors the Greeks, Celts, Germans and Slavs. It is the oldest and most natural form of human religion, as religion itself is a seeking of the light. As such, solar religion is also the religion of the future as we return once more to our spiritual roots in the coming ages of light.

The Sun is a grand symbol, a profound psychological and spiritual archetype. The Sun is the visible form and presence of the deity. It is the image, the face of Truth itself. The Sun is God, the Divine incarnate in nature. The Sun is the Deva, the deity. To the ancients the Sun was the One God, which was the unity of truth. In our birth charts the Sun shows our divinity, our unity and point of focus, our center and central purpose in life. According to the solar religion of the *Vedas*, the Sun is the Atman, the Self of the entire universe. The Sun is the Divine Being who dwells in the hearts of all beings as the true Self. The Sun symbolizes cosmic intelligence, pure consciousness or the enlightened Mind.

The winged disc of the Sun was used throughout the ancient world to symbolize the soul and its transcendence of time. The Sun was worshiped in human representation as the cosmic person made of gold, representing the true human being that contains all the Gods within himself. This solar person was the basis of the image worship of the Hindu religion, particular the form of Vishnu or Surya-Narayana.

The savior worshiped in ancient cultures was the son of the Sun, the presence of the Sun on Earth, the incarnation of the Divine light of truth. This symbolism is found even in Christianity, where Christ is born on the winter solstice, the day the Sun is reborn, as the days once more begin to get longer. It is found in Buddhism, where the Buddha as the enlightened or solar being turns the wheel of the law, the Sun wheel.

The first man, the father of the human race, the Hindu Manu, is also the son of the Sun. He was not a fallen Adam but a rishi or enlightened master. The Sun is our spiritual father, our origin and final place of rest. At death the ancients prayed that they might merge into the Sun, to follow the path of light to the Gods and to the supreme light.

The human being is meant to manifest the Divine light on Earth, to bring the light of truth into the material realm. As such, we are all children of the Sun, doing the cosmic labor of manifesting the light. We are portions of the sunlight projected on Earth to further the will of the Divine Sun in its creative play. To be conscious as souls, we must awaken to this duty.

The Sun dwells within the hearts of all of us as our inner Sun, our inner light and life. Without this inner light, no perception could be possible. Without this inner life, we could not even breathe. Just as there is the movement of the outer Sun through the constellations of the zodiac, so there is the movement of the inner Sun through the chakras of our subtle or astral body which reflects our birth chart.

Nor is the Sun merely the luminary of our local solar system. The Sun is our local manifestation of the cosmic or universal light. It brings to us the light, life and love from all the stars, whose children we are. It reflects the light from the galactic center, the central Sun of our galaxy. It is connected with the Suns in subtle realms as well as this physical world. It is a doorway to all the domains and powers of light. All the planets shine with the reflected light of the Sun; they represent different solar rays. There is only one real light, which is the Sun, which is all lights, and which is inwardly the light of the mind.

In Vedic astrology the Sun is the most important factor for determining the spiritual life. It represents the soul, the causal body or reincarnating entity whose will is behind our fate. It is also the mind or the mental principle on a lower level as reason, discernment, clarity and illumination.

A well-placed Sun gives intelligence, perception, and strength of will and character. It affords endurance, stamina, vitality, positive spirit, direction, courage, conviction, confidence, leadership, independence and straightforwardness. Without it, whatever we may do or accomplish in life will not be ours and will not give us inner strength or peace. A poorly placed Sun gives lack of intelligence, poor perception, weakness of will and character. It creates lack of endurance, low vitality, melancholy, fear, dependency or servitude, deviousness or dishonesty.

A malefically disposed Sun creates pride, arrogance, and tyranny. When it is too strong, it creates many of the same problems as Mars. It can give a deceptive charisma and a manipulative personality. When the Sun is strong we outshine everyone else, for good or ill depending on whether its disposition is benefic or malefic.

A weak but spiritually disposed Sun makes us receptive, self-effacing and eager to do good. But we lack confidence and come under the rule of other people. We seek to sacrifice ourselves but do not know what to give ourselves over to.

The Sun rules the heart, the organ of circulation and vitality, and a weak Sun may give problems with that organ. Inwardly the heart is the seat of intelligence that regulates the life, breath, aspiration and perception. The Sun in the chart shows what we really are in our hearts. The Sun shows who we are in ourselves as individuals, quite apart from how we may appear or what roles we may play.

The Sun indicates the level of our self-manifestation. On the lower level, the Sun represents the ego. It shows our impulses towards power, prestige, fame, honor, respect, authority and control — all the things that give value and preeminence to our individual selves. It shows where we shine, how we shine and in what we shine, how we illumine.

On the higher level, the Sun as our soul shows our aspirations, our creativity, our seeking for light and truth. The Sun is who we really are, and the Sun in the birth chart focuses on the problem of identity, the search for the true Self, the great enquiry "Who am I?" The Sun directs us towards the yoga of knowledge for the revelation of our inner being.

In terms of family relationships, the Sun represents the father. We can read through it the life of our father, our relationship to him and his influence upon us. It is the role of the father to shape our sense of self, to provide us with direction and self-worth in life. The absence, weakness or failure of the father in modern culture is behind the identity and self-image problems so many of us suffer from today. The son needs a beneficent father to give him a sense of self-strength, self-mastery and capacity to function capably in the world. The daughter needs a good father to give her the sense of self-worth, integrity and the capacity to be herself in the world. We can judge this by the Sun in the birth chart.

The Sun shows the kinds of authority and the values that shape our lives. The Sun represents the king, the president or political leader. It can indicate the government in general and whatever favors or promotions come through it. It represents law and order on lower or higher levels, rule and reason.

The Sun can represent spiritual authority and, along with Jupiter, can help us understand the nature of the guru or the spiritual teaching we are most likely to follow. It shows our guiding light, principles, values and precepts.

The inner purpose of the Sun in the chart is to aid in our transcendence. It takes us beyond outer things, negating their limitation. It may raise us to a high level in life, but it will push us inwardly beyond that. It operates to negate all things into the self. The Sun tends to deny the ordinary activities of life, but only to command the extraordinary, the highest and the best.

The Sun gives the power of independence, the capacity to become a value or a light unto ourselves. It promotes the growth of intelligence. While destructive of form and expression, it elevates the being and the intrinsic worth of things. It does not always give abundance, but it does give quality. It gives power, fame, mastery and glory, but not always wealth or emotional happiness.

In Sanskrit, there are innumerable names for the Sun. Most commonly he is called *Surya*, which means the father, progenitor, or enlivener, the source of energy, motivation and inspiration, like the Greek Sun god Apollo. He is also called Savitar, which has a similar meaning and further indicates the Divine will in creation.

The Moon

The Moon is watery and airy (kapha and vata) in constitution,
she is intuitive and has a round body; she has a
luminous countenance, sweet speech, is changeable and moody.

Parashara 3.24

As the Sun represents the cosmic masculine force, the Moon indicates the cosmic feminine force. The Sun is the God or Deva and the Moon is the Goddess or Devi. The Sun is the spirit and the Moon is its creative force, which becomes matter; the Sun is Shiva and the Moon is Shakti. Together, they represent the great primal duality as masculine and feminine, active and passive, mind and body, day and night, will and love. As the Sun is the Divine Father and creator, the Moon is the Divine Mother and creatrix. As the Sun rules time, the Moon governs space; as the Sun rules fire, the Moon rules water.

As the Sun is the Self, the Moon is the mind. According to the *Vedas*, the Moon was born from the mind (Sanskrit *manas*). Yet the Sanskrit term for mind has a different meaning than the usual Western one. Manas includes emotion and means feeling — consciousness in general, that which reflects upon things. It is often a general term for the entire mental field. As the Self is the point of central clarity and perception, the mind is the field of conception and manifestation. Its action is thought, care, and consideration, as well as musing, dreaming, and imagining.

The Sun represents the Self, which is our independent, directly perceiving consciousness. The Moon shows the mind, which is our dependent, reflective, usually conditioned consciousness. As the Sun represents who we are in ourselves, the Moon shows how we relate to others, our social consciousness. As the Sun represents character or individuality, the Moon indicates our personality.

The Sun shows the causal body that indicates the will of the soul to be achieved in incarnation. The Moon shows the astral body, the field of impressions or past karma operative behind the present incarnation. Hence the Moon is an important karmic indicator.

The Sun represents the present and future, the Moon indicates the past. The Sun shows what we are and are meant to be. The Moon shows who we have been and what we bring with us from the past. It can show positive resources from the past which give us greater consciousness in life, or it can show negative influences from the past that bind us to regressive patterns of behavior.

Afflictions to the Moon show personality disorders, difficulties in relating to other people, and emotional disturbances. A badly placed Moon gives wrong imagination, hallucinations, and psychological turbulence. It creates lunacy, as our language reflects. A badly afflicted Moon shows poor heredity, poor family background, bad education and other traumas to the emotional nature, which can be difficult to overcome.

The Moon shows our capacity to receive, to be affected. Of all the planets, it is the most easily hurt and indicates our general vulnerability. A strong Moon shows sensitivity, receptivity, caring for others and a nurturing attitude in life. It gives emotional maturity, responsibility and the capacity to have a beneficial effect upon society.

The Moon, like the Sun, is a sattvic or spiritual planet. It gives faith, love, openness, surrender, peace and happiness. It imparts the grace of the Goddess, the Divine Mother. It makes us pliable, sensitive and contemplative. It causes us to do good for the sake of others and to be obedient to higher principles. People with such a spiritual Moon usually have a strong connection with a traditional religion and may have had monastic past lives. They have sweet, tolerant and humane dispositions which can become saintly. They are among the easiest people to be around and the least critical, seeing the good in all.

The main weakness of the religious lunar type is that such people can become too orthodox. They may rely unquestioningly on an authority that does not represent the truth. They like organization, ritual and tradition and represent the best of it, but when that tradition has become negative, they are often unable to question it, much less break away from it. They may be more concerned about being good than about finding the truth.

As a sensitive and mutable planet, the Moon can be easily influenced and overcome by other planetary energies. Saturn can darken or depress it, or give it detachment. Rahu can cloud it or cause us to lose power over our minds, which it rules. Mars brings conflict and aggression into the lunar mind.

The Moon represents inertia as well as responsiveness. Through our lunar sensitivity we can become accustomed to a life of pain, sorrow or ignorance, as well as to one of joy and truth. The Moon is our capacity to endure in any environment, which can become a negative factor through which we accept subordination, subservience or degradation.

The mind is a dependent consciousness. It has no real nature of its own. As such, it can function in one of two ways: it can reflect the inner nature of things or it can merely reflect the outer appearance. It can mold itself after the inner light of truth, the spiritual Sun, or after external influences and authorities, the outer or social lights (which the planets can project upon it).

In its higher nature as pure, receptive awareness the mind is one with the Self, the Moon and Sun are one in function, and the consciousness of the human being is integrated. Such a well-placed and spiritual Moon is often found in the charts of yogis and other conscious individuals. Functioning in its lower nature as impressionability to mass influences and collective traumas, an ill-placed and malefic Moon may frequently be found in the charts of criminals, the insane, or those suffering from neurological disorders.

As an indicator of the feminine nature in general, the Moon gives beauty and attractiveness. It can make for a good wife or homemaker. When more intellectually disposed, it gives a broad grasp of many fields of knowledge and, like Venus (which resembles it), affords artistic accomplishment or religious devotion.

On the level of human relationships, the Moon represents the mother. Through it we can read her nature, her influence and her longevity. It also shows our birth, and through it we can read the difficulty or ease of our birth and the factors that brought it about. The Moon indicates the home, or where we feel at home. It shows happiness and the state of the emotions. It shows where we place our care and affection.

The Moon has love and friendliness for all. Such a benefic Moon is found in the charts of doctors, healers or psychologists, as well as good mothers and wives. It gives the ability to focus our attention on the needs of others.

While the Sun stands alone, the Moon is the friend of all. The Moon measures our popularity, our social status and capacity to influence the masses. In this capacity it is, like the Sun, an important planet for political influence. Like the Sun, a strong Moon can give power or preeminence. It can outshine the other planets, sometimes even the Sun. Whereas the Sun creates the king or strong-willed leader, the Moon creates a good administrator or a leader open to the needs of the masses.

The Moon is our social nature and indicates our social concerns of interchange and communication. It shows our general propensity for relationship, how we receive others and view society. It gives creativity and expression to the mind, the capacity to influence others as well as to be influenced ourselves.

While the Sun projects the seed, the Moon gives birth. While the Sun stands alone and overcomes any planet with which it is associated, the Moon brings together and accepts into herself any planetary energy with which she is conjoined.

Lunar people are friendly, caring, and nurturing, but not always honest, consistent or clear. While lunar people work through cooperation and mutual help, family and friends, solar people rely upon the power of their own character, the strength of their own will. As solar types may become egoistic, lunar types may become circumscribed within a family, clan, or group and be unable to work with anyone outside it.

The Moon governs water — water as a psychological symbol, water in our own body, or water in the world. She sustains our fluidity of body and mind. She allows us to flow. As such, she is she creative flow of life, the stream of awareness, the waters of creation from whose well we must drink to find contentment in life. She is the water of delight that bestows happiness in life. In her influence is love and communion.

The main name for the Moon in Sanskrit is *Chandra*, the giver of delight and rhythm as the great cycles of nature, like the tides, reflect her. The Moon is also called *Soma*. This refers to our inner nectar of happiness that alone has the power to calm the mind and refresh the nerves. The Moon gives the inner contentment through which alone longevity and rejuvenation can proceed. She is the general beauty, bliss, communion and communication from which the more specific energies of Mercury and Venus arise.

Mars

Mars is cruel, has blood-red eyes, is ill mannered yet generous,
is bilious (pitta) *in constitution,*
is prone to anger and possesses a thin waist and body.

Parashara 3.25

Mars is the great planet of energy. As Venus governs our affections, our emotional and vital impressionability, Mars relates to our passions, our emotional and vital capacity for self-projection. We could say that Venus governs our incoming emotions, our capacity to receive emotion; Mars rules our outgoing emotions, our capacity to project emotion.

Mars is the male and Venus is the female. They are the positive and negative, the active and passive sides of our feeling nature. Venus is emotional sensitivity, which can become refinement. Mars is emotional excitability, which can become violence. Thus, generally, Venus represents the benefic and Mars the malefic side of the emotions.

Whereas the Sun and Moon represent our masculine and feminine natures generally, Mars and Venus do so specifically. They are the planets of sexuality and the relationship between the sexes can be read through them, whereas the luminaries have a parental influence stemming from a male and female nature which is more general. When the influences of Mars and Venus combine, particularly in fixed signs, the sexual drive can become very strong and may dominate the person.

Mars is the planet of power, strength, courage, and aggression, which measures our ability to project force in life. A strong Mars provides us the energy, independence, will and self-confidence to carry out our endeavors, qualities it shares with the Sun. Without it we have no real interests, passions, motivations, or determination, no ability to carry anything out to its full accomplishment.

On the negative side, this same aggression brings about competition, argument, and conflict — a placing of our own personal will-to-power over the good of others. Mars has always been known as the great God of War. He can make a person militaristic or violent, turn them into a soldier, or even into a criminal if malefically disposed. He can cause us to inflict death on others. He can also, if he afflicts the factors representing the self in the chart (like the Ascendant and its ruler) bring injury and accident upon us.

The malefic nature of Mars is well known in most instances of violent death, whether accidental or intentional. Mars can also indicate premature death in a chart, as with the loss of the partner, particularly the loss of a woman's husband. He is the general significator for injury, accident, and conflict. Mars creates misunderstandings, arguments, and litigation. In this regard Mars is the selfish will that does not take into account the views and needs of others.

Yet these difficulties come about because Mars insists upon greater independence, differentiation and clarity of views. He makes us certain about who we are and who our friends are. He causes discontent and seeking until we discover the real source of power within us.

Mars is the significator of brothers, friends and alliances. These include any association of common interests to achieve a common goal. In a lower sense, this is the alliance of soldiers or even thieves. But the Mars energy of working together in discipline is necessary for any common endeavor. Mars is the leader or the central energy of determination, upon which the right organization of forces depends. All energy requires a focus for its proper application. Mars grants this direction.

Mars indicates arms and muscles and gives physical prowess. A good Mars is necessary for physical strength and athletic performance. It gives sexual vitality to the male. A weak Mars can cause impotence or lack of manly characteristics and make any accomplishment difficult.

Mars is a critical, perceptive and discriminating planet. On the positive side, he gives good skills at speech and oratory as well as good logical faculties. The lawyer, politician and scientist need such a strong Mars. Mars similarly gives mechanical skills. He is the machinist, engineer, miner, chemist, or electrician. He invents things to help us get the job done better.

Mars rules tools, weapons, machines and their usage. He is the planet of research and development. Modern culture is based upon technology and thus has a strong Martian influence; hence our tendency towards war and monstrous weapons. Technology and war go together as aspects of Mars energy we have not yet understood or controlled properly. Mars causes us to develop energy but it does not necessarily give us the wisdom or love to use it properly. It tends to regard power as an end in itself whereas it is really only a means.

On a higher level, Mars directs us to the yogas of knowledge and energy, and gives self-discipline and asceticism. A strong and spiritual Mars is good for the practice of rituals and yogic techniques, methods of directing occult and spiritual energies. We find such a Mars in the charts of those drawn to energetic yogas or Tantric practices. Mars types like a more dramatic, challenging and daring path in all fields of life.

Mars is the son of the Earth in Hindu mythology. He is called *Kuja*, "the one born from the Earth." He is the secret flame hidden in matter. His energy demands manifestation in material form. But he can also bring out the negative or dark sides of the Earth energy, the titanic primordial powers, the asuras or demons of the abyss who wish to destroy the creation and bring things back to the state of raw chaos. This inertia or tamasic quality behind Mars energy must not be forgotten.

Combined with Jupiter, the positive side of Mars comes out as the capacity to make great achievements in life in harmony with law and truth. Combined with Saturn, its negative side usually predominates, creating selfish, perverted or criminal tendencies, particularly when there are no balancing factors. Where balancing factors do exist, this combination creates discipline and the capacity for great accomplishments.

Mars is the planet of goal-oriented action. As is one's ultimate goal and highest value in life, so is one's action. It is important to subordinate our Martian energy, which is indispensable for a creative life, to spiritual principles and to the influence of spiritual planets. In this way Mars affords the practical application of energy on a spiritual level in yoga and meditation. It can give insight and inquiry on an inner as well as outer level.

In short, most of the qualities of Mars relate to his nature as fire. He can burn or give warmth, give light or create smoke, disturb or illumine, but unlike the Sun, who is self-luminous, Mars requires some fuel in order to burn. We must make sure that we use our own limitations as fuel for the fire, rather than something we have taken from others.

Mercury

Mercury has the best appearance, is witty, fond of jokes and laughter, and is learned. He takes upon himself the nature and constitution of the planets with which he is associated.

Parashara 3.26

Mercury, as the great messenger of the Gods, represents speech, communication and commerce. In his lower function he organizes and articulates material resources. On a higher level he connects us with our inner capacities, the deeper powers of the mind.

As Jupiter represents the higher or abstract mind, Mercury indicates the lower or concrete mind, the intellect or informational mentality. However, Mercury is not limited to this. He also shows the higher mind in its discriminating ability and connects us with the Divine Word or word of truth. Mercury governs names. On a lower level, these are the outer appearances of title and personality, which are illusory. On a higher level, they are the names of God that connect us to the universal aspect of things.

Mercury governs writing, education, calculation, and directed thought. He is the fastest moving of the planets and thus is indicative of quick comprehension, facility, ease and plasticity in expression. Mercury provides for the quick correlation of ideas, the fast interchange of information or of things of value. He is mental and nervous energy in its articulate activity. Therefore Mercury in the chart shows our intellectual powers and the degree of mental development in life.

Mercury is a child and indicates the state of childhood generally, particularly the period between infancy and adolescence. Afflictions to Mercury can cause health problems in childhood, troubles in the home life or difficulty at school. The mind and nervous system may suffer, as well as the lungs.

As a planet of commerce, Mercury represents trade or articles of trade, including money. He is helpful in both acquiring and keeping wealth, as he helps us organize it. He is necessary whenever there is an exchange of ideas or commodities. He sees the value of open markets and free communication and is not restricted by boundaries of race, nation, caste or belief. However, he can be attached to his own opinions and calculations, his own gains and losses.

Mercury breaks down barriers between people and reveals a common humanity and common human needs. As such, he possesses a certain compassion and sense of equality based not so much upon sentiment as upon objectivity and practicality. Afflicted, he is willing to exploit people, though he will often improve their outer condition in the process.

Mercury is an important factor for determining our vocation, for that is what we do in life to communicate with others; our vocation is our interchange with society. Mercury shows how we appear and how we function in the network of transactions that makes up the world of things and ideas. In this regard, his representation of our education or training comes into play. He is the child that is the father of the man. Our Mercury establishes our values in life. Material values like prices and standards of measurement, artistic values, and spiritual values are different aspects of Mercury.

Mercury is the most mutable of the planets. He easily takes upon himself the nature of the other planets with which he is associated, for good or for ill. He tends to value communication and public opinion more than truth, and become dependent on whatever is the strongest environmental influence. He is the mind that has no real nature of its own but reflects whatever it considers to be the reality, which may be no more than the impressions of the senses.

A weak Mercury makes us rationalize things to suit our purpose. It creates immaturity, naivete and folly. It can create dishonesty, a lack of properly defined boundaries. This may make a person a thief — not because he is cruel, but because he does not respect anything as belonging to another. Such individuals take what they need according to a childish view of life that the world should provide for them. They have no objective perception and are caught in childish fantasies and may even believe that what they have taken was really given to them or merited by them.

In this regard, Mercury is like the Moon — who, in Vedic astrological tradition, is said to be his father. Mercury is the rational conscious mind that is only the most articulate part of the subconscious mind (the Moon). He is the thinking mind that does not perceive of its own accord, but merely organizes ideas. If the mind orients itself toward the perception of truth, the vision of the eternal, then it will see the falseness of the external world and the reality of the inner consciousness. If it orients itself to the images of the senses as reality, then it will see the outer world as real and create a materialistic view of life. If, however, it orients itself to our selfish fears and desires as reality, it will create illusion, a neurotic or even schizophrenic view of life.

In Sanskrit, Mercury is *Budha*, which means intelligence or cognition, and relates to the *buddhi*, the faculty of determination whereby we discern the real from the unreal (and which, when fully awakened, creates and "enlightened one" or Buddha). When this faculty judges reality not by appearances but by discerning the transient from the eternal, then it functions rightly and the higher power of Mercury is revealed. When it discriminates names and forms, we become caught in the apparent reality of the external world.

In the higher sense, Mercury is this faculty of truth determination that discriminates the truth from illusion. This is the most precise and perfect functioning of the mind. In this higher activity Mercury, the mind, is Vishnu, the pervasive consciousness who is also the Divine son, the guiding cosmic intelligence and source of the great teachers and avatars.

A good Mercury gives good humor and psychological balance. He imparts a mental adaptability that is also playful. He is the trickster but can become deceptive. When afflicted Mercury becomes the fool, the idiot. Sometimes, even when wise, he will play the fool to express his adaptability and wit and to learn what would otherwise be hidden from him. Under a strong negative Saturn influence Mercury can lose its power and show lack of intelligence.

Afflictions to Mercury do not always give lack of intelligence or intellect, however. They may cause some other harm, like speech defects, nervous system disorders or neurosis. Other planets, like Jupiter, can give good intelligence, but without a strong Mercury there will be difficulty in expressing it, particularly through the written word. Mercury determines our expression in life. Of what value is what we do or who we are if it cannot be in some way communicated or shared?

Mercury is very important in modern culture and represents one of its most beneficial powers — the need to establish open communication that must lead to a world culture. Telephone, radio, television and computers are products of Mercurial needs, aligned with the engineering capacity of Mars. Yet so far we remain caught in the lower domain of Mercury and are only sharing superficial wealth and information, not communing with our deeper Self. We are swamped with massive and usually trivial data through the development of the lower Mercury principle through the mass media.

The practice of astrology requires a strong Mercury for its needs of calculation and communication. As our principle of balance, Mercury is often the point at which we can change our lives for higher purposes.

Jupiter

Jupiter has large limbs, is heavy, has yellow hair and eyes; his constitution is phlegmatic (kapha), he is intelligent and endowed with all the branches of learning.

Parashara 3.27

Jupiter is well known as the most helpful, generous and benefic of the planets. The votaries of astrology have always sought his grace. In Sanskrit, he is called Guru, the spiritual teacher or the guide. He signifies dharma, the law of our inner nature, which is the law of creative evolution and self-realization. He shows our principles in life, our guiding light of truth. The extent and nature of one's principles can be measured by the disposition of Jupiter in the chart.

Jupiter indicates such domains of principle as law, religion and philosophy. He is a spiritual and ethical (sattvic) planet, which insists upon the pursuit and support of the good. He establishes our good in life and, through his influence, that goodness comes to us.

Jupiter is the planet of intelligence — not the intellect that depends upon information or refined discernment (and which is more generally indicated by Mercury), but the formless intelligence that goes back to eternal laws and ultimately to the eternal itself. He represents our sense of the enduring and the extent to which we are aware of and live according to cosmic intelligence. He represents the immanent Divine spirit that establishes and upholds the laws of nature.

Jupiter is the planet of creativity. He signifies outer creativity, such as our children. From Jupiter the state of our children is to be ascertained — their number, sex, health, and our relationships with them. Yet he is also creativity in the inner sense. He gives powers of expression that can produce anything from philosophies to institutions (though he seldom produces art, for this is under Venus). Creativity springs from our inner principles, which are determined by Jupiter. He is expansive and loves to share; his delight is in ever greater unfoldment.

As Mercury tends to show our outer career in life, how we relate to society on a practical level, Jupiter indicates our inner career, where we really find our personal fulfillment and what we enjoy doing. He indicates our spiritual mission in life, while Mercury represents our outer expression. With a good Jupiter but without a good Mercury, one may be wise inside but will outwardly appear unwise. Unlike Mercury, Jupiter does not give much attention to detail, and so may not allow us to articulate ourselves with clarity. His concern is more with doing the work right than with explaining how it is rightly done.

Jupiter represents joy in living, the positive spirit. He is the great optimist who always sees the good. In him all sorrow, depression and melancholy are overcome or turned into a learning experience. Jupiter is the planet of luck, grace, favor and fortune. He gives wealth, abundance, prosperity and success. In the lower sense, he gives fortune on the material plane, for it is the daring optimist who succeeds in the end. He is also indicative of good karma, unexpected rewards. Those who win at races or lotteries or have great inheritances usually have a well-placed Jupiter.

In the higher sense, Jupiter is the Divine grace that can fulfill all of our needs without our seeking. He gives religious merit and spiritual beneficence. When Jupiter is with us, all life and the entire universe is with us because he is that cosmic beneficence. On a physical level, Jupiter is the planet of positive health. He makes us active in a healthy way and attunes us with the joy of nature. He gives vigor, vitality and a strong immune system.

On the negative side, however, we can become overly optimistic through the expansive Jupiter nature when it is afflicted. We will imagine the best and not guard ourselves properly. We will be vulnerable to the deceptive schemes of others. We can over-extend ourselves, go beyond our resources, be overly generous or spend too much. Our speculations will prove faulty. We will try to do too much and succeed in doing nothing. We may suffer from unexpected bad luck, bad karma, trouble with authorities and institutions, or loss in litigation.

A Jupiter which functions too outwardly can make us materialistic, enamored of wealth and caught in conventional values and beliefs. We may become self-satisfied, too content and caught within the status quo. Jupiter is a joyous planet, but when wrongly placed it can get us caught in the pursuit of pleasure and luxury, much like Venus. While the pleasure of Venus is largely sexual, that of Jupiter more often concerns groups and crowds.

Jupiter likes music and can indicate musical talent. He likes shows, ceremonies, parades and rituals. He can make us into showmen. On a lower level, he likes parties and can make us self-indulgent. With his love of expansive energy, his influence can make a good entertainer. His happiness is in sharing, even when unspiritually oriented; he will cause us to drink with our friends and pay for the drinks.

On a higher level, Jupiter indicates the priest and is concerned with propriety, formality and hierarchy. He can make us enamored of ceremony, ritual and display. In Sanskrit he is also called *Brihaspati*, the original priest or Brahmin. Jupiter is the great planet of aspiration. He shows our faith in life and can indicate the religion we follow or the form of the Divine we are naturally inclined to worship.

Jupiter shows our devotion and dedication in life. As such, it often signifies the husband in a woman's chart. It will show his nature, his health, and her relationship with him. However, these significations are more relevant to Hindu society, where marriage has followed family and religious sanction. In the West, where marriage is a matter of choice or passion, Mars is often more indicative of a woman's partner.

Jupiter reveals the expansiveness of our spirit, just as Saturn indicates our capacity to contract or concentrate. It is no wonder that people all over the world have always sought the energy of this planet for inner as well as outer prosperity and creativity. It is the energy of grace in our chart that we can use to further our aims in life, which should be the aim of life itself for the overflowing of beneficence and love.

Jupiter's influence functions better if tempered with that of the Sun or Saturn, which are more stern and realistic. All planets, even Jupiter, represent energies that are one-sided and require proper balancing for true harmony.

Venus

Venus is joyful in spirit, possesses a beautiful body, is splendorous and has lovely eyes; she is the inspirer of poets, is watery and airy in constitution (kapha and vata), and has curly hair.

Parashara

Venus manifests the feminine spirit; she is well known as the Goddess of love and beauty. Our Venus shows our affection and sense of harmony in life. In the chart of the male, she represents the wife or lover. She is our appreciation of the beautiful and as such represents our aesthetic sense.

Venus is the significator of art, poetry, painting, music and dance. She is our muse in life, our sense of the beloved that draws out our creative expression. She indicates our sensitivity, refinement and gentleness.

On the lower or outward level, Venus shows our seeking for pleasure, comfort and luxury. She represents the pleasure of the senses and the comforts of the body. She gives sexual attraction and serves to make either the woman or the man more appealing to the opposite sex. She brings wealth as an adornment. She is beauty, style and elegance; the refinement of wealth and not just crude accumulation. Her concern is not just with quantity but with quality and good taste. She likes gems, antiques and things of special value. She wants things not just for the joy of possessing them, but to have the adulation of others.

Yet Venus is also inclined to be vain, superficial and affected — her loveliness can become a mere show. She likes not only to exhibit herself and her beauty, but also to display the adornments which serve to embellish her. She demands that we please her and that we be pleasing to her. She can become the pleasure that dissipates, exhausts and debilitates, the self-indulgence that can destroy us.

In this regard, Venus is the seductress. Her web can catch our energy like a spider and drain away our fire, our positive will in life, as we pursue her favor, which is fickle or hard to get and impossible to keep. She is dreamy, wispy and elusive, and controls us simply because we are always seeking her. She may never let us attain her, for her joy is in being desired, not in being possessed.

Inwardly, Venus is the morning star, the light of inspiration that is the first spark of the Sun of truth. Venus is our aspiration to the good, the beautiful and the pure, our devotion to truth. She is our love, which in its true nature is the love of truth. She is our sensitivity, which becomes sensuality through its impressionability; but her basic nature is good.

Such a pure Venus comes out in association with Jupiter and Mercury. Saturn also can help refine and spiritualize Venus. Her vain side manifests itself in alliance with Mars, which causes an excess of passion, emotion, sexuality and sensuality.

Venus shows our natural tendency to beautify things, to make things reflect their pure or astral forms. Our Venus works on our world to bring it into harmony with its inner meaning as a play of delight. For Venus all is play (which on a lower level means all is show), and it is the pathos, the drama of the play that matters to her, and not any practical or objective results. Venus gives the sentiment that would sacrifice a kingdom for one's true love. The astral gods are Venusian creatures and through them arises the play of beauty in the world.

Venus represents the astral light. She opens us up to the kingdoms, the realms of beauty of the Gods. These include not only the realms of art and myth but also psychic abilities, powers of visualization and creative direction of the mind force. On the highest levels she opens us up to the heavens of devotion in which we can commune with the Divine in the form that most appeals to us. Tantra falls in the field of Venus, with the lower or sexual Tantra reflecting lower Venus energies and the higher or devotional Tantra reflecting the higher Venus force.

The Sanskrit name for Venus, *Shukra*, means "brilliant light" and "heat" and also indicates the reproductive fluid. In Hindu mythology Venus, the sage Shukra, is the teacher of the demons or titans, the asuras, because to subdue and influence them cannot be done by force but only by charm and grace. Venus also gives power. It is not only the power that fascinates but also the power to move and to motivate.

A strong Venus gives sexual power which, on inner levels, can be transmuted into astral or spiritual power and strength of will. A strong Venus can give charisma or power of personality. This may be a capacity to inspire or a giving of enthusiasm. But it can also be the power to hypnotize and deceive. Venus can be the sorceress, and has many forms of subtle power and allure to entrap us.

Venus was the main planetary deity of Egypt and Mexico, where Atlantean influences persisted the longest on this planet. Their calendars were based in part upon the cycles of Venus. The positive and visionary side of Venus came out in Atlantis with the use of gems, colors and music and an understanding of the creative power of astral forces. But the negative side also came out when the culture of Atlantis declined into black magic and an occult abuse of the forces of nature.

Modern culture is bringing out aspects of a negative occult Venus in the mass media, with its cult of sex and violence. However, we will probably avoid the destruction that Atlantis suffered, though we will experience some major difficulties from our ignorance. It is important that we use this glamour force in the right way. It can heal if used consciously or destroy if used selfishly.

A strong Venus is very helpful in any chart, as it indicates our capacity to love and our sense of refinement, beauty and purity. Love is the strongest power, and in this regard Venus possesses the power to overcome even Mars. Venus gives vitality, the energy of delight. She is our portion of the Ananda, the Divine bliss in creation.

Yet an afflicted Venus is one of the most difficult things to overcome, because it allows us to be taken in by appearances. This lower side of Venus is much in evidence in our culture with its emphasis on sensory pleasures. Even the artistic side of Venus has been reduced to this today with our emphasis on loud music, bright colors and showmanship.

We must discover Venus as the love of truth to overcome Venus as the love of appearance. For this we must seek the deepest nature of our love and not accept an image of glamour for it.

Saturn

Saturn has a tall and thin body, has yellow eyes and is airy (vata) in constitution; he has large teeth, is lazy, lame and has coarse hair.

Parashara 3. 28-29

Saturn is traditionally the most difficult of the major planets, the legendary king of the malefics. He has been feared throughout the centuries as the great God of Death — the significator of death, disease, poverty, separation, ugliness and perversity. Though Saturn possesses a higher and more beneficent side, at least from the standpoint of the spiritual life, even this is stern and exacting, a power of discipline, asceticism and solitude.

Saturn brings about limitation and obstruction, hindrance in self-expression and in self-manifestation, which may become oppression and adversity. As Jupiter indicates the process of creation and expansion, Saturn causes contraction and destruction. As Jupiter is the great affirmer, Saturn is the great negator. As Jupiter is the God of joy, Saturn is the God of sorrow. As Jupiter is the optimist, Saturn is the pessimist. Jupiter is the positive teacher of the soul; Saturn is the negative guide. As Jupiter tells us that "all is God," Saturn drills into us that "nothing is Divine," that nothing is truly real in the outer world.

Saturn is the significator of disease, old age and death; the great enemies of human life, which overcome all life bound by time. As the furthest in orbit of the major planets, his is the major influence we all must face in the end. Saturn's place in the chart reflects the ultimate issues of our life and destiny, the hard facts or stern reality that we must eventually face.

Though Saturn's power to limit or destroy should not be underestimated, its positive value must not be forgotten. Destruction is the necessary counterpart for creation, as decay and death are required for new life and growth. The limitation on our material fate is necessary: all material things must come to an end, what is put together must come apart, and all things must return to their component elements. The Four Noble Truths of the Buddha and his doctrines of impermanence and universal suffering reflect the wisdom of Saturn.

Our fear of Saturn measures the degree of our attachment to the material world and our inability to face the ultimate issues of our existence. Saturn shows us the limitation of this realm, which is the necessary but painful lesson we must learn to find our way into the unlimited. Saturn is the death which takes us beyond the limitations of mortal life and which is the gateway to the eternal, though straight and narrow as the razor's edge.

Saturn gives bad luck, misfortune, difficult karma, or an unfortunate destiny. Yet these afflictions do not necessarily come upon a soul because it has been evil or slow to evolve in past lives. Some souls, particularly those more advanced, may seek such things as a means of quicker spiritual growth. Anyone can resort to the Divine in prosperity, but who can do so under great adversity? Such is the measure of a great soul. Saturn is also the suffering that makes us grow inwardly.

The influence of Saturn is to delay and withhold. As the slowest moving of the planets, he retards things and holds back their development. His Sanskrit name, *Shani*, means "he who moves slowly." Those who are retarded in mind or speech usually have a strong Saturn affliction. He can make us deaf and blind, stunted or deformed.

Saturn is the significator of old age, the God of time who brings on the degenerative processes of aging, the failure of our faculties and our powers. A badly placed Saturn causes premature aging. Saturn takes away our vitality, whether on a physical or on a mental level. He causes depression, melancholy, and self-pity and gives rise to worry and anxiety.

As a nervous planet, Saturn obstructs nerve functioning. He may cause numbness, paralysis or degenerative neurological disorders. His obstructing and repressing influence on the mind promotes neurosis or insanity. Saturn is behind most diseases, particularly chronic, degenerative diseases, including arthritis and cancer. As representing decay, he can cause an accumulation of waste materials in the body and is a point of devitalization in the chart.

Saturn causes poverty, deprivation and want. He keeps us in bondage or servitude, under the domination of others. Yet Saturn also causes us to retain what we possess. Saturn indicates property, land, or fixed assets. Those who obtain wealth through a well-disposed Saturn will carefully hold on to what has been acquired through so much difficulty.

In the lower sense, Saturn is the planet of selfishness. It indicates our most deep-seated and obstinate ego drives. Saturn is our survival instinct, our need to maintain our separate existence, which is even stronger and more basic than our sexual drive. Most of our materialistic values, like the need for wealth, are little more than glorified survival values and bear Saturn's limitation and poverty of vision. They are caused by the influence of Saturn but, being circumscribed by it, they are also destroyed by its disintegrating effect in the end.

As the planet of the ego, Saturn is the planet of fear upon which the ego is based. Saturn creates fear and darkness in the mind. It makes us feel that we cannot overcome things, that life is against us. It makes us doubt ourselves and become prey to fears, fantasies and phobias.

Saturn represents the darker side of the mind and the baser elements of life: crime, perversity, and paranoia. It indicates the underworld, the lower astral realms. Its influence works through ugliness, terror and fright, through abuse, degradation and debasement. Saturn can not only cause separation from loved ones, he can also cause sexual perversions. Saturn can cause us to pursue gross pleasure or even violence, finding pleasure in seeing others in pain.

A strongly malefic Saturn is prominent in the charts of criminals or the insensitive. Its negative side comes out particularly in association with Mars, another cruel planet. On a lower level Saturn represents the gross body and the senses, the elemental forces which dominate us. It is the gravity that pulls us down and gets us attached to what is inferior. Saturn is the God who eats his own children. He raises people up, but eventually casts them down in a precipitous fall. Those who live under the spell of his base values eventually get destroyed.

As the power of darkness and obstruction, Saturn is the enemy of the Sun and the Moon, and has an eclipse-like effect upon them. Only Jupiter has the power to really balance out his influence, though Venus and Mercury can refine it to a great degree. As Saturn is limiting, Jupiter is unlimiting. As Saturn is miserly, Jupiter is generous. Both together allow for an equalized movement of expansion and contraction, creation and destruction, in which there is true growth. As Jupiter elevates Saturn, Saturn gives Jupiter a greater detachment and more objective perception.

Yet Saturn is not only the lowest of the planets; it is also the highest. Its lesson is the most difficult but the most rewarding. Saturn is the grandfather spirit and lawgiver, our guiding ancestor. He also represents the positive spirit of the past that brings order and consistency to our lives.

In Hindu mythology Saturn is the son of the Sun. The Sun moves in a chariot directed by Saturn. Saturn is the darkness, death and sorrow we must overcome for the revelation of the true light. He is the guardian of the mysteries of true awareness — which is only possible through a precise and exacting cultivation of attention.

Saturn is the yogi in meditation. He can give complete detachment and independence. He is the one who stands alone and goes beyond the limitations of the masses. He shows the way of transcendence, though necessarily difficult, through which all limitations can be overcome by resorting to our true and unlimited Self. In this respect the power of Shiva, the lord of the yogis and god of transcendence, works through Saturn.

A well-placed and strong Saturn is necessary for the spiritual life. In fact, it is necessary for creating anything of enduring value in any domain of life. Saturn gives the concentration, sense of detail, discipline and seriousness necessary to deal with the great challenges of life.

Saturn is the significator of life itself. It indicates fate, term of life and longevity. A strong Saturn protects the life. Saturn is the planet to be propitiated in old age. He indicates the regimen necessary for full life and longevity, violating which we suffer from premature decay and death.

Rahu and Ketu

Rahu creates smoke, has a dark body, resides in forests and engenders fear; he is airy (vata) in constitution. Ketu is similar to Rahu.

Parashari 3.30

In addition to the seven planets, the nodes of the Moon are very important in Vedic astrology. The north node is called *Rahu* or the Dragon's Head; the south node is called *Ketu* or the Dragon's Tail.

Rahu and Ketu are regarded as secondary or shadowy planets. Astronomically, they represent the points at which the Moon's orbit crosses the ecliptic, the celestial equator. At these places at which the Moon crosses the point of the Sun's orbit, eclipses can occur. The lunar nodes show the times when the solar and lunar forces obstruct each other or cancel each other out. They show the potential for short-circuiting, as it were, our solar or lunar energies. They are thus very sensitive points that cause repercussions in the total field of planetary forces.

Rahu, the north or ascending node, is the point at which the Moon crosses the ecliptic to the north. Ketu, the south or descending node, is where it crosses to the south. The influence of the north node is thus ascending, expanding, externalizing, but it expands or externalizes a force which is largely negative. The south node is descending, contracting and internalizing. Hence in the Vedic system the south node is less negative than the north.

Eclipses of the Sun and Moon can occur in proximity to either of the nodes. The nodes were regarded as the two halves of a dismembered demon that swallows one of the luminaries and causes the eclipse. As such, the nodes have the power to overcome the Sun and the Moon, and in this sense can be stronger than any of the planets. In Vedic astrology, the conjunction of any planet with either of the lunar nodes is regarded as a kind of eclipse of that planet, in which its energy is in some way obstructed, negated or liberated. As eclipses are points of energy transformation, they can transfer or augment planetary influences for good or ill.

Western astrologers have correlated the north node (Rahu) with Jupiter and the south node (Ketu) with Saturn. They see the north node as generally benefic and the south node as malefic. They interpret the north node as a point of easy expansion of energy, leadership potential and good luck. The south node appears to them as a point of obstruction, limitation, thwarting of self-expression, loss of power or misfortune. However, recently a new thinking about the nodes has also emerged among Western astrologers that only takes this view as a first step and not the last word on these shadowy planets.

Western astrologers regard the nodes karmically. The north node is seen as a point of good karma from an unselfish past life, in which the individual used his or her energies for the general good. The south node is regarded as a point of difficult karma from a past life, in which the individual furthered his selfish interest at the expense of others.

However, the influence of the north node in excess can result in a dissipation of energies. It may cause us to become carried away by mass trends and collective influences (something like a badly placed Jupiter). The south node, on the positive side, can develop strong concentration and mastery of abstruse or arcane subjects (something like a well placed Saturn).

The lunar nodes in Vedic astrology are a more complex and studied phenomenon than in Western astrology. Their meaning is usually different, though it is sometimes similar to that of the Western system. The nodes are generally regarded as the most malefic forces in the chart. The north node, Rahu, is said to be like Saturn, while the south node, Ketu, is compared to Mars. Yet the nodes have a subtler, more psychic and difficult to neutralize force than these two malefics. Of the two, the north node, Rahu, is regarded as more malefic, often the most malefic force in the chart.

That the two nodes are malefic is quite logical. They indicate the factors that cause eclipses, which block out the light of the great luminaries, the Sun and the Moon. For this reason they are more often indicators of bad karma than good. They show those times when collective karma shadows the individual's life, and in this regard they can represent collective catastrophes. The south node, as completing this karmic cycle, is more generally fortunate than the north node that begins it, because the energy is being internalized and withdrawn.

Vedic astrology does recognize that the lunar nodes (more commonly the north node) can function in a positive, Jupiterian manner, when associated with a strong planet or in a strong position. As shadowy planets, they take on and magnify the power of the planets with which they are combined. Rahu in the tenth house, for example, boosts up our career influence, particularly if the tenth lord is also strong.

Rahu is regarded as the main planetary factor behind insanity, neurosis, neurological disorders, possession by negative entities and other such abnormal sensitivities of the mind and nervous system. This is particularly true when Rahu influences the Moon and other factors representing the mind, like Mercury and the fourth house. It can heighten our astral sensitivity, which weakens our soul's grip upon the physical body.

I have studied the influence of Rahu on many charts and seen the high instance of Moon-Rahu combinations in insanity, nervous disorders or criminal action. Rahu's manifestation is not always quite so severe, and may be counteracted by other forces, as with anything else in astrology. Yet its basic effect is usually as predicted in traditional Vedic astrology, and seldom Jupiterian.

The key to most nervous, psychological and emotional disturbances, susceptibility to drugs and psychic influences, mysterious diseases like cancer or neuromuscular disorders, as well as inexplicable general mental unhappiness and malaise, can usually be traced to the influence of these nodes, especially Rahu. This is particularly true when they combine with the negative force of other malefics like Saturn.

Ketu creates doubt, disturbance, and willfulness, a critical and narrow vision in life that leads to conflict and argument. While Rahu shows an individual carried away by mass trends, Ketu shows the individual caught in his own contracted energies, isolated, alienated, and obstinately separate.

As the factors that determine eclipses, the nodes are the shadows of the Sun and Moon (speaking here symbolically, not astronomically). The north node, Rahu, is the shadow of the Moon, or the negative Moon. It has the power to obstruct, negate, cover or darken the Moon (the mind). The south node, Ketu, is the shadow of the Sun or the negative Sun. It has the power to cover or darken the Sun (the self).

As the negative Moon or the negative side of the mind, Rahu represents illusion, hallucination, trance, psychosis, paranoia and other such negative mental states. As the negative Sun or the negative side of the self, Ketu represents self-doubt, lack of self-confidence, and lack of self-worth, which can lead to self-aggrandizement or megalomania.

While Rahu has the power to overcome the Moon, Ketu has the power to overcome the Sun. The nodes can limit other planets as well, Rahu by an uncritical expansion and Ketu by an overly critical contraction. Similarly, Ketu can obstruct the Moon, creating a psychic sensitivity that may bring an attraction to the lower or macabre side of life, alcoholism or something of that order. Rahu can obstruct the Sun, creating confused imagination, indecision, or illusions about oneself, with the tendency to lose oneself to collective or psychic influences. But Rahu is more dangerous to the Moon and Ketu to the Sun. As having the power to overcome the Sun, Ketu may be the most powerful planet in the chart besides the Sun.

On the positive side, Rahu puts us in harmony with positive social trends and gives popularity, prestige, fame and power. It imparts an almost psychic sensitivity to mass trends and a capacity to use them. Ketu, in the positive sense, imparts great powers of concentration and powerful perception, with psychic and spiritual powers. In terms of yoga and the spiritual life Ketu is the significator of liberation itself (*moksha karaka*). Aligned with Mercury it grants good insight and helps in the pursuit of subjects like astrology.

Rahu usually functions best when placed in a strong house, like the ninth or tenth, with the ruler of that house powerfully placed elsewhere, preferably in an angle or trine. Then Rahu can give fame, status and prestige (Raja Yoga). It may give these things when strongly located in the first or fourth house.

Ketu means "a flag." It has the power to boost up the effects of strong planets with which it is conjoined. A planet located in its own sign or exalted while conjoined with Ketu gains considerable power. Venus in the second house in Libra conjoined with Ketu, for example, will give wealth or talent. With Mars in Scorpio in the third house, Ketu can give military prowess.

A strong Rahu gives worldly powers and success, the fulfillment of outer desires, but not usually inner fulfillment. It can give rise to worldly desires that can never be fulfilled, however successful the individual may be. Its outer good luck is combined with an inner unrest. Ketu gives sudden and unexpected results for good or ill, depending upon its placement. Well-placed, it makes the individual strong but not necessarily sensitive to others. Yet as the two nodes are always opposite each other, when one is strong or weak the other usually is as well.

In the spiritual realm Rahu gives psychic powers and a mediumistic capacity, but also danger from drugs, possession and black magic. Ketu gives wisdom and psychic sensitivity but can be narrow or self-righteous in its effects. Mastering the nodes is perhaps the key to spiritual growth.

The positive influence of the nodes is less common than the negative, and both nodes tend to have a debasing effect. Both represent forces that are difficult to handle and their positive side may only come out through overcoming great obstacles in life.

Mars

Dressed in red, with a red body, who has four arms, the son of the Earth, whose vehicle is a ram, who carries a trident, spear and mace in his hands, with a coral crest jewel on his head, making the gesture that grants boons — may Divine Mars ever grant us his grace.

6

The Signs

How the Planets Transmit the Influences of the Stars

Vedic astrology employs the same twelve signs of the zodiac as does Western astrology. The meanings are similar, but their locations are determined sidereally.

THE TWELVE SIGNS OF THE ZODIAC

	English	Sanskrit	Symbol	Ruler
1.	Aries	Mesha	Ram	Mars
2.	Taurus	Vrishabha	Bull	Venus
3.	Gemini	Mithuna	Twins	Mercury
4.	Cancer	Kataka	Crab	Moon
5.	Leo	Simha	Lion	Sun
6.	Virgo	Kanya	Virgin	Mercury
7.	Libra	Tula	Balance	Venus
8.	Scorpio	Vrishchika	Scorpion	Mars
9.	Sagittarius	Dhanus	Bow	Jupiter
10.	Capricorn	Makara	Crocodile	Saturn
11.	Aquarius	Kumbha	Pot	Saturn
12.	Pisces	Mina	Fishes	Jupiter

The signs reflect the meaning of the planet that rules them. The key to sign rulership is that it reflects the orbits of the planets around the Sun.

Cancer and Leo represent the orbit of the Sun. Around these two signs are Gemini and Virgo, which represent the two halves of the orbit of Mercury, the nearest planet to the Sun. Then follow Taurus and Libra, the two halves of the orbit of Venus, the next planet out from the Sun. Then come Aries and Scorpio, the two halves of the orbit of Mars. Then follow Pisces and Sagittarius, the two halves of the orbit of Jupiter. The zodiac ends with Aquarius and Capricorn, the two halves of the orbit of Saturn, the most distant planet from the Sun.

Each planet rules two signs. The odd numbered sign represents the positive half of its orbit around the Sun, where it is increasing and expressing its energy; the even numbered sign represents the negative half of its orbit, where it is decreasing and withdrawing (interiorizing) its energy. Cancer and Leo represent the positive and negative halves of the Sun's rotation on its own axis. By this system, Vedic astrology cannot accept Uranus, Neptune or Pluto as ruling signs, as they do in Western astrology. This would destroy the sequence of orbits and the logic of sign rulership.

The Sun and Moon are in essence one planet. The Moon is the feminine side of the Sun that has been emanated to the proximity of the Earth to nourish and promote life. The Moon is the incarnation of the Divine Mother who dwells in the Sun. It is no mere astronomical coincidence that the Moon and Sun have the same relative size from the Earth. It is part of the working of cosmic law. Eclipses of the Sun and the Moon can only occur because of this. They are not accidental, but are points of energy transformation necessary for the development of life on Earth. The Sun is approximately 108 solar diameters from the Earth, while the Earth is about 1/108 the size of the Sun. Meanwhile the Moon is about 108 Earth diameters from the Earth. No wonder 108 is such an important number in Vedic thought!

The interrelationship of the Sun and the Moon is necessary to maintain the balance of positive and negative, masculine and feminine, yin and yang energies on Earth. Without the Moon being the same apparent size and balancing the influence of the Sun, life on Earth would be impossible. The homeostasis necessary for life could not be maintained. The Moon allows the Earth to hold water and is responsible for the maintenance of the oceans. Through the oceans it allows for life, for the rains that nourish plants, and for maintaining fertility in creatures. Its energy allows for the building up of our bodies and minds.

ODD AND EVEN NUMBERED SIGNS

Odd numbered signs reflect the positive, masculine or active signs; the even numbered are their negative, feminine, and passive counterpart. For example, Aries, sign 1, is the positive or masculine sign of Mars, where its energy is outgoing, expressive, and manifest. Scorpio, sign 8, is the negative or feminine sign, where its energy is internalized, hidden, and acting behind the scenes. Planets are generally stronger in positive signs; that is, they can accomplish more. Odd signs have a more yang or solar nature, and even signs have a more yin or lunar nature. Odd signs are more energetic or rajasic; even signs are more resistant or tamasic.

Both positive and negative signs are necessary; no distinction of good or bad is implied. The negative side of a planet is embodied in that portion of its orbit where it is gathering in cosmic energy, while the positive side is where it is releasing it.

The planets exist to bring into the solar system their respective portion of the sevenfold cosmic energy from the stars. The planets are the dynamic principles, whereas the signs are the fields or tissues maintained by their movement. The solar system is an organism. The zodiac reflects the relationship of the solar system with the galaxy. The planets are transmission stations that bring in the seven rays from the galactic center and project these for the evolution of the solar system and the development of life on Earth.

We see, therefore, that the signs do not exist apart from the planets. Gemini, for example, is nothing but the energy channeled by Mercury in the positive side of its orbit; while Virgo is its energy channeled in the negative half. The energy sustained by the orbit of each planet is projected through two signs of the zodiac, two thirty-degree sections of the sky relative to the Earth.

QUALITY OF SIGNS

Each sign relates to one of the three major qualities, which in Western astrology are called *cardinal*, *fixed*, and *mutable*. In Sanskrit they are called *chara*, or moveable, *sthira*, firm or immovable, and *dwiswabhava* or dual natured.

These qualities relate to the manner in which the individual directs his or her energy and are reflected in the nature of the character. In terms of electrical charges they are much like positive (cardinal), neutral (fixed) and negative (mutable),. No quality is necessarily better than the other. Each has its energetic pattern and characteristic imbalances that must be mastered by any individual dominated by it.

MOVEABLE (CARDINAL) TYPES

Moveable signs show the dynamic, initial or guiding phase of the element. Moveable quality gives impulse, direction and expression but may cause disturbance and agitation along with too forceful or frequent changes.

Individuals with planets predominantly in moveable signs are people of action. They are positive, expressive, and outgoing, with a high sense of achievement and accomplishment. They are willful, aggressive, and dynamic and often become leaders. Yet while they can accomplish a great deal and get what they want, they may lack in sensitivity. They may impose themselves on others or harm others along the way.

Moveable types may have trouble sticking with jobs or relationships, which can harm their potentials. They can overextend themselves or burn themselves out through excess movement and stimulation. Their outer lives are also mobile. For example, planets in moveable signs cause us to move or change our residence.

Moveable types need to develop more consistency and stability. They must make sure that what they are directing their energy toward reflects their deepest will and aspiration and not merely action for its own sake. If they can do this, their capacity for inner development in life can also be very high.

FIXED (IMMOVABLE) TYPES

Immovable or fixed signs show the stable or enduring phase of their respective element. The immovable quality is the condition of form or substance that gives continuity and consistency, but may also cause inertia, resistance and stagnation.

Fixed types are firm, stable and determined in who they are and in what they do. They like to sustain, preserve and uphold things. They are settled in themselves and unwilling to modify their opinions or to question themselves. Their characters are firm and can be unyielding. They are consistent, have strong faith and seldom waver in their beliefs. They prefer what is conservative or traditional and do not like to change. They are often possessive and may accumulate much in life, finding it difficult to let go. Their lives will be fixed outwardly as well, with little change of residence or profession. They hold on to whatever they gain and are unwilling to part with it.

When highly evolved, they are souls who hold to the truth and have great faith. When less evolved, they may be insensitive, attached or resistant. They can be emotional, sentimental or have a strong feeling nature. Sometimes they are thoughtful but go more deeply into the ideas they already have rather than develop new ones.

Fixed types need to develop more initiative and attempt new activities, particularly new ways of looking at things. At the same time they need to be more sensitive, adaptable and open. They must make certain that what they are holding to is really the truth and not just some pattern of inertia.

MUTABLE (DUAL-NATURED) TYPES

Mutable signs show the transitional, unstable, or malleable phase of their respective element. As the name dual-natured implies, they can go either way. They can move or stand still. They are ambivalent, unpredictable, and go back and forth. Mutable signs are ruled by Mercury and Jupiter, which are planets of the mind and give much mental and emotional sensitivity (particularly Virgo and Pisces).

Mutable types are flexible and adaptable and have many talents, interests, and skills. They are prone to be indecisive and may find it difficult to act. They like to think, calculate, worry or reflect and can be too introverted or preoccupied with themselves. They typically suffer from mental or nervous disorders, immune system derangements and allergies.

Mutable types are talkative and communicative, though not consistent in what they say. They can be good businessmen because of their ability to exchange things. They can be successful as performers because they can modify what they appear to be. When highly evolved, they are capable of great sensitivity and broad comprehension. When less evolved, they can be erratic, unreliable and neurotic. Outwardly, their lives are also characterized by ambiguity and by extremes.

Mutable types need more initiative, daring and willingness to act. They should set aside their thoughts and work through their actions. They also need firmness, consistency and peace. Above all, they must learn to use their sensitivity consciously as a tool rather than have it react against them.

SIGNS AND THE ELEMENTS

Each sign relates to one of the four elements of Earth, Water, Fire or Air, in one of the three modes of these major qualities. As the signs show the field in which the planets operate, their elements show their different levels, the layers or densities of our being through which we function in life.

EARTH SIGNS

Planets in earth signs give a sense of form, order, and utility, and cause us to seek material manifestation or expression. They indicate much work to do with the Earth, the body or physical matter. For example, we can find earth sign individuals in such professions as gardeners, doctors, bankers or farmers, or any other line of work which deals with something tangible in the material world.

Planets in earth signs show work with the hands, or work with the practical, informational or earthly side of the mind. They keep us in the realm of the senses and require that we use our senses in a clear manner. They demand that we develop mastery of the body. They can have a certain gravity or heaviness about them.

On the higher level, earth located planets give us the capacity to realize our inner potentials in the material world. We find them in the charts of old souls who have much connection with traditional cultures (like India or Mexico) and who may be completing their cycle of evolution. Those who follow Earth or nature religions, like Taoism or the Native American path, may be of this type. On a lower level, earth signs tie us to the world and to the body and place a shadow over us. Many souls just coming into this world, or up from the animal kingdom, can be dominated by coarser earth influences.

Well-placed planets in earth signs give practical efficiency, physical purity and the capacity for work. Poorly placed planets in earth signs constrict and block us and keep us tied to the harsher side of life.

WATER SIGNS

Water signs bring our planetary energies into the realm of feeling and give love, affection and attachment. They can be instinctual or intuitive, depending on how we use them, and usually cause us to seek emotional regard and recognition. They show work to do with our psychology and with human relationships. They can give strong vital natures. They indicate that our main fulfillment will come through relationship, which may be embodied in family, friends, social recognition, or even spiritual relationships.

Individuals with many planets in water signs usually have many people around them and often provide a place in their house for people to come together or just hang out. They may find it hard to create boundaries between themselves and others and may lack clarity. Their lives may be in the sea, as it were.

On a higher level, water signs give wisdom, faith, devotion and compassion. They are connected with astral worlds of art or devotion. On a lower level, they give sentimentality, greed and attachment. We may get drowned in the emotional issues we are not able to work out or do not want to let go of. We should note that while water is creative, it can also cause decay. Well-placed planets in water signs give positive feelings, love and creativity; negatively placed planets breed deep seated emotional turmoil or stagnation.

FIRE SIGNS

Fire signs show strong will, ambition and determination, as well as good perception and a critical mind. People with fiery planets seek power and like a display of force and drama. Their focus is more on their own self and character than upon interchange with others. They like to be popular but they also like to dominate, not to be on the same level with others. They show that our main field of activity in life is in the realm of the will. Fire signs give us the need to develop real independence, clarity and understanding, not just to shine over or rule over others.

On a higher level, planets in fire signs give independence and insight, strong judgment and high values. Those with strong planets in fire signs are able to penetrate into things and understand the underlying energy, motivation or force behind them. Fire signs give leadership, the capacity to make alliances, the ability to project warmth, light and beneficence. On the lower level, they may make us destructive. Our will may clash with those of others and bring us into argument and conflict. They may cause us to be vain, proud or self-promoting.

Well-placed planets in fire signs give illumination, freedom and enlightenment. They show the soul coming forth in its manifestation. Wrongly placed planets in fire signs can be burnt up and show the will in turmoil and complication.

AIR SIGNS

Air signs show versatility of movement and change, generally on a mental level. People with airy planets are often intellectuals or at least mental types. They seek communication and realization of ideas and ideals; their love is usually of knowledge. They are speculative and not concerned with practical results. Air sign types live in their ideas, calculations, plans, and projections. Planets in air signs show much work to do in the realm of thought and communication. People with these placements may seek to ascend but may not have the foundation for it. Their energies may get scattered or diffused.

On a higher level, planets in air signs increase idealism and aspiration and the longing to go beyond this world. They make us philosophical or humanitarian in outlook. On a lower level, they keep us confused and ungrounded, not willing to face the facts about life or about ourselves. We want to change things according to our own notions, which may not correspond to anything real.

Well-placed planets in air signs give comprehensiveness, balance and sensitivity. Wrongly placed planets in air signs have their energy dispersed. They show disturbance, uncertainty and lack of consolidation, and may cause mental or nervous problems.

For a complete understanding of the elements in the chart we must examine the elements represented by the planets themselves, particularly that of the strongest planet in the chart. For example, one may have many planets in earth signs, but if they are predominantly fiery planets and strongly placed, especially an exalted Mars in Capricorn, one will have much energy, enthusiasm and motivation (fire) to accomplish things in the material or practical realm (earth). Such people, we could say, are like "fire operating in the field of the earth." Their force or the quality of their nature would be fiery, but their realm of manifestation would be earthy. Even their physical constitution would usually be fiery (pitta), though they would be active through the body or the concrete side of the mind.

DESCRIPTION OF THE SIGNS

Western astrology focuses on the Sun sign. In Vedic astrology, the Ascendant is the most important factor, the Moon sign comes second, and the Sun sign is only third. This is logical, because the Ascendant is the most quickly changing of all planetary factors. It changes signs in two hours, compared to two and a half days for the Moon and a month for the Sun. Hence it more directly reflects our individuality. As it is the point of orientation of the Earth to the heavens, it also more directly reflects the meaning of our particular incarnation on Earth.

The following delineation of the signs is general, mainly according to personality types. Their qualities are described here primarily as Ascendants that, but the same indications apply as Moon signs or Sun signs.

Aries ♈

Aries is the positive sign of Mars, cardinal fire, the beginning of the zodiac and the head of the Cosmic Person (time personified), a ram. As sign 1, Aries gives independence, force, self-expression and a strong personal orientation in life.

Aries types are dynamic, aggressive and competitive, and possess much initiative. They often live in their heads and can have a penetrating power of perception. They have scientific and logical abilities and may be good at research and invention. They are independent, adventurous and skillful in whatever they do. While they possess strong emotions and passions, they usually remain in control of them.

Aries people are willful, impulsive or headstrong and can be critical or opinionated. Yet they can make good psychologists once they learn to examine themselves. Less evolved Aries types may be angry and manipulative, pushing their way through life and imposing their ideas and energies on others. Their martial energy is expressed more through the mind than the body. They are prone to argument but do not often resort to violence.

Aries types can be self-centered and are not always sensitive to others. They benefit from relationships to balance them out. They are usually initiating a new phase of manifestation. Their key to spiritual growth is to use their sharp minds and strong energies to discover truth, not to promote themselves.

Taurus ♉

Taurus is the negative sign of Venus, fixed earth, the face and neck of the Cosmic Person, a bull. As sign 2, it gives a strong sense of relationship, partnership and communication of feeling. Taurus types seek balance and harmony in the organization of their immediate environment.

Taurus types are stable, enduring and fixed in their ways. They have a good sense of form and beauty and may become artists and poets. They are often attractive, particularly when young, and like to adorn themselves. Taureans are possessive and may become businessmen or bankers and may accumulate property. They are apt to be materialistic and sensual and like comfort, luxury or adornment. Yet they easily develop taste, refinement and grace. They communicate well with others and associate readily with foreigners.

Taureans tend to become obstinate and do not like to move from a position once they have accepted it as their own. They are slow to anger but also slow to forgive and can be cruel or insensitive to those outside of their circle of association. They possess good memories but may become sentimental or cling to the past. They like to live in their bodies and their senses.

Taureans usually value stable and happy homes and married lives. They can be very romantic and devotional and are often votaries of the idea that all is love. They are attached to the earth, often work with their hands and leave their mark of form on their practical environment. Their mode is to acquire, preserve and refine. Spiritually they are also devotional and like tradition and ritual.

Gemini ♊

Gemini is the positive sign of Mercury, mutable air, the lower neck and shoulders of the Cosmic Person, twins, or a couple (a man and a woman). As sign 3, it gives an energetic nature with a seeking of change and interchange, motion and invention.

Those in whom the influence of Gemini predominates are nervous, restless and agitated. They possess quickness and adaptability of body and mind but can exhaust themselves through excessive activity. They have good intellects, along with excellent powers of speech and a good command of language. They may be writers, journalists, or poets, or secretaries or computer programmers. They are good with information and statistics and may be scientists. There is a speculative side of their minds, however, and they can pursue ideas for their own sake or get caught up in their own unrealistic fantasies or worries.

Geminis are as mobile in human relationships as they are in mind and tend to marry more than once or have several partners. They may be strongly sexually oriented, but must be careful because their vital energy is not always as high as their imaginations. They love stimulation and novelty and can easily become addicted to media or computer influences. They like anything that excites their nervous system or increases their velocity in life but can become hypersensitive or neurotic. Their agility of mind may cause them to become deceptive or unreliable.

Geminis can be indecisive and never bring anything to fruition. They are the most changeable of all types and always on the go until their energy fails them. Once they come to seek inner knowledge rather than outer knowledge and sensation, they can become quite spiritual, as their energy is the most subtle and volatile of all the signs.

Cancer ♋

Cancer is the sign of the Moon (an even or negative sign), cardinal water, the chest of the Cosmic Person, a crab. As sign 4, it shows a need for mental and emotional stability and happiness.

Cancer people are usually friendly, sympathetic, caring and nurturing, as they are under the sign of the mother. They value human relationship and the exchange of feelings, particularly on an intimate and personal level. They have many people in their homes or friends coming and going, and they like to cook or care for them.

Cancerians seek popularity and are sensitive to the moods of the masses, through which they can gain social influence and recognition. Yet they may be emotionally sensitive, shy, and dependent. They love their home and family, but sometimes to the point of narrow mindedness. In the same way, they can love their community, country or religion with an enclosure of feeling.

Cancerians are devoted, loving and intuitive, sensing immediately the feelings of others. They have powerful imaginations, yet may be bound by subconscious fixations and attachments. They are gentle and non-harmful but may become defensive or cowardly. They are just and frugal, but may be lacking in will, initiative and courage. They are receptive and can become contemplative when they open up to the spiritual life. They are usually of a devotional bent of mind, yet they will represent and project the beliefs they follow to the world at large. Once they feel connected they gain confidence, initiative and power and can shine over others like the Moon. Once they learn how to be receptive to truth, they can do great service and act with great power.

Leo ♌

Leo is the sign of the Sun (positive), fixed fire, the solar plexus of the Cosmic Person, a lion. As sign 5, it shows a need for order and harmony around a central will and character influence.

Leo individuals possess a strong sense of self, character and will. They know who they are and want others to recognize it. They are proud, bold, ambitious and aristocratic. They respond strongly and personally to things and are dramatic, sometimes vain, in their self-expression. They like to shine in social situations and may dominate others. Leos prefer to be the center of attention and value honor, respect and prestige. They are often strong souls and possessed of fine principles and good intelligence. They can be refined in their manners or philosophical in their outlook on life.

Leos have strong and noble hearts but can suffer from too powerful emotions or too much need for attention. They do not always do well in partnership and tend to form alliances with inferiors or to subordinate their partners to them. They may suffer from their children as they do not always give them enough independence. They like to turn others into satellites that rebel against them. If they can control their pride they can develop much power of character that can take them through all the highs and lows of life and grant them a spiritual perception. Inwardly they can develop greatness of the soul. As they have a high standard for themselves, Leos can become very dejected if they fail or do not succeed as much as they wish.

Virgo ♍

Virgo is the negative sign of Mercury, mutable earth, the intestines of the Cosmic Person, a virgin. As sign 6 (2 x 3), it shows the need for balancing energy, particularly between body and mind.

Like their Gemini counterparts, who are also mutable and ruled by

Mercury, Virgo types possess good intellects, command of the language and nervous sensitivity. They make good teachers and have a strong sense of the facts. As earth signs, Virgos also project the healing ray of Mercury. They make good doctors and healers and can be good at hatha yoga. They are more physical than Geminis, have a liking for exercise, and may excel as athletes, particularly when young. Their knowledge has a practical or informational side and they are often good at trivia. They are possessed of good and factual memories. They are helpful and service oriented and become good workers, but they can suffer from overwork or lack of recognition in what they do.

Virgos make good craftsmen, draftsmen or artists, as they have a strong sense of form, line and detail. They may become actors, as they can easily learn how to discipline their expression and project their emotions. Virgos are more technical actors than charismatic types, however.

Owing to their sensitive changeable minds and nervous systems, Virgos easily become neurotic. They suffer from a nervous or variable digestion and elimination. They are usually the weakest of the signs physically. They are more likely come down with disorders or chronic diseases that are difficult to treat, particularly problems involving the nervous system. Their body-mind coordination tends to be weak. Sexually they tend to be shy when young but are prone to excessive sexual activity when older, though it is seldom open or freely expressed.

Virgos are fussy, discriminating and exacting about details and like cleanliness and order. For this reason they can be hard to live with and never seem pleased with anything. Yet their discrimination sometimes has a spiritual orientation and they can be good at philosophies which are built on purity and discrimination, like Vedanta.

Libra ♎

Libra is the positive sign of Venus, cardinal air, the lower abdomen of the Cosmic Person, the scales or balance. As sign 7, it gives leadership, power and command of ideas.

Libra has a somewhat different meaning in the Vedic system than in the Western. It is the sign of reformers, revolutionaries, prophets, idealists and fanatics. Libra individuals have a strong sense of harmony, justice and balance, particularly in the realm of ideas. They want to see heaven on earth. They are sensitive and humanitarian, with the power to arouse and influence the masses. Their orientation is often political, in which sphere they often become leaders, even great generals.

Librans love the truth and are devoted to their ideals but may go too far in their zeal and become propagandists. Their idealism may also express itself through art and drama, which for them becomes a vehicle of social change. They like fame and recognition, seek an audience for their ideas, and have a strong social sense.

Librans are usually attractive and have a charisma that may become sexual. They are not much concerned with home and family but, being under the rule of Venus, they do like to have beauty around them. They like to have circles of beautiful or famous friends. They often live in the clouds and have strong connections with the higher astral plane. They can attune themselves to the love of truth and quickly learn to transcend the world.

Because of their sociable nature, they are often successful and want to make a mark upon the world. They like business situations that give them administrative power or the ability to influence others. Yet they can lose themselves in their goals and projects. They ever seek an ideal balance and harmony, even if they have to cause disharmony to get it!

Scorpio ♏

Scorpio is the negative sign of Mars, fixed water, the sexual organs of the Cosmic Person, a scorpion. As sign 8 (2 x 4), it shows a need for balance and stability on a deeper or psychic level.

Scorpio is a profound and mysterious sign. As the negative or physical side of Mars, Scorpio people are often soldiers, policemen or athletes. They like to use their martial power on a physical level and can be prone to the use of force. They usually have good muscles and like to exercise. When mentally developed they have a good capacity for research and inquiry and may become chemists or surgeons.

More evolved Scorpio types like to explore the depths of the mind and may have an interest in the occult and yoga (Tantra). Their kundalini can often be easily aroused for good or ill. They may like trying to work with or overcome negative forces, and they may see life as a battle between light and darkness, with which they may become obsessed. They are often fascinated with techniques or technologies for directing energy, either outwardly or inwardly.

Scorpios can be very intelligent and perceptive, but prefer to remain behind the scenes. They do not express themselves quickly, not because they are slow but because they are cautious. They can be good orators or debaters, and may become good poets, artists or actors due to their ability to express powerful emotions. They are usually passionate and can be very attached sexually. When unevolved they are prone to vice, perversity or the underworld side of life and can become emotionally or physically violent.

Scorpio types are intense, secretive, introverted and sometimes troubled. They have an active subconscious and must keep their emotions clear and pure, free of envy and attachment, or they can get stuck on an emotional level. Yet because of this sensitivity, they may develop a philosophical disposition and profound insight that the other types rarely attain.

Sagittarius ♐

Sagittarius is the positive sign of Jupiter, mutable fire, the hips of the Cosmic Person, a horse, centaur or archer. As sign 9, it indicates grace, beneficence, completion and full harmony (3 x 3), the manifestation of the will in action.

Sagittarius individuals project the positive side of Jupiter. They have a positive attitude in life, an expansive spirit, and a moral, religious or philosophical disposition. They have a strong sense of principle, law and justice. They are usually warm and friendly, dramatic and seek to develop their principles in life. They make themselves noticed and can easily become active or involved with the expansion of the social forces to which they open up. On the other hand, they can be too conventional, law-abiding and moralistic, caught in some dogmatic idea.

Sagittarians may become lawyers, religious leaders or successful businessmen. They like to be generous, but they also like to stay within the conventions of the society, group or organization with which they are involved. They possess critical minds and strong opinions but are prone to become self-righteous. Their minds may be too discriminating and fault finding and they may be unable to see their own limitations.

Sagittarians are often athletic, though not always competitive; they like the outdoors, enjoy the wilderness, and are lovers of nature. They have a sense of play or even partying, which may become self-indulgence or group indulgence. They find it hard to settle down. They are lucky in life and things often come easy for them. The world often responds quickly and favorably to them. They can inherit much from father or family. They are a helpful presence in any enterprise, as they bring much enthusiasm and make good and devoted friends. Yet, however successful they may be in the material world, Sagittarians usually retain some sense of higher aspiration and are attracted to religion or the spiritual life.

Capricorn ♑

Capricorn is the negative sign of Saturn, cardinal earth, the knees of the Cosmic Person, a crocodile. As sign 10, it shows the state of power, order and complete organization.

Capricorn is often the lowest and the highest of the signs in terms of achievement in life. It is the sign of practical realization. On the material level, this can create much worldliness and obstinacy and make people selfish. Less evolved Capricorn types may be sons of the earth, farmers who know little beyond their farm. Somewhat more evolved is the hardheaded Capricornian businessman who saves everything for some eventual great gain. On the spiritual level, Capricorn can give the capacity to manifest spiritual principles in daily life and practical work.

Capricorn types are hardworking, persevering, and tenacious and have the power for eventual great accomplishments. They usually work for themselves and learn to value everything that comes through their own effort. They start slowly in life, often encounter many obstacles along the way, but thereby create the energy for long-term success. They are ambitious but often narrow in their goals and rigid or cutting in their opinions. They can be shrewd at business and are often good in science and technology, with a strong mathematical sense. They tend to be traditional and may have much past life karma in traditional and Oriental cultures.

Capricorns need to learn more self-surrender; to take themselves less seriously and to be less concerned about outer forms. They are often detached from their emotions, either by lower sensate or higher intellectual or spiritual values, or by conventionality or just being caught in the senses.

Aquarius ♒

Aquarius is the positive sign of Saturn, fixed air, the lower legs of the Cosmic Person, a pot or water bearer. As sign 11, it indicates the group and the needs of the masses.

Aquarius individuals are the most self-negative of all types. On a higher level, they have more faith and capacity to surrender the ego to the Divine. On a lower level, they believe in others and denigrate themselves. For this reason, they tend more towards sexual deviation than the other signs. They are prone to do what they are told not to do and to befriend those they are told to avoid. In this way their energy can be blocked, dissipated, confused or darkened.

On a higher level, Aquarians are willing to sacrifice themselves for the good of all and are strongly humanitarian. On a lower level, they may accept a subservient, servile or even degrading role in life, and not protest against the injustice inflicted upon them. They like to take the side of the oppressed, the outcaste or disapproved elements of society. They often have much guilt and like to blame themselves. They act selflessly in relation to those things in which they repose their faith. If that is the Divine, they may become saintly. If it is some criminal group, they can even become underworld leaders.

Aquarians may be eccentric and scattered in what they do, unclear as to who they really are. They lack charisma and often fail to attract the masses as political leaders. Yet by their faith and devotion, they are often successful as religious leaders and teachers. The water they bring is that of truth from their intuitive perception.

Pisces ♓

Pisces is the negative sign of Jupiter, mutable water, the feet of the Cosmic Person, the fishes. As sign 12, it shows the complete display of all possibilities but not necessarily their proper integration.

Pisces individuals are emotional, expansive, intuitive and imaginative. They are enthusiastic but not always wisely so. They like to influence others but are themselves easily influenced and may be vulnerable or impressionable. They are friendly and communicative and can relate to a variety of people. They can easily become dependent or make others dependent upon them.

Pisceans are sentimental and easily moved by feelings, including those that are not genuine. They are friendly and compassionate but can be too easily moved by sympathy and pity. When frustrated in life, they often develop self-pity. They are usually attached to the past for good or ill and may accept the values of the culture and religion into which they are born. However, they are susceptible to missionary type influences and like demonstrations of faith. They like ceremony and ritual, enjoy music, and make good musicians.

Pisceans often lack boundaries and may not have enough clarity and practicality. They can be amorphous, hard to pin down, and will appear in such a way as to please others or reflect the influence of the moment. As a mutable and emotional sign, they are prone to emotional disorders and may have sensitive digestive and nervous systems. They are not often good leaders but make good followers or promoters.

Pisceans can lack in self-confidence or have too many impractical ideas about themselves, though they wish to achieve a great deal in life. They can become dependent on or addicted to sugar or alcohol and often need special acknowledgment or approval. Pisces types need to control their imaginations and develop more discrimination. Once they do this, they can reflect the creative joy of the soul.

EXALTATION AND DEBILITY

Each planet has one sign in which it functions at its optimum, called its exaltation. Except for Mercury, which both rules and is exalted in Virgo, this sign is different than the signs ruled by the planet. In Vedic astrology, there is a specific degree where the exaltation is highest. These points of exaltation are different for every planet. Planets occupying their degree of exaltation are preeminently strong.

Exaltation Positions of Planets

Sun	10°Aries
Moon	03° Taurus
Mars	28° Capricorn
Mercury	15° Virgo
Jupiter	05° Cancer
Venus	27° Pisces
Saturn	20° Libra
Rahu	20° Taurus
Ketu	20° Scorpio

According to some Vedic astrologers, Rahu and Ketu are both said to be exalted in Gemini and Virgo, the signs of Mercury.

Exaltation is an important factor in determining the strength of a planet and its sign location. By some systems, the strongest planet in the chart is the one closest to its degree of exaltation. The sign opposite that of exaltation is referred to as a planet's fall or debilitation. The degree opposite its degree of exaltation is the degree of its fall. Planets in their fall are weak and cause difficulties.

Planetary debility can be cancelled out by special factors. A planet with its debility cancelled can give very good results, even better than exaltation. The first of such cancellation factors is when the debilitated planet is located in an angle from the Ascendant or the Moon. A second factor is if the ruler of the sign in which a planet is debilitated is itself exalted. For example, if the Moon is located in its fall in Scorpio, but Mars as ruler of Scorpio is located in its exaltation in Capricorn, this can cancel the debility of the Moon. To a lesser extent, if the ruler of the debilitated planet is strong or in its own sign, the debility can be reduced. For example, if the Moon is in Scorpio but Mars is in Aries, the strength of Mars in Aries would help counter the weakness of the Moon.

Another helpful factor is if the debilitated planet has a planet exalted in one of the signs that it rules. For example, if Mars is in its debility in Cancer in a chart but the Sun is in its exaltation in Aries, which is ruled by Mars, the strength of the Sun will reduce the weakness of Mars. A less important factor is if a debilitated planet is retrograde. Generally, debility must be cancelled in at least two ways to be effectively countered. Even then, the person may have to undergo great difficulties before having great achievements.

MULATRIKONA

Mulatrikona means root trine. These are special areas where a planet functions very well, almost as well as in exaltation. They usually consist of some portion of the positive sign ruled by the planet. In the case of the Moon, however, the mulatrikona is part of its exaltation sign, as the Moon does not have a positive or odd numbered sign. With Mercury it is part of its own and exaltation sign Virgo, as it has no special sign of exaltation.

Mulatrikona Positions of Planets

Sun 04–20° Leo	Jupiter 00–10° Sagittarius
Moon 04–20° Taurus	Venus 00–15° Libra
Mars 00–12° Aries	Saturn 00–20° Aquarius
Mercury 16–20° Virgo	

PLANETARY RELATIONSHIPS

The strength of a planet in a sign depends upon its relationship with the ruler of the sign in which it is located. Planets are strong in their exaltation, mulatrikona or own signs. For other signs, there is a system of planetary relationships for measuring the connection between planets.

Planets are strong in signs of their great friends or friends. Planets are neutral in strength in neutral signs. They are weak in the signs of their enemies or great enemies, and more so in their fall (opposite exaltation).

Planetary relationships are twofold as permanent or temporary. Permanent relationships depend upon the natural status of the planets.

Temporary relationships are similar to aspects and are another kind of relationship by position in a particular chart. In terms of permanent planetary relationships, planets fall into two major groups: *Sun, Moon, Mars and Jupiter are the first group of friends. Mercury, Venus and Saturn are the second group of friends.* Planets in each group tend to be inimically disposed to planets in the other.

The list of Permanent Planetary Relationships shows the more specific scheme that evolves from this. The Moon, for example, is a friendly planet and is inimical towards none. Hence planets with which it would be enemies are mainly neutrals. The Sun and Mercury are always close together. Hence Mercury is a neutral to the Sun, and the Sun is a friend to Mercury, rather than inimical as would be expected. Other exceptions exist but usually do not extend beyond a group friend or a group enemy becoming a neutral. Rahu and Ketu are sometimes given relationships similar to Saturn, but, since they are not primary planets, most astrologers do not consider them.

Permanent Planetary Relationships

Planet	Friends	Neutrals	Enemies
Sun	Moon, Mars, Jupiter	Mercury	Venus, Saturn
Moon	Sun, Mercury	Venus, Mars, Jupiter, Saturn	None
Mars	Sun, Moon, Jupiter	Venus, Saturn	Mercury
Mercury	Sun, Venus	Mars, Jupiter, Saturn	Moon
Jupiter	Sun, Moon, Mars	Saturn	Mercury, Venus Sun, Moon
Venus	Mercury, Saturn	Mars, Jupiter	Sun, Moon,
Saturn	Mercury, Venus	Jupiter	Mars

Temporary Planetary Relationships

Rule: Planets located in the second, third, fourth, tenth, eleventh and twelfth signs from the sign in which a planet is located in a chart (counting that sign as the first) are to be regarded as its temporary friends. Planets in the same sign, or in the fifth, sixth, seventh, eighth and ninth from it, are to regarded as its temporary enemies.

In other words, friendship occurs according to the quarter of the zodiac preceding and the quarter succeeding the particular sign in which a planet is located. They are in proximity but not on top of each other. Enmity occurs when a planet is distant from a particular planet or occupying the same sign. They are either too close or too far away for their rays to combine harmoniously.

Composite Planetary Relationships

The factors of both natural and temporal friendship have to be combined to get an accurate measure of the relationships between planets in any specific chart.

Permanent friend	+	Temporary friend	=	Best Friend
Permanent friend	+	Temporary enemy	=	Neutral
Permanent neutral	+	Temporary friend	=	Friend
Permanent neutral	+	Temporary enemy	=	Enemy
Permanent enemy	+	Temporary friend	=	Neutral
Permanent enemy	+	Temporary enemy	=	Worst Enemy

The correct ascertainment of planetary relationships is essential for determining the value of planetary location or the effect of aspects. An aspect between friends proves beneficial but one between enemies gives difficulty. Moreover, planets in a relationship of friendship function well for each other, even if not in any aspectual relationship, just as those in a relationship of enmity function adversely.

Example of Planetary Relationships: Paramahansa Yogananda

Pis. Ju Ma	Aries Ra	Tau.	Gem.
Aqu.			Can.
Cap.			Leo Mo ASC
Sag. Su Me	Sco. Ve	Libra Ke	Virgo Sa

January 5, 1893, 8:38 pm LMT, 83E23 26N47

Ascendant 06° 31' Leo	Sun 23° 12' Sagittarius
Moon 03° 14' Leo	Mars 13° 18' Pisces
Mercury 00° 55' Sagittarius	Jupiter 23° 51' Pisces
Venus 24° 44' Scorpio	Saturn 20° 13' Virgo
Rahu 12° 40' Aries	Ketu 12° 40' Libra
Uranus 17° 41' Libra	Neptune 16° 37' Taurus Rx
Pluto 17° 21' Taurus Rx	

The Sun is in Sagittarius, a sign of Jupiter, a natural friend, and is located in the tenth house from that planet, a friendly position. Friend plus friend equals great friend. The Moon is in Leo, a sign of the Sun, a natural friend, and is located in the ninth house from it, an inimical place. Friend plus enemy equals neutral. Mars is in Pisces, a sign of Jupiter, a natural friend, and is located in the same sign with it. Natural friend plus temporal enemy equals neutral.

Mercury is in Sagittarius, a sign of Jupiter, a natural neutral, and is located in the tenth house from Jupiter, a friendly position. Neutral plus friend equals friend. Jupiter is in Pisces, its own sign. Venus is in Scorpio, a sign of Mars, a natural neutral, and is located in the ninth house from Mars, a temporal enemy. Natural neutral plus temporal enemy equals enemy. Saturn is in Virgo, a sign of Mercury, a natural friend, and is located in the tenth house from Mercury, a temporal friend. Natural friend plus temporal friend equals great friend.

THE 27 NAKSHATRAS

	Nakshatra	Starting Point	Ruler
1.	Ashwini	00 00 Aries	Ketu
2.	Bharani	13 20 Aries	Venus
3.	Krittika	26 40 Aries	Sun
4.	Rohini	10 00 Taurus	Moon
5.	Mrigashira	23 20 Taurus	Mars
6.	Ardra	06 40 Gemini	Rahu
7.	Punarvasu	20 00 Gemini	Jupiter
8.	Pushya	03 20 Cancer	Saturn
9.	Ashlesha1	6 40 Cancer	Mercury
10.	Magha	00 00 Leo	Ketu
11.	Purva Phalguni	13 20 Leo	Venus
12.	Uttara Phalguni	26 40 Leo	Sun
13.	Hasta	10 00 Virgo	Moon
14.	Chitra	23 20 Virgo	Mars
15.	Swati	06 40 Libra	Rahu
16.	Vishakha	20 00 Libra	Jupiter
17.	Anuradha	03 20 Scorpio	Saturn
18.	Jyestha	16 40 Scorpio	Mercury
19.	Mula	00 00 Sagittarius	Ketu
20.	Purvashadha	13 20 Sagittarius	Venus
21.	Uttarashadha	26 40 Sagittarius	Sun
22.	Shravana	10 00 Capricorn	Moon
23.	Dhanishta	23 20 Capricorn	Mars
24.	Shatabhishak	06 40 Aquarius	Rahu
25.	Purvabhadra	20 00 Aquarius	Jupiter
26.	Uttarabhadra	03 20 Pisces	Saturn
27.	Revati1	6 40 Pisces	Mercury

This is the cycle of the 27 lunar constellations or *nakshatras*. They are most often used for marking the qualities of the Moon, whereas the signs relate more to the Sun. However, both signs and nakshatras can be used to read the properties of all the planets. A planet benefits by being in its own nakshatra.

Each nakshatra marks an area of the zodiac of 13 degrees and 20'. They come in three groups of nine: Ashwini to Ashlesha rule the first third of the zodiac, Magha to Jyestha the second third and Mula to Revati the last.

A twenty-eighth lunar constellation is sometimes marked, called Abhijit, placed between Shravana and Dhanishta (constellations 22 and 23).

The nakshatras are used for determining personality types, like the Sun signs in Western astrology. They are used in compatibility readings, with the compatibility between lunar nakshatras being a key factor in relationship compatibility. An elaborate point system called the kuta system exists to determine the exact degree of compatibility. The nakshatras are also important in horary and electional astrology to determine favorable times for action. The main usage of the nakshatras that we will examine here is for determining the planetary periods. The other factors, which are quite extensive and intricate, require a complete book in itself. Note the recent book *The Nakshatras: The Lunar Mansions of Vedic Astrology*, by Dr. Dennis M. Harness.

7

The Houses

DOMAINS OF PLANETARY ACTION

After planets and signs, the most important factor in all systems of astrology is the houses. The signs are a fixed twelvefold division of the zodiac that is the same for all charts. The houses are a changing twelvefold division, as the point from which they start varies according to each chart. The houses reflect the position of the Earth in its daily rotation relative to the heavens. As the Earth rotates during the course of the day, the whole zodiac gradually rises in the east and sets in the west. Depending on the time of birth during the day, any point in the signs may mark the different houses. The term "house" arose because each of these areas delineates a specific domain of our life. The Sanskrit term is *bhava*, which means a mode of being, essence or feeling. This shows how house location colors the effects of planets and determines their results.

The houses are oriented to the cardinal points. The point of the zodiac rising on the eastern horizon becomes the cusp or the determining point for the first house or Ascendant. The point of the zodiac overhead becomes the Midheaven or the cusp of the tenth house. The other houses are determined mathematically from these.

The Ascendant, or *Lagna* in Sanskrit, is the most variable of the major factors used in astrology. The Sun passes through one sign in a month and the Moon in two and one-half days, but the Ascendant sign changes every two hours. The Ascendant is the most important factor in prediction in Vedic astrology, with the Moon-sign second and the Sun-sign a distant third. This is logical, as it is the most specific factor in differentiating charts. Two people born the same day but at different times will have different Ascendants, though the other planets will change little. A difference in Ascendants makes a major difference in chart interpretations because it determines which houses planets will be located in and what domains of life they will affect.

The Ascendant is a spatial factor and reflects geographical position, particularly latitude. Two people born at the same time but at different places will have different Ascendant degrees, the more so the greater the distance between their places of birth.

The Ascendant shows the orientation of the Earth in the astrological chart. As such, it determines the outer domains of life and our action in the material world. We could say that the Ascendant represents the Earth as a planet in our chart. The Ascendant indicates our physical incarnation and how we project ourselves into the world at large. The twelve houses delineate the different domains of life and our potentials within them.

The signs reflect more our nature or character, the houses how we express and manifest it. The deeper and more cosmic aspects of our mind and soul relate to the signs and the stars. The more personal and outer expression of who we are comes through the houses and the Earth. In Vedic astrology we judge personality types not by the Sun sign but by the Ascendant. As the Ascendant determines the entire field of action for the individual, it becomes the lens through which we interpret all the different aspects of life.

HOUSES AND SIGNS

The houses in Vedic astrology have the same basic meanings as in the Western system, with a few important variations. Generally, the houses follow the analogy of the signs.

1. The **first** house, like the first sign Aries, shows the head, the ego and one's sense of self.
2. The **second** house, like the second sign Taurus, relates to the gathering and holding of personal and material resources.
3. The **third** house, like the third sign Gemini, governs curiosity and research.
4. The **fourth** house, like the fourth sign Cancer, relates to the mother, home and emotional happiness.
5. The **fifth** house, like the fifth sign Leo, relates to our soul nature and creative intelligence.
6. The **sixth** house, like the sixth sign Virgo, relates to health and disease, work and service.
7. The **seventh** house, like the seventh sign Libra, indicates relationship and partnership.
8. The **eighth** house, like the eighth sign Scorpio, shows sex, death, the occult, and the dark or hidden side of life.
9. The **ninth** house, like the ninth sign Sagittarius, shows our religious,

philosophical or ethical principles or opinions.

10. The **tenth** house, like the tenth sign Capricorn, indicates our public status and our achievement in the material world.
11. The **eleventh** house, like the eleventh sign Aquarius, refers to our aspirations and goals, as well as intelligence and friendship.
12. The **twelfth** house, like the twelfth sign Pisces, shows our subconscious and our hidden emotional nature.

The Vedic system departs more from this analogy than its Western counterpart, mainly for its interpretation of the third and eleventh houses. The meaning of the houses cannot simply follow the signs, as it is dividing up a different kind of space.

DIFFERENT SYSTEMS OF HOUSE DETERMINATION

The main difference between Western and Vedic astrology lies in the interpretation of the house cusps. Both agree that the cusp is the most important and powerful point in the house, and that planets located at the cusp have the strongest effect and most typical meaning in terms of the house. However, while Western astrologers make the cusp the beginning of the house, in the Vedic system the cusp marks the middle of the house. The first house in Vedic astrology will contain half of the Western system's twelfth house, and so on. Naturally, this gives rise to some different interpretations. In a Vedic chart, therefore, planets will not only go backwards the better part of a sign, they will also go back up to half a house.

Some Western astrological studies have found that planets have the strongest effect if placed 8 degrees prior to the Ascendant or Midheaven. This gives credibility to the Vedic view that would place these points in the first and tenth houses, not the twelfth and ninth, which are not thought by anyone to be powerful locations.

Several different systems exist for determining the location and extent of the houses. The problem shared by both Vedic and Western astrology is how to determine the location of the house cusps. All agree on using the Ascendant as the cusp of the first house. Some like to use the Midheaven, the point in the zodiac directly overhead, as the cusp of the tenth house.

As house orientation is relative to position on the globe, this becomes more variable the further from the equator the place of birth may be. It is rarely that there are exactly 90 degrees between the Ascendant and the Midheaven, except near the equator or at the time of the equinoxes.

In other words, the Earth's orientation to the zodiac does not divide it equally, except at the equator. As we move away from the equator it divides it in more and more unequal sections. The Sun appears overhead at the equator but lower in the sky the further away from it we move. Hence a twelfth of the day will not see a twelfth of the zodiac rising, just as the days vary in length the further we go from the equator. In arctic regions, with their long periods of darkness or light lasting days or months, some signs will not rise at all for long periods of time.

MIDHEAVEN BASED HOUSE SYSTEMS

If we use the Midheaven, the simplest method is to divide up the difference between the Ascendant and Midheaven equally. If, for example, the Ascendant is 20° Libra and the Midheaven 2° Leo, a difference of 78°, then we divide that by three. In that case, we get an extent of 26° for each house. Therefore the cusp of the eleventh house is 28° Leo and that of the twelfth is 24° Virgo. This is the method most often used in Vedic astrology, the Sripati system.

However, one may ask: If the difference between the cardinal points of the houses is not equal, why should it be divided up equally? For this reason, other house systems have been formulated, like the Placidus houses commonly used in Western astrology. This point certainly has its validity. We can use whichever system we find to be most accurate, as the difference is not always that great. As India is close to the equator where such differences are less, this issue did not require as much consideration as in Europe, which is much further north.

EQUAL HOUSE SYSTEMS

Owing to the variability that arises in Midheaven house systems, simpler systems have arisen that do not consider it as the cusp of the tenth house. They regard the Ascendant as the cusp of the first house and place all other house cusps an equal thirty degrees from it. If 5° Gemini is the Ascendant, the cusp of the second house will be 5° Cancer, that of the third house will be 5° Virgo, and so on. These are called *equal house* systems.

The advantage of these systems is that they are easier to calculate. They are also easier to read for aspects, as aspects are determined by degree position in signs, not by the angles as visible from the Earth. For example, a planet in the cusp of the tenth house in the equal house system will always be in a 90° or square aspect to the Ascendant. In non-equal house systems no such aspect may be formed. A planet conjunct the Midheaven may not be at any angle aspect to the Ascendant. Aspects cannot be determined by sight in such systems, but require examining the exact degrees of planetary locations.

Equal house systems become more important in extreme latitudes, north or south, where several houses may occur in one sign or several signs in one house, which would otherwise make chart interpretation very complicated. The disadvantage of the equal house systems is that they do not adequately consider the Midheaven, a powerful point in the chart. For this reason, it is wise to still add the Midheaven as a special point even in equal house systems. In equal house systems the Midheaven may fall in the ninth, tenth or eleventh houses.

HOUSE AND SIGN CHARTS IN VEDIC ASTROLOGY

Vedic astrology usually employs two different systems of house determination. First, it has a special chart, called the *bhava chakra* or "house chart," which specifically measures the houses. It can be done in two ways, either as a Midheaven or as an equal house system. It resembles the house systems used in Western astrology.

Second, it considers the houses in the *rashi chakra* or "sign chart." This we find more commonly used. In this chart it is not just an equal house system that is used, it is an *equal sign* system. In this system, for example, if any degree of Taurus is the first house, then Gemini will be the second house, Cancer the third, and so on. This is true even if it is 1° of a sign or 29°. This is the most simple and general method of house determination, in which primacy is given to the signs over the houses.

Houses are determined generally according to the rashi chakra and specifically according to the bhava chakra. The bhava chakra is thus a whole other chart. In it the positions of the houses are given, not the signs, though the exact sign positions of the cusps are placed along with the chart, as well as the points at which the houses begin and end.

HOUSES FROM THE MOON AND SUN

Vedic astrology considers the Moon as another Ascendant. For this purpose, it considers the location of the Moon at birth as the first house. It uses mainly an equal sign system, with the Moon-sign as the first house, the next sign the second house, and so on.

If a certain house from both the Ascendant and the Moon is aspected, then the results will be more certain. If the fifth houses from both the

Ascendant and the Moon are aspected by Saturn, the inability to have children would be more likely than if only one of them were so afflicted. In Vedic astrology we always examine houses from the Ascendant and the Moon. For example, for career we also look to the tenth from the Moon.

In the same way houses can be counted from the Sun as well. Sometimes a chart is drawn up using all three Ascendants, the regular Ascendant, Moon and Sun, noting planetary and house positions from each. This is called *sudarshana chakra.*

DIFFERENT HOUSES AS ASCENDANTS

Vedic astrology considers other houses as Ascendants for different purposes. In judging the affairs of the wife or partner, one can count the seventh house as the Ascendant for the wife and examine the other houses from that point. For example, the eighth house from the seventh (the second house in the usual order) can be examined as representing her longevity. Similarly, the fourth house can be considered the Ascendant for the mother, the ninth house for the father, the fifth house for children, and the third house for siblings.

Planets located in malefic houses from a particular house, like the sixth, eighth or twelfth from it, will adversely affect it. The opposite can be said for planets in benefic houses relative to a particular planet or house, like the fifth or ninth. Whatever house we regard as the Ascendant for whatever purpose can be examined just as the Ascendant in the birth chart. Vedic astrology also notes the houses, particularly the Ascendant, in the divisional charts (see chapter).

Houses have greater intricacy and importance in Vedic interpretation than in the Western system. The houses are treated as a system of moveable coordinates that can be applied in various ways. However, the houses from the prime Ascendant and from the Moon are the most important — the others are for fine-tuning.

House systems that do not consider the Midheaven in effect regard the Ascendant as a planet, marking the Earth in the chart. If we regard the Ascendant as a planetary point then we can see how the houses can be used relative to any planet. The twelve house system can be used independently of its connection to the Ascendant as another system of determining planetary influences. It is this freer use of the houses as a system of coordinates that is characteristic of Vedic astrology.

USE OF THE HOUSE (BHAVA) CHART

As Vedic astrology considers the houses in the rashi or sign chart from the Ascendant, Moon and divisional charts, often the more specific bhava or house chart is not used. Very accurate readings can nevertheless still be given. Yet while many Vedic astrologers only look to the sign chart, others give great important to the house or bhava chart and consider house rulerships from it as well. They see the house chart as adding more accuracy to the sign chart, so the bhava chart should not be overlooked. To approach Vedic astrology we must first learn to apply the houses in terms of the rashi chakra or sign chart. Once these are understood we can consult the house chart for more specific indications.

The house chart is oriented towards the outer affairs of life while the signs are more representative of the inner nature or soul. The more specific systems of house determination should afford us a better view of our actions in the outer world, while the sign-oriented systems should provide better knowledge of our inner nature.

Let us take an example. In a particular horoscope, a planet is located in the eleventh house of the house chart or bhava chakra, but in the sign chart or rashi chakra it is in the twelfth house. This would mean that in terms of outer actions the individual would accomplish a great deal, an eleventh house meaning. Yet in terms of their inner nature, they would be solitary or self-effacing, a twelfth house meaning. Hence, once we have understood the basics we can blend the meaning of different ways of looking at houses to afford us deeper insight.

Just as the signs are categorized according to qualities and elements, the houses have similar correlations. We will examine these main factors in the following section.

HOUSE QUALITIES

Angular Houses

Most important are the angular or *kendra* houses, houses 1, 4, 7 and 10 that mark the angles from the Ascendant. Planets situated in angles are strong and active to accomplish their potential. Angular houses are similar in character to moveable signs. They are sharp, energetic, and decisive. They give power for achievement and a strong will in life.

Of these, the tenth is the strongest angle, followed by the seventh, fourth and first. Planets in the tenth house dominate the chart and overpower even the Ascendant, making their imprint strongly on the life and character of the person.

Malefics in angles cause difficulties and inflict much damage, while benefics in angles afford much luck, grace and protection. Angular houses are said to be Lakshmi houses, named for Lakshmi, the Goddess of fortune. They give fortune of body (first house), home (fourth house), marriage (seventh house), and career (tenth house). They are like the pillars of the chart. When they are strong, the entire chart is propped up.

Succedent Houses

Succedent or *panapara* houses are 2, 5, 8 and 11. Planets here are moderate in strength. Succedent houses are similar in meaning to fixed signs, showing the accumulation of resources and maintaining what we have. Of these, the fifth is the strongest succedent house, then the eleventh, second and eighth.

Succedent houses generally relate to income. The fifth gives gains through speculation, the eleventh through income, the second through one's personal work, and the eighth through inheritance. They are also houses of the mind and self-expression. The fifth governs intelligence, the second relates to speech, the eighth gives insight, and the eleventh shows communication of our ideas to the world at large.

Cadent Houses

Cadent or *apoklima* houses are 3, 6, 9 and 12. Planets here are weak, uncertain, or hidden in their action. Cadent houses are similar to mutable signs. They give mental sensitivity and general adaptability that can grant a high intelligence, but they also tend toward instability and insecurity and are prone to mental and nervous problems. They can be good for spiritual development. Of these the ninth is the strongest, then the third, sixth and twelfth. The sixth and twelfth are difficult houses for health and happiness. The ninth and twelfth are more spiritual houses. The third and sixth give conflict and striving.

In order for a chart to give success in life, it is usually better to have some angular planets. If we examine the charts of famous or powerful people in any field, they will usually have some strong angular planets in their charts. For this reason the chart design used in north India is based upon the angular houses as the most important factor. A chart without good planets in angles is regarded as without distinction or power. A chart with bad planets in angles is like a ship with holes in it. Good benefics like Jupiter in an angle cancel numerous afflictions.

Trine Houses

Trine (*Trikona*) houses are 1, 5 and 9. Their locations form a triangle relative to the Ascendant. Residency in a trine house is a source of strength, like placement in an angle, though angles are a little stronger than trines. Jupiter does well in trines because its trine aspect comes into play in them. Once Jupiter is in one trine, it aspects all the others. The Moon also does well in them. Benefics are good in trines but malefics spoil the good effects of these houses and cause many difficulties.

In this regard the ninth house, though a cadent house, is very good, as it is the best trine. The fifth also gets boosted by this factor and becomes the best succedent house. Planets here, though not as strong for outer action as angular ones, are more important for spirituality and character. The lords of these houses also become very auspicious for the chart. Trine houses are called Vishnu houses, from Vishnu, the God of dharma. They promote dharma, the ninth our collective dharma, the fifth our creative dharma, and the first our personal dharma.

We notice by these different house factors that planets do well when located above the horizon, near the Midheaven in houses 9, 10 and 11. These houses represent how we affect the world in terms of our values (ninth house), actions (tenth house) and goals (eleventh house). Opposite them, houses 3, 4 and 5 represent our self in terms of our vital energy (third house), emotional state (fourth house) and intelligence (fifth house). Planets high in the chart tend to dominate those located below.

Upachaya and Apachaya Houses

Houses 3, 6, 10 and 11 are called *upachaya* or increasing houses. Planets located in them increase in strength through time and give progressively better results as one gets older. Natural malefics like Mars and Saturn do well in these houses, and give the power to overcome difficulties. The lords of these houses (except the tenth), however, are usually inauspicious and can cause harm because they are too impulsive in nature.

Of these houses, the tenth and eleventh are the best locations, though the tenth is more specifically an angular house. The eleventh is a good place for any planets because malefics do very well here and benefics do not fare badly either.

Houses, 1, 2, 4, 7 and 8 are said to be *apachaya* or houses of decrease. Planets located in these houses lose their strength through time and malefics do not do well in them. Of these the eighth is the worst, probably the most unfortunate house in the chart. This is another special grouping of houses unique to Vedic astrology.

Dushthanas or Difficult Houses

Houses 6, 8 and 12 are difficult or malefic houses (*dushthanas*). These houses are difficult points because they are places of transition, located on either side of the Descendant or seventh house (houses 6 and 8) and just above the Ascendant or first house (house 12). Planets located in them, particularly benefics, are weakened and can cause problems. This is particularly true if they are under malefic aspects. The Moon in particular suffers in these houses and harms the health of the person during infancy.

Malefic planets in the sixth may be good for power because the sixth is an upachaya house, but they can still cause disease if afflicted. Benefics in the sixth can be good for intelligence but can also cause disease. Mars in the eighth can cause death or harm. Saturn in the eighth, however, can aid in longevity, though it may not give prosperity. Benefics in the twelfth can give a spiritual nature or good rebirth. Venus is exceptional in that it can be good in the twelfth house and give comfort and prosperity. Ketu does well in the twelfth and can give spiritual insight and the ability to ward off negative psychic influences. Rahu is similarly good in the sixth. It can give freedom from enmity and success through foreigners, though it can still contribute to nervous system disorders.

HOUSES AND THE FOUR GOALS OF LIFE

Houses are related to the four goals of life. Houses 1, 5 and 9 relate to our basic nature, vocation or career (*dharma*). The first shows our basic character in life, the fifth our creative expression, and the ninth the higher aspiration that we are seeking.

Houses 2, 6 and 10 relate to work, wealth and possessions (*artha*). The second house shows our basic possessions in life, the sixth the work and difficulties they cause, and the tenth what we are able to achieve through them.

Houses 3, 7 and 11 relate to our desires (*kama*). The third house shows our basic vital energy, the seventh the ways we wish to enjoy it, and the eleventh the goals we wish to achieve through it.

Houses 4, 8 and 12 relate to liberation (*moksha*), our seeking of transcendence. The fourth shows our basic seeking of peace and happiness, the eighth the struggle we have to go through to find it, and the twelfth the sacrifices we have to make to arrive at it.

HOUSES AND THE ELEMENTS

Houses relate to the elements, like the signs, but this is a secondary factor. Yet a fiery planet in a fiery house will receive some boost thereby. Many planets in the twelfth, for example, can be found in the charts of those who drown.

Houses 1, 5 & 9, like Aries, Leo and Sagittarius, represent *fire.*
Houses 2, 6 & 10, like Taurus, Virgo and Capricorn represent *earth.*
Houses 3, 7 & 11, like Gemini, Libra and Aquarius represent *air.*
Houses 4, 8 & 12, like Cancer, Scorpio and Pisces represent *water.*

- Fiery houses are dharma houses and relate to the *kshatriya* or warrior temperament.
- Earthy houses are artha or wealth houses and relate to the *vaishya* or merchant temperament.
- Air houses are kama or desire houses and relate to the *shudra* or servant temperament.
- Water houses are moksha or liberation houses and relate to the *brahmin* or spiritual temperament.

DESCRIPTION OF THE HOUSES

First House

The first house relates to the self. It indicates our basic self-expression in life and our appearance in the material world. In Sanskrit it is called *tanur bhava,* which means "the house of the body." The first house is the main factor in determining our physical constitution, but it also shows our orientation to life as a whole. As the beginning of the houses, it is the house of birth and shows our origin. Strongly afflicted, it produces difficult birth or even infant mortality. It indicates our congenital physical vitality, so that when weak it is a primary factor in ill health.

The Sun shows who we are, our basic character or individuality. The Moon shows how we relate to others, how we appear on a social level to friends and family. The Ascendant or first house indicates how we project ourselves on a public level — our initial and general appearance to the world at large. Therefore it determines the whole structure of our outer manifestation, our personality as well as our body. Afflictions to it cause psychological as well as physical disorders.

For any significant accomplishment in life, a strong first house and its lord are necessary. It aids us in all our actions, particularly career, vocation and dharma, because it establishes our self-identity. Much like the tenth house, it is important for honor, integrity, fame or recognition.

Whatever the first house is associated with becomes central to our manifestation in life. Aligned with the ninth house, it gives an ethical nature or spirituality; with the sixth or eighth house it gives disease, with the second or eleventh house it gives wealth, and so on according to the nature of the house factors with which it is connected. Through it, the influences of the planets are able to enter into us and become part of our lives. The Ascendant is our general significator in the chart, our vehicle in manifestation. It is the most important factor in the chart and its strength or weakness can override anything else.

Second House

The second is the house of livelihood. It relates to our earning capacity, our ability to provide for ourselves in life. It does not indicate career per se; rather, it shows how much financial success we attain in our career, and whatever accrues to us through our own labor.

Relating to the face, it can show how we appear in life. Relative to the mouth, it shows our appetite and may indicate taste, not only in food, but also our taste in art or ideas. As the house of speech, it shows intellect and the capacity for communication, including communication of an artistic and poetic kind. It represents education and, as immediately following the first house, shows the period of childhood (between infancy and puberty). Afflictions to it can show unhappiness as a child or separation from the parents.

The second house shows how we operate and express ourselves in life, our capacity for communication and commerce on all levels. According to its strength it may give wealth, social prestige, or powers of speech and writing. Afflicted, it shows excessive spending or harsh speech.

Third House

The third is the house of brothers, *bhratri bhava,* indicating also friends and companions, how we act as members of a defined group of equals. It shows the people we like to do things with, the alliances that we make to achieve particular goals.

In Vedic thought the third is a martial house, a house of prowess symbolized by the arms. It shows our basic energy in life — the impulses and intentions that drive us, our will and ambition. It reveals our passion or zeal, along with our courage and boldness, which may become rashness and impulsiveness.

The third house shows our motivation and indicates our main interests, whether physical or mental — what we really like to do. It shows whims and interests, sports and hobbies. Well-placed planets here give a capacity for profound interest, deep research and scientific thinking. They can also give artistic capacities, including for the fine arts.

These meanings are a little different than those of the third house in the Western system, which relate more to the informational mind, rational thought and logic, factors which are often found under the third house's curiosity aspect in the Vedic view.

Fourth House

The fourth is the house of the mother, *matri bhava*, and is used to judge her influence in one's life. It also shows our house and environment, both outwardly and inwardly (the mind). Thus it relates to our basic emotional nature, our heart or feelings. Upbringing, education and refinement in life can be seen through it. It indicates the masses and, consequently, our popularity, particularly on a public level.

The fourth house shows land and property, and our ability to acquire them. As the general house of property it shows the vehicles we possess, like automobiles.

On a psychological level, the fourth shows how happy we are at home or in our emotional nature. It also relates to our capacity for rest and relaxation. It is the psychological house per se, and afflictions to it show emotional and mental disorders. It is probably the most sensitive of all the houses, and afflictions to it can be hard to overcome.

Spiritually, the fourth house indicates our faith and our family religious background. It shows our capacity for devotion and contemplation. It marks the nadir, the lowest point in the chart, and hence what is internal, hidden, or personal. Benefic planets here are good for meditation and peace of mind.

Fifth House

The fifth is traditionally the house of children, *putra bhava*. It represents our capacity to have children and shows the kind of relationship we will have with them. Afflicted, it either denies children or limits happiness through them (though for women the fifth house from the Moon is often more important for children than the fifth from the Ascendant).

The fifth is the house of creativity in general. On a higher level, it shows creative intelligence, our capacity for original thinking. It indicates our capacity to give good advice and to counsel others. In this regard it is important for lawyers and politicians. Generally, the fifth is the most important house for judging our level of intelligence (*buddhi*). Afflicted, it gives wrong judgment and emotional distortions to the thinking mind.

On the spiritual level, the fifth is the house of the *Ishta Devata*, the form of God that we choose to worship in life. It shows our devotion, the truth which is our guiding star. Like the ninth, it is a house of grace and good karma. It indicates the resources or merits (or lack of them) we bring into life, our past life karma. It is the house of mantra and shows our proficiency in using our words and thoughts with spiritual power.

The fifth is a house of love, higher or lower. It indicates romance and is the house of the beloved (not necessarily the marriage partner). It is a house of pleasure, enjoyment, and recreation, and shows what we love to do. It is also the house of positive health and vitality.

The fifth is another house of wealth and fortune. It shows our capacity to gain through speculation (like the stock market), how we can gain through our productions, creations, recreation and imagination.

Sixth House

The sixth relates to disease and enmity. It is the house of enemies, *shatru bhava*, and indicates opposition, difficulties, and obstacles in life.

Because the sixth is a house of disease, planets here tend to cause physical disorders according to their nature, particularly relative to the digestive system. Influences here, like those to the Ascendant, are important for showing our physical constitution in life. Specifically, the sixth house represents the immune system. Unafflicted it provides a strong immune system, but afflicted it makes us prey to many diseases.

The sixth is a house of injury and shows wounds and accidents. It is a house of power and impulse, and shows the negative effects of abuse of power, which may be directed against us or which may come through us. It shows our own martial prowess or that of our enemies, and the dangers that come from any use of force.

Malefics here, like the Sun, Saturn or Mars, are strong and show our ability to defeat our enemies, but they still tend to give health problems (unless they are without afflictions) and much struggle in life. As indicating enemies, the sixth indicates theft or litigation and can cause poverty. It shows where we should place our caution in life.

The sixth house relates to work and service, our capacity for karma yoga and for discipline and austerity. Well-placed planets here aid in our spiritual evolution. Benefics here make us service oriented, gentle, without enmity or self-negating. Yet planets in the sixth may also indicate overwork or cause subservience. The sixth is a house of effort and shows our capacity to do great labors. It also shows our relationship with foreigners or distant relatives.

Seventh House

The seventh is well known as the house of the partner, *kalatra bhava,* showing the wife in a man's chart and the husband in that of a woman. It is the main house for judging marriage and male/female relationships. As the house opposite the Ascendant or self, the seventh house or Descendant represents one's opposite or complement, the other.

The seventh is a house of love and passion, and planets here give a strong sexual nature. Yet it represents long-term committed relationships rather than romantic infatuations, which are better indicated by the fifth house. The seventh indicates partnership in general, even on an impersonal level.

As reflecting our relationship with the other, the seventh shows our social nature and general capacity to affect others. It can indicate political power or power over others, particularly if malefics like Saturn or Mars are located here. Such malefics may also render us disturbed in our sexual relations.

Planets in the seventh, even benefics, usually do not favor personal relationships. Mercury here tends to cause quick or superficial relationships. Mars causes conflict but gives personal power. Saturn causes separation, detachment and selfishness but also gives power. The Sun causes domination or control. Venus gives attraction but can cause excess desire. Even Jupiter can make us too expansive in relationship.

Eighth House

The eighth is the infamous house of death, *mrityu bhava.* It indicates destruction and dishonor and can show negative, criminal or violent aspects of the character. It represents chronic diseases or injury leading to death. It can indicate those people in life that we are likely to lose to death. Planets here cause us to suffer relative to the affairs that they represent in the chart.

On a positive side, the eighth house indicates wealth that is gained through inheritance or legacy.

The eighth is a very deep and mysterious house and can give profound insight to the mind, an understanding of life and death. It gives a strong and piercing but not always benefic intelligence and can show genius. It indicates research or invention, including mathematics and philosophy. It can give proficiency in Tantric type yogas and occult knowledge. The eighth shows distant travels or strange adventures, both in body and mind. It is the house of transformation for good or ill.

The eighth house shows our connection with the dark or underworld side of life. Drugs, prostitution and the power to manipulate others are shown here. The eighth gives a strong sexual passion and a good deal of sexual attractiveness, but often lacks the concern for partnership shown in the seventh house.

The eighth is the house of longevity, indicating our span of life. Showing the nature of our death, it also indicates the factors that tend to keep us alive. The negative and positive implications of this house are major factors for determining the ultimate meaning of our lives.

Ninth House

The ninth is the house of dharma, *dharma bhava*, and shows our prime values, principles and ideals. It is the house of the father, and his fate can be read from it. It shows the authorities that guide and inspire us.

The ninth is the house of religion, philosophy and law, and indicates our spiritual and ethical disposition. It is a good gauge of our potential for spiritual or yogic practices. The ninth relates to the deeper and philosophical side of the mind and our capacity for abstract thinking. It shows our higher education as well. As showing our values, it helps reveal our profession, particularly if we are teachers or religious figures, roles which are ruled by the ninth house.

The ninth is the prime house of grace, fortune and luck, and gives sudden and unexpected gains. Those who win lotteries or races usually have good influences from this house. Good planets here can go very far to counteract any negative influences in the chart.

The ninth house gives honor, prestige and power in life, usually of a beneficent nature. It gives easy recognition and acceptance, and through its strength our principles are able to operate in the world and shape the course of events.

Tenth House

The tenth is the house of karma, *karma bhava*, which means action. It is the main house for showing our effect upon the world and relates to career or vocation. The tenth house does not in itself determine the career; for this the first house and other factors must be considered as well. But it does show success in career and the status that we are able to achieve in life.

The tenth is a house of skill, achievement, honor, recognition and prestige. It shows the position we are able to attain in life and the power that goes along with it. It is an important house for determining political, social or worldly power. The tenth house measures our mark upon the world and whether we bring good or bad karma to it. It indicates pilgrimages and religious charities through its good karma side.

Because the tenth house is the highest point in the chart, planets here are strong and serve to raise us up in life. The tenth gives us the favor of the government or established authorities. It causes us to be visible and to gain respect and acknowledgment. Hence it can make us worldly or politically minded. Whatever we do through it will be noticed. The danger is that it will make us too outgoing and achievement oriented.

Eleventh House

The eleventh is the house of gains, *labha bhava*, and shows income or that which brings us increase. It indicates anything that we may possess much of or find increase through. It relates to goals, aspirations, will and ambition. It measures our individualistic motivation that can lead to impulsiveness and egoism. On the other hand, the eleventh house indicates the realization of our ideals and desires. In terms of family relationships it represents elder brothers and sisters and their fate is read through it.

The eleventh is a house of abundance, in which all planets are usually strong and favorable, both malefics and benefics. Whatever planet is located here will tend to possess its qualities in great measure. Venus here can indicate several partners. Jupiter here gives wealth. Mercury gives a good mind and success in communication ventures. The Sun shows the fulfillment of our prime goals in life.

The eleventh gives material gains, but there is a tendency to be overly presumptuous about them and to overextend ourselves. It is not only the place of abundance but also of excess. On a higher level, the eleventh gives spiritual gains and shows the development of an expansive and articulate intelligence. In this respect it resembles the fifth house, its opposite point in the chart. As the fifth is our intelligence, the eleventh is our ability to project that intelligence into the world. As the fifth house relates to writing, the eleventh is publishing.

Twelfth House

The twelfth is the house of loss, *vyaya bhava*, as the eleventh is that of gain. It is a house of expense, as the eleventh is that of income. It shows decrease, wastage and decay.

We tend to lose or waste away the traits of the planets located in this house. The Sun here shows a loss of self-confidence or a poor reputation. The Moon here shows emotional drain and moodiness. Saturn here causes weakness of the nerves and worry or anxiety. Jupiter here causes excessive or wasteful generosity. In general, planets here make a person weak or tired as their energy becomes suppressed.

The twelfth is the house of sorrow, disappointment and resignation. It indicates confinement or adversity, sometimes imprisonment. It is a secretive house and shows work behind the scenes, as in a hospital or a monastery. Yet the twelfth is also a house of passion, luxury and dissipation, the secret pleasures of life.

The twelfth house represents the past (as the ninth house does the future) and shows the past karma or past influences we are under. It can indicate guilt, regret, and grief. It shows the subconscious, where our rational mind and ego are dissolved, and it can indicate fantasy, mental disorders, or trance. It is an astral house and shows how we connect with the subtle planes, including our after-death state.

The twelfth house represents the end of the life-cycle. Yet as the negation of life, it indicates liberation, the denial of ego, renunciation and surrender. This makes it a house of yoga and meditation. As a house of isolation or separation it shows one alone, negated by adversity into a state of sorrow, or negated by inner peace into enlightenment.

The twelfth is the house of foreign countries, particularly those distant or overseas. Those who work with foreign countries or gain success in foreign lands, including politicians and diplomats, commonly have planets in the twelfth house.

KEY HOUSE SIGNIFICATIONS

1. self, body, general prosperity and well-being
2. livelihood, speech, youth
3. power, brothers, friends, motivation, interest
4. happiness, home, property, mother
5. creativity, intelligence, romance, children
6. disease, enmity, foreigners
7. partnership, marriage
8. death, destruction, longevity, research
9. dharma, grace, fortune, father
10. skill, achievement, success
11. gain, aspiration, impulse
12. loss, sorrow, limitation, liberation

PLANETARY SIGNIFICATORS FOR THE DIFFERENT HOUSES

Both Vedic and Western astrology judge the affairs of a house by noting the influences on the house and its ruler. To this the Vedic system adds another planet as the general house significator. These planets are the same for all charts. Their position in the chart should be considered in regard to the affairs of the particular house.

Planetary Significators of Houses

First House	Sun — self
Second House	Jupiter — earning capacity
	Mercury — childhood, speech, education
Third House	Mars — energy and prowess
Fourth House	Moon — mind, emotions, mother
Fifth House	Jupiter — children, creativity, intelligence
Sixth House	Mars — enmity, injury and theft
	Saturn — disease
Seventh House	Venus — wife for male;
	Jupiter — husband for female
Eighth House	Saturn — death and longevity
Ninth House	Jupiter — dharma; Sun — father
Tenth House	Mercury and Jupiter — profession
	Sun — fame and prestige
Eleventh House	Jupiter — gain
Twelfth House	Saturn — loss
	Ketu — liberation

Some planets are significators of more than one house: Jupiter relates to houses 2, 5, 7, 9 and 11, Saturn to houses 6, 8 and 12. This can help us discriminate the effects of a planet. For the indications of children in the chart, we can examine Jupiter and the fifth house; for dharma (religion or spirituality) we can examine Jupiter and the ninth, for income Jupiter and the eleventh and for livelihood Jupiter and the second. For disease, we can examine Saturn and the sixth, for longevity Saturn and the eighth, and for sorrow and liberation Saturn and the twelfth.

Rahu and Ketu, the lunar nodes, can be treated as joint significators with their planetary counterparts — Rahu with Saturn, Ketu with Mars. Yet Rahu is a special significator of foreigners, judged relative to the sixth house. Ketu is the special significator of liberation, judged relative to the twelfth house.

All planets are significators of different things. Some of these cannot be defined in terms of only one house. Venus is the significator of art. Yet poetry would be judged by the second house and craftsmanship by the third house. The capacity for emotion would be indicated by the fourth house, with the fifth house as a measure of general creativity.

It is often not good if the planetary significator of a house is itself located in that house. For example, Jupiter in the fifth is not considered good for children.

8

House Lords

Astrology presents us with the archetypal forces at work in life, the great powers of the cosmic mind. On one hand, these extend into the cosmic unconscious, the teeming inconscient ocean of ignorance in which great elemental forces struggle. It is here, in the dark sea at the beginning of the world, that the inertia of the lower forms of life persist tenaciously with their primeval fears, desires, aggression and attachment. On the other hand, these same forces extend upward into cosmic consciousness, the infinite ocean above the world, which contains in its great creative matrix the potencies of all redemption and transformation. As the lower ocean is, mythologically speaking, the domain of the demons or titans (Asuras), the higher ocean is the domain of the Gods or Devas. These two domains are ever in conflict or opposition, the Gods with their ascending or evolutionary force and the demons with their descending or de-evolutionary force.

Through the great elements of earth, water, fire, air and ether these two forces clash: the Gods aspiring to transform the chaos of the elements into a vision of cosmos, the demons straining to return them to the dull sleep of chaos. Yet these two warring forces are also related and, in some ways, complementary.

The planets project both forces of evolution and de-evolution, ascent and descent. These two powers are one — the undivine is the inversion or reflection of the Divine. The planets in their higher or harmonized nature function as deities to carry us up into the light. In their lower or conflicting nature, they become the demons that drive us into darkness and despair. It depends upon how we use their energy. Using it consciously through self-knowledge, it moves us upwards. Taking it unconsciously, not regarding the cosmic powers in our life, it drives us downward, putting us under a negative spell of illusion.

The planets as great Gods and great demons are the lords of great power that we must respect. They may create or destroy, further or restrain either the ascending or descending force. As each planet is the natural lord of certain forces, according to basic nature and sign rulership, so each planet is also a *temporal lord* or temporary ruler of certain forces through time according to the principles of house rulership. According to this principle of house rulership, the great power of the planets comes out for good or ill.

One of the unique and most important principles of Vedic astrology is this principle of house rulership — that the nature of planets changes according to which houses each planet rules relative to the Ascendant. A good planet for one Ascendant may be a malefic for another. Vedic astrology does not ascribe to planets a simple fixed nature, but modifies planetary nature according to each Ascendant. This principle is of particular importance for understanding how planets project their effects through time.

Planets possess certain qualities relative to the houses they rule. The lord of the fifth rules over children. When Saturn, a sterile planet, rules the fifth, it becomes a creative force and loses much of its natural sterility. When Mars, an unspiritual planet, becomes ruler of the ninth house of spirituality, he gains in spiritual force. The disposition of planets as house lords is as important as their natural disposition. For the prediction of events in planetary periods, it can be more important. The art of Vedic astrology revolves around the ability to combine the natural and temporal statuses of planets for an integral interpretation.

Many yogas or planetary combinations are stated purely in terms of house lordship. For example, when the lords of the second and eleventh houses combine it is very auspicious for wealth, as both rule houses of income. It is only of secondary import whether the planet involved is Jupiter, a natural significator of wealth, or Saturn, a natural significator of poverty. Jupiter would enhance the yoga by its natural status. Saturn would cause the yoga to manifest more slowly, with difficulty, or through such Saturnian domains as property. But the house lordship is the overriding factor.

In this way the meaning of the planets varies for each Ascendant. Each Ascendant has its own rules and the planets function uniquely relative to each. That is why the Ascendant is so important — it determines not only the basic nature of the person, it determines the general meaning of all the planets. Saturn for a Libra Ascendant, where it is a strongly benefic house ruler, has a radically different value than Saturn for a Leo Ascendant, where its house rulership is highly malefic.

In Vedic astrology, therefore, we must learn not only the meaning of each Ascendant but also how the planets function relative to them. The Ascendant colors the meaning of all the planets, which depends as much upon the Ascendant as upon their own nature. Each Ascendant is a different astrological game and requires a unique shifting of astrological rules.

LAWS OF HOUSE RULERSHIP

Planets are classified as temporal or temporary malefics or benefics according to the houses they rule relative to the Ascendant. Those that rule benefic houses become temporary benefics; those that rule malefic houses become temporary malefics. In this way a naturally benefic planet like Jupiter may become functionally malefic in a chart if it does not rule any benefic houses.

Lords of trine houses, 1, 5 and 9 are always considered to be auspicious. Lords of angular houses, 4, 7 and 10 are regarded as auspicious if they are natural malefics, like Mars and Saturn. Yet they are deemed inauspicious if they are natural benefics, like Jupiter, Mercury, Venus.

In other words, rulership of angular houses reverses the normal benefic or malefic status of planets. Rulership of trines, on the other hand, only makes planets benefic.

Lords of malefic houses 3, 6 and 11 are generally inauspicious, as these are houses of egoism, power, violence and disease. Lords of malefic houses 2, 8 and 12 are generally malefic but functionally neutral. Their nature depends upon what other houses their planet rules. In this context, the stain of rulership of house 8 is greater than that of house 12 or 2. While it is more dangerous for planets to be located in difficult houses like 6, 8 and 12, the lords of houses 3, 6 and 11 project a more negative force.

Planets rule two houses, except for the Sun and the Moon, which rule one house each. For this reason the temporal status of planets has to be interpreted according to the meaning of both the houses that the planet rules.

Planets often rule both a benefic and a malefic house, which makes their influence mixed. It will be good for the effects of the positive house it rules, but bad for the effects of its negative house. The planets in this way reflect the ambiguity inherent within the Ascendant and within life itself.

Saturn for Virgo Ascendant rules houses 5 and 6. As the ruler of the fifth house it will be good for children, creativity, intelligence and gains through speculation. As ruler of the sixth it will give bad effects in terms of health or enmity. This reflects the nature of the Virgo Ascendant, which is on one hand disciplined in its action but tends towards disease through too much sensitivity.

When a planet rules two houses, one benefic and one malefic, the house that is stronger or more important determines whether the overall effects of the planet are primarily helpful or harmful. Rulership of certain houses outweighs rulership of others.

The ruler of the Ascendant is always generally auspicious even if the other house that the planet rules is the sixth or eighth. Yet this malefic rulership does taint its status.

The ruler of the twelfth house generally gives the effect of the other house that the planet rules. Venus as the ruler of houses 5 and 12 for Gemini Ascendant is very auspicious and gives mainly the results of the fifth house. The negative effect of twelfth house rulership is most evident if the other house a planet rules is malefic. Saturn as ruler of houses 11 and 12 for Pisces Ascendant is very inauspicious because the eleventh is a difficult house.

In this regard we must consider the mulatrikona sign of the particular planet. Planets give predominantly the effect of the house ruled by their mulatrikona sign. Saturn rules houses 8 and 9, the worst and best houses, for Gemini Ascendant. Yet as Saturn's mulatrikona sign Aquarius rules the ninth house, its effects will be on the whole more positive than negative. For Virgo Ascendant Saturn is less auspicious, as its mulatrikona sign governs the malefic sixth house.

Another important factor is the natural friendship or enmity of a particular planet with the lord of the Ascendant. Though Saturn rules malefic houses for Mercury Ascendants (Gemini and Virgo), as a natural friend of Mercury it tends on the whole to give more favorable than unfavorable results. If such a house lord is a temporal as well as natural friend of the planet, the effects of malefic lordship will be further reduced.

Also important is which sign is stronger in terms of aspect or occupancy. If Saturn is in Capricorn in a Virgo Ascendant, its fifth house influence will become more important than its sixth house effect.

THE SUN AND MOON

The Sun and the Moon rule only one sign each. Two systems have come into being to deal with this. The first treats them as one planet. They rule the same houses as Saturn, relative to opposite Ascendants. Hence by the laws of house rulership they are auspicious for Aries, Cancer, Leo, Scorpio, Sagittarius, and Pisces Ascendants and malefics for the rest.

By the second system they are treated as separate planets, the Sun as a malefic and the Moon as a benefic. As a malefic the Sun is auspicious ruling angles and trines; the Moon as a benefic is only auspicious ruling trines. The problem with this system is that the generally benefic Moon, the friend of all the planets, becomes more often malefic than benefic as a house lord. For this reason we may not want to count the Moon as a negative house lord for ruling angles. Yet we do see it giving bad results as the lord of the sixth, eighth or twelfth houses. This is particularly true when it is under malefic influence or is the dispositor of malefic planets.

However, the Moon is regarded as an Ascendant in itself and is thereby generally auspicious for all charts. When houses are counted from the Moon, the lord of the Moon-sign becomes auspicious from that perspective, just as the lord of the Ascendant in the usual order.

SPECIFIC INDICATIONS OF HOUSE LORDS

Planets as house lords have specific meanings relative to the houses they rule. For example, the lord of the eleventh house, though generally malefic in terms of health and prone to make the character impulsive, is still the lord of the house of gains and as such is good for material acquisitions. It also gives good intelligence and the capacity to work with groups of peoples (these being the indications of the eleventh house).

When Mercury is the lord of the second and eleventh houses for a Leo Ascendant, it is a ruler of two houses of gain and income and as such becomes a double significator of wealth and income. Hence, apart from its generally somewhat malefic nature for this Ascendant in terms of health or judgment, it is particularly good for wealth.

The rule is that a planet is good for the affairs of the houses it rules, even though it may not be so for the Ascendant or the chart as a whole. This is because houses only represent one aspect of life and some rule over negative things in life. The lord of the twelfth in this way is good for giving losses, that being the power of its house that it boosts up, but it is not good for the Ascendant as a whole. The lord of the sixth is good for promoting disease, or giving power to our enemies, as that is what he rules. The lord of the eighth can give death, negativity or devitalization and so on.

House rulership is one of the primary methods of ascertaining the power and effect of planets. It is as important as the basic meaning of planets and signs and helps fine-tune those indications. The meaning of both natural and temporal statuses of planets must be blended properly. The basic rule is as follows:

Natural benefics, even when temporarily malefically disposed, will do some good, while natural malefics, even when temporarily benefic, will do some harm. When a planet has the same significance both naturally and temporally, the effects will be clear, unmixed and relatively easy to predict.

RAJA YOGA

When a planet rules both a trine and an angular house (apart from the Ascendant), it gains a special power. It becomes a *Raja Yoga Karaka* or significator of great power. It can confer status, power and prestige. The union of trine and angular house rulership is a union of Vishnu and Lakshmi or the God and the Goddess, giving great karmic rewards. Trine houses (1, 5, 9) as houses of dharma and spirituality represent Vishnu. Angular houses as home (4), relationship (7) and status (10) represent Lakshmi or fortune. In the astrological context, the word yoga refers to a special combination of planetary influences caused by one or many planets. We will discuss this principle more in the next chapter.

In the literal sense, Raja Yoga has the power to make one a king or to put us in a position of political or social power, as raja means "king." This idea includes any great position of fame and power, like a judge, mayor or administrator. Most political leaders have such combinations. It also gives general success in life in terms of the chart's basic orientation, including knowledge or spirituality However, these combinations are not rare and should be reinforced by several factors to be really strong.

For most Ascendants, one planet by itself can produce Raja Yoga. Such a planet is a doubly powerful temporal benefic. Saturn for Gemini and Libra Ascendants, Venus for Capricorn and Aquarius, and Mars for Cancer and Leo have such power.

For Aries and Scorpio, Raja Yoga is produced by the combination of the Sun and the Moon. Other combinations of rulers of trine and angular lords can create Raja Yoga, particularly exchanges between the ninth and tenth house rulers. How strong this yoga is will depend upon supporting factors in the chart.

POWER OF DIFFERENT ASCENDANTS

According to this principle of house rulership some Ascendants are better than others. Libra is sometimes regarded as the best Ascendant to have, because Saturn, ruling houses 4 and 5, becomes a Raja Yoga planet, a great benefic, while the main malefic becomes Jupiter, ruling 3 and 6, otherwise the most benefic of planets and one which usually cannot do much damage. Some astrologers consider that Jupiter actually gives good results for the Libra Ascendant. Moreover, Libra is a cardinal sign, which gives strength. However, while Libra may be a good Ascendant for our capacity to affect the world, it is not necessarily the best for all other things.

On the other hand, Aquarius is sometimes regarded as the worst of Ascendants because the ruler of the Ascendant, Saturn, is itself a difficult planet and also rules the twelfth house, the house of loss. Aquarius types seldom develop much fame, prestige, or charisma and often end up losers (Walter Mondale was a typical example in the political world). Yet at the same time, Aquarius is often regarded as the best sign for spiritual growth, the twelfth house also indicating liberation (as, for example, Ramakrishna).

By a similar principle of house-sign correlation, we can see that certain Ascendants are difficult. Virgo, for example, as the sixth sign, has the negative indications of the sixth house, the tendency towards disease. Scorpio as the eighth sign has eighth house properties as relating to death, vice or negativity. Pisces as the twelfth sign suffers from emotional confusion.

Cardinal signs generally do well as Ascendants, particularly for outer affairs, like Libra and Cancer. Mutable signs do not always make strong Ascendants, particularly Virgo and Pisces, yet are good for mental and spiritual sensitivity. Trine signs like Leo and Sagittarius are usually auspicious as Ascendants.

However, a chart with an Ascendant that is not inherently strong but with strongly placed planets is better than a strong natured Ascendant with a chart characterized by weakly placed planets. Stronger Ascendants give high potentials or expectations in life, which if not met can give us a great sense of failure.

PLANETS BY ASCENDANT

The laws of house rulership allow us to differentiate Ascendants and adjust the meaning of planets relative to each. Each house represents a particular field of activity, while the ruler of a particular house represents the lord of that field.

For example, if the lord of the self (first lord) is located in the field of destruction (eighth house) and the lord of destruction (eighth lord) is in the field of the self (first lord), then the individual is apt to have a short or difficult life. By rulership of certain houses each planet becomes a temporal indicator of certain affairs in life, the most important of which are mentioned below.

INDICATORS OF POWER/RAJA YOGA KARAKAS

This status has already been discussed. By ruling over two houses of power (an angle and a trine), a single planet gains this strength.

INDICATORS OF WEALTH

When a planet rules over houses of wealth, it gets this status. Strongest is when a planet rules over houses 2 and 11 (the houses of livelihood and gain). Mercury for Leo Ascendants and Jupiter for Aquarius gain this status.

Planets that rule houses 2 and 5 or 2 and 9 gain this power to a lesser extent. Such are Mercury for Taurus Ascendant, Jupiter for Scorpio, Venus for Virgo, and Mars for Pisces.

INDICATORS OF KNOWLEDGE/JNANA KARAKAS

Jnana is spiritual knowledge. Jnana Yoga Karakas give spiritual and other profound knowledge. Planets that rule both houses 9 and 12 (the houses of religion and liberation) acquire this status. These are Jupiter for Aries Ascendant and Mars for Libra.

Planets ruling houses 2 and 9 gain this status secondarily, like Venus for Virgo Ascendant and Mars for Pisces. These give Divine grace or favor in life.

Planets ruling both houses 5 and 8 (intelligence and research) give extraordinary mental powers if strong. Such planets are Mercury for Aquarius Ascendant and Jupiter for Leo. Again, any combinations of such house rulers has similar meanings.

INDICATORS OF DISEASE AND DIFFICULTY

The sixth house represents disease, as does the eleventh house as the sixth from the sixth. Planets ruling both houses 6 and 11 become powerful disease significators. These are Mars for Gemini Ascendant and Venus for Sagittarius. Mars is worse, as it is naturally a difficult planet.

The eighth house represents death and chronic diseases. The eighth from the eighth is the third. Planets ruling houses 3 and 8 become strong significators of death and disease. These are Mars for Virgo Ascendant and Venus for Pisces. Such planets are also significators of longevity, as both of these are houses of longevity.

Planets which rule houses 6 or 8 along with other malefic houses (3, 6, 11, 12) become significators of disease. Such are Mercury for Aries Ascendant, Jupiter for Taurus, Saturn for Cancer and Leo, Jupiter for Libra,

Mercury for Scorpio, Saturn for Sagittarius, Jupiter and the Sun for Capricorn, Mars and the Moon for Aquarius, and Saturn for Pisces.

INDICATORS OF EGOISM

Houses 3, 6 and 11 indicate egoism and excess use of force, along with a tendency towards a manipulative, aggressive nature and ulterior motives. When a planet rules these houses it can make an individual overly impulsive and self-promoting to the point of blindness or violence.

Such significators of impulsiveness include Mercury for Aries Ascendant, Mars for Gemini, Jupiter for Libra, Venus for Sagittarius.

Considering the tenth house in this context, we also have Saturn for Aries. Saturn for Leo can function this way as well, ruling houses 6 and 7 (as the seventh is the tenth from the tenth). Mars for Aquarius Ascendant and Venus for Leo are also very impulsive and power seeking, ruling houses 3 and 10.

INDICATORS OF LIFE AND LONGEVITY

Houses of longevity are 1, 3 and 8. Planets that rule two of these houses have special power in this area. Mars for Aries Ascendant and Venus for Libra, ruling houses 1 and 8, have this status to the highest degree. Mars for Virgo and Venus for Pisces have this to a secondary degree.

INDICATORS OF PASSION

Houses of passion and sexuality are houses 5 (romance), 7 (marriage) and 12 (secret pleasures). A planet ruling over two of these houses can give a strong passionate or sexual nature. Such planets are Mars for Taurus and Sagittarius Ascendants and Venus for Gemini and Scorpio. Venus and Mars are also naturally passionate planets anyway.

Additional indications can be derived through understanding the different meanings of the two houses that a planet rules. Mars for Capricorn and Venus for Cancer rule 4 and 11. Hence they can indicate gain (eleventh house influence) through property (the fourth house). Or they can indicate violence or inclination to injure (eleventh house influence) in the mind (the fourth house). A planet must be viewed according to the houses it rules and their meaning on all levels. The Sun and Moon can be more easily interpreted as they rule only one house at a time and will give their influence in a more unmixed way. The Moon, however, should always be judged as an Ascendant as well.

The following is an examination of house rulership by Ascendant. Note that this classification is general. Planets are not just simply good or bad, different factors have to be discriminated within this framework. So don't take this system too rigidly.

House Rulership Table, Temporal Disposition of Planets

Sign	Sun	Moon	Mars	Mercury	Jupiter	Venus	Saturn
Aries	5 A	4 A	1, 8 A	3, 6 I	9, 12 A	2, 7 I	10, 11 I
Taurus	4 N	3 I	7, 12 I	2, 5 A	8, 11 I	1, 6 A	9, 10*
Gem.	3 I	2 N	6, 11 I	1, 4 A	7, 10 I	5, 12 A	8, 9 N
Can.	2 N	1 A	5, 10*	3, 12 I	6, 9 A	4, 11 I	7, 8 I
Leo	1 A	12 N	4, 9*	2, 11 I	5, 8 A	3, 10 I	6, 7 I
Virgo	12 N	11 I	3, 8 I	1, 10 A	4, 7 I	2, 9 A	5, 6 N
Libra	11 I	10 N	2, 7 I	9, 12 A	3, 6 I	1, 8 A	4, 5*
Scor.	10 A	9 A	1, 6 A	8, 11 I	2, 5 A	7, 12 I	3, 4 I
Sag.	9 A	8 N	5, 12 A	7, 10 I	1, 4 A	6, 11 I	2, 3 I
Cap.	8 I	7 N	4, 11 I	6, 9 A	3, 12 I	5, 10*	1, 2 A
Aqua.	7 I	6 I	3, 10 I	5, 8 A	2, 11 I	4, 9*	1, 12 A
Pisces	6 N	5 A	2, 9 A	4, 7 I	1, 10 A	3, 8 I	11, 12 I

A = Auspicious, I = Inauspicious, N = Neutral,
* = Very Auspicious, Raja Yoga Karaka

HOUSE CORRELATION

A unique principle of Vedic astrology is that of house correlation, called in Sanskrit *bhavat bhavam*, meaning "from house to house." By this principle, a house which is the same number of houses away from a particular house as that house is from the Ascendant will possess similar effects.

For example, the tenth house is a house of power and prestige. The tenth house from the tenth house (counting the tenth itself as the first house) is the seventh house. So the seventh will also be a house of power and prestige.

The ninth is a house of grace, luck and fortune. Thus the ninth house from the ninth, namely the fifth house, also shares these traits.

The eighth house is a house of death, destruction and longevity. The eighth from the eighth, the third house, will also indicate these. For longevity, then, we would examine not only the eighth house but also the third. If both are afflicted, it would much more likely indicate short life than if only one were afflicted.

The sixth is a house of disease, injury and enmity. The sixth from the sixth, or the eleventh house, will also relate to these factors. Hence if a planet is the ruler of both the sixth and the eleventh houses, it is doubly a significator of violence.

The fifth is a house of children, creativity and intelligence. The fifth from the fifth, or the ninth house, can similarly be examined for determination of the state of children.

The fourth house relates to the emotional state of the person, home and happiness. The fourth from the fourth, or the seventh house, can also be considered conjointly with the fourth for determining these affairs.

Other applications of the principle of house correlation exist. For example, the twelfth house is the house of negation, representing the end of life. Applying this principle generally, the twelfth house from any house will be its negation.

The ninth house is the house of fortune, grace, honor and luck. The house twelfth to it, the eighth house, will be the negation of these traits; it will represent misfortune, disfavor, dishonor and bad luck.

The seventh house represents relationship. Twelfth from it is the sixth house, which will represent enmity, conflict or the denial of relationship.

Most importantly, the third and eighth are houses of longevity. The houses which twelfth from these, 2 and 7, become death causing or *maraka* houses.

This principle can also be used to show the negation of negative houses. The sixth house is a house of disease. Twelfth from it is the fifth house, which indicates the negation of disease or the positive condition of health.

We can apply the principle of house correlation to different houses as Ascendants as well. For example, the fourth house is the house of the mother. Her longevity will be indicated by the house located eighth from the fourth house, which is the eleventh house.

JAIMINI PLANETARY SIGNIFICATORS

There is another system, called Jaimini planetary significators (*Jaimini karakas*) and named after the great ancient astrologer Jaimini, by which planets become significators of different domains in life. This is determined by how many degrees they occupy by sign in the chart. To figure these out, we take the positions of the seven major planets in the chart and, not noting the signs, place them in order of their degrees and minutes.

The planet with the highest number of degrees in any sign becomes the *atmakaraka*, the significator of the self or self-indicator. This, like the lord of the Ascendant or a final dispositor, may become the most powerful planet in the chart. It is often the most important planet to consider in judging the spiritual nature of the individual, particularly relative to its position in the navamsha chart. We can take its position as the Ascendant in the navamsha and other divisional charts and read the indications of the chart according to it.

The planet second in its number of degrees in any particular sign becomes the *amatya karaka*, the significator of the confidant, symbolically the minister to the king, the one to whom we are closest. On an inner level it represents the mind or intellect.

The planet third in the sequence becomes the *bhratri karaka*, the significator of brothers. On a psychological level, it represents will, energy and motivation. It has a meaning like that of the third house or house of brothers.

The planet fourth in the sequence is the *matri karaka*, the significator of the mother. On a psychological level, it represents our emotions, of which the mother is the main indicator. It has a meaning like the fourth house or house of the mother.

The planet fifth in the sequence is the *putra karaka*, the significator of children. On a psychological level, it represents our creativity. It has a meaning like the fifth house or house of children.

The planet sixth in the sequence is the *jnati karaka*, the significator of relatives. On an inner level, it shows our capacity for interchange with society generally. It has a meaning like that of the sixth house, which indicates distant relatives as well as enemies and diseases.

The planet seventh in the sequence becomes *dara karaka*, the significator of the wife or spouse. On a psychological level, it indicates our capacity for relationship and partnership, our love and affection in life. It has a meaning like that of the seventh house of marriage.

It is good to examine the conditions of these significators for the domains that they represent. This is particularly true of their positions in divisional charts, mainly the navamsha, but also the divisions that relate to them (like the significator of brothers and the drekkana).

Mercury

Dressed in green, with a green body, who has four arms, the incarnation of Vishnu, who is a yogi, whose vehicle is a lion with an elephant's trunk, who carries a sword, shield and book in his hands, the son of the Moon, with an emerald crest jewel on his head, making the gesture that grants boons — may Divine Mercury ever grant us his grace.

9

Planetary Aspects and Yogas

All systems of astrology, East and West, base their predictions on the aspects that exist between the planets in the chart. By the theory of aspects, planets project their influence from their given position in the zodiac to certain other points. These are determined by the angle of arc of the zodiacal circle relative to the planet's position. The Vedic term for aspect is *drishti*, which means sight, showing the planets as conscious forces adjusting to one another.

Imagine the zodiac as a circle and the locations of the planets as points along that circle. Draw a line from the points of the planets to the center of the circle. If we then compare the positions of any two planets, a certain angle or arc of that circle will be created. This can be measured in terms of degrees. Some of these degrees, like 90°, 120° or 180°, create various aspects according to the different systems of astrology.

Western astrology carefully considers the exact degrees between planets in its calculation of aspects. It has major aspects like the square or trine, 90° or 120° aspects. These aspects are regarded as effective when the planets are within a certain number of degrees or "orb" of each aspect. Western astrology ascribes a different nature to the different aspects. Some aspects tend to be malefic or difficult (like the square); others tend to be benefic or easy (like the trine), whatever the planets involved.

Vedic astrology uses aspects in a different way than Western astrology, which may be difficult to comprehend for those who are familiar with the Western system. First of all, it judges aspects not according to the exact degree of angle between the planets involved but relative to sign. In the opposition or 180° aspect, the main one used in Vedic astrology, a planet aspects the sign opposite it (not just the degree). The aspects are not between planets, but from planets via the signs they occupy to other signs of the zodiac and to whatever may be contained in them.

For example, Jupiter in Aries would aspect the sign Libra by its opposition aspect, as well as the house ruled by the sign Libra and any planets located in that sign. If Jupiter is located at 5° Aries and Saturn at 25° Libra, the aspect would still count (though it would be too wide an aspect by the standards of Western astrology, being 20° from a direct opposition).

Vedic astrologers consider aspects to be stronger the more they approach the exact distance of arc. They may regard such aspects to exist independently of signs. If Jupiter is at 1° of Aries and Saturn at 29° of Virgo, the planets are not in opposite signs but the angle of their aspect is 178°, close to an exact opposition. Vedic astrology may still count this as an aspect, particularly when examining the house or bhava chart.

Imagine each sign to be like a separate room and the planets to be like lights. Wherever the light may be in the room, it will still light up the whole room. The first and last degrees of signs are like doorways. At these juncture points the planets can influence both signs but once out of these small doorways, they have little influence on adjacent signs.

Aspects by sign are easy to figure out and do not require knowing the exact degrees of planets. They do not have to be calculated in addition to the chart. For this reason, Vedic charts do not have the list of aspects which most Western charts require. And with aspects counted by sign, Vedic astrology uses fewer aspects than western astrology.

Vedic astrology does not ascribe any particular quality to different aspects. Aspects are distinguished only by their strength as major or minor. All aspects represent a relationship between planets. The nature of that relationship depends upon the nature of the planets, not upon the type of the aspect. The Vedic system does not regard oppositions or squares as necessarily bad or difficult, or trines as intrinsically good or easy. It depends upon the planets involved. An opposition of a badly disposed Sun in its fall in Libra may prove very difficult, but when well disposed, exalted in Aries, it may prove beneficial. A square from Mars in Aries, its own sign, to Jupiter in Cancer, its sign of exaltation, can be good, as both planets are well placed.

All the information on judging planetary nature is useful for determining the effects of aspects. An aspect from a great malefic like Saturn tends to be difficult whatever it is. An aspect from a great benefic like Jupiter tends to be helpful whatever it may be. The detailed way of determining the status of planets by nature and house rulership provides a similarly detailed way of judging aspects. Once we have ascertained the nature of a planet and its action in the different domains of life, its aspects will reflect that.

Vedic astrology ascribes certain aspects only to certain planets. While all planets share a general scheme of aspectual influence, some planets possess special aspects which other planets do not have, except as minor aspects.

Trines, 120° aspects, are regarded as a special full aspect for Jupiter, which other planets possess only as a minor aspect. Squares, 90° aspects, are given as full aspects only for Mars (forward in the zodiac) and Saturn (backward in the zodiac). This may be the basis of the Western astrological consideration of trines as good and squares as difficult, as trines are related to benefic Jupiter and squares to malefic Mars and Saturn. Vedic astrology regards the influence of planets in aspects as only thrown forwards in the zodiac, whereas Western astrology usually sees an aspect as coming from both planets. If Saturn is at 3° Gemini and Mars at 3° Pisces, Saturn would have an aspect of 270° (tenth house aspect) to Mars and Mars 90° (fourth house aspect) to Saturn.

In Western astrology aspects are regarded as a relationship between the planets. In the Vedic system, planets aspect houses as well, even if there are no planets located in them. They do so by aspecting the sign on the cusp of the particular house. Their aspect on houses improves or detracts from the affairs of the house, depending upon the nature of the planet.

The main rule in chart judgment is to examine an issue according to the house that relates to it, the ruler of the house, and the house significator, and to examine houses not only from the Ascendant but also from the Moon. Aspects to all these factors are considered.

For spirituality or religion, for example, we consider the influences on the ninth house, its lord, and Jupiter, and also the ninth from the Moon. In this regard we do not merely consider the aspects between planets, but the entire network of aspectual effects on all the factors in the chart that relate to a particular issue in life. Vedic astrology may sometimes consider aspects upon houses as more significant for judgment than the aspects between the planets themselves.

From the standpoint of Western astrology, the aspects of Vedic astrology appear general and non-specific. A few major aspects by sign seems very limited compared to its diversity of aspects by degree. Such a Western astrologer may wonder how Vedic astrology can be accurate with such limited aspects. Yet we must not overlook the fact that Vedic astrology also judges the aspects in its series of divisional charts. This allows for many subtler aspects and a finer analysis of exact degree relationships between planets. In addition, Vedic astrology judges planetary relationships by an extensive system of which aspects are only one part. This includes planetary friendships and various yogas.

Major Planetary Aspects

Sun, Moon, Mer., Venus	7th
Mars	4th 7th 8th
Jupiter	5th 7th 9th
Saturn	3rd 7th 10th

The primary rule is that all planets aspect the seventh sign from the sign in which they are located. This is similar to the opposition or 180° aspect in Western astrology.

Mars, Jupiter and Saturn, the distant planets, possess special aspects. Mars, in addition to the regular seventh sign aspect, aspects the fourth and the eighth signs. The fourth aspect is similar to an approaching square or 90° aspect in Western astrology. The eighth aspect is like a quincunx or 150° aspect in Western astrology, but it only throws this aspect on planets behind it in the zodiac, so the real angle is 210°.

Jupiter has special aspects on the fifth and the ninth signs from it. These are the same as trines in Western astrology, operating both forwards and backwards in the zodiac. Saturn has special aspects for the third and the tenth signs from it. Its aspect on the third is like a sextile or 60° aspect in Western astrology but only operates on planets in front of it in the zodiac. Its tenth aspect is a square, but only operates backwards, hence its angle is really 270°.

Rahu and Ketu are generally not given special aspects but a few Vedic astrologers, like J.N. Bhasin, give them aspects like Jupiter on the fifth and ninth. The Rahu-Ketu axis, however, is always important. Any planet conjoined with one of the lunar nodes will be in opposition to the other.

SAMBANDHA/ COMPLETE CONNECTION BETWEEN PLANETS

For most purposes, only full aspects are used in Vedic astrology. When planets are in mutual full aspect, they are said to be in *sambandha*, which means "complete connection." This complete connection or sambandha may exist due to other factors as well. When planets exchange signs, for example when Jupiter is in Aries, a sign ruled by Mars, while Mars is in Pisces, a sign ruled by Jupiter, this is also a complete connection, like a mutual full aspect. It is called *mutual reception* in Western astrology and is one of the most powerful connections possible between planets.

CONJUNCTION

Planets in close proximity are said to be in conjunction. This is a kind of intimate association. In Vedic astrology conjunction is not considered to be an aspect, as aspects are only regarded as possible when there is a certain distance between planets. Yet, along with aspects, it is counted as a kind of planetary relationship, a full planetary relationship like a full mutual aspect, and thus constituting sambandha.

Vedic conjunctions, like aspects, are counted by mainly by sign, though the closer in degrees the planets are to each other, the stronger the effect of the conjunction becomes.

MAJOR AND MINOR PLANETARY ASPECTS

All planets aspect the seventh sign with a full influence or sight. They aspect the fourth and eighth signs with a three-quarters sight or influence. They have one-half aspect on the fifth and ninth signs. They have one-quarter aspect on the third and tenth.

For Mars its special aspects, which are generally given three-quarters influence, are regarded as full. For Jupiter the usual one-half influence aspects, its special aspects, are regarded as full. For Saturn the one-quarter influence aspects, its special aspects, are counted as full. The rest of the additional aspects for these planets are like the other planets.

Minor aspects are usually not used in reading charts. Their main place is as another factor for determining planetary strengths, as part of the system of shadbala (see chapter).

COMBUSTION

Planets in close conjunction with the Sun become "combust" or "burnt up." They are weakened and may be rendered powerless. They are particularly difficult for the human element that they rule. For example, if the Ascendant lord is combust it is bad for the health of a person, while if the seventh lord is combust it is bad for the partner.

For Mars, Jupiter and Saturn, the orb of conjunction for combustion is 8° 30'. For the Moon, a larger planet, it is 15°. For the inner planets it is less, 4° for Venus and 2° for Mercury. Some Vedic astrologers make these orbs wider. Others consider that if planets are in close conjunction, less than a degree, with the Sun they merge with its rays and cease to suffer from the negative effects of combustion. However, if a planet is in a favorable sign or house the effects of combust can be mitigated.

Generally all planets function better if located some distance from the Sun. This is particularly true of the Moon, Mercury and Venus, which are subject to waxing and waning. Just as the Moon is strongest when full and becomes weaker as it approaches the Sun, so Mercury and Venus are strongest when at maximum distance from the Sun and become weaker as they approach it. To a certain extent, this is also true of the other planets.

The logic behind combustion is that, when in proximity to the Sun, the rays of planets are overcome by the power of the solar light. So conjunction with the Sun must be generally regarded as a negative for the energy of any planet.

PLANETARY WAR

When two planets are in conjunction of one degree or less, they are said to be in a *planetary war*. There is a clashing of the forces of their respective rays. The planet with the lower degree of longitude becomes the winner of this planetary war. For example, if Mars is at 23° 35' Sagittarius and Venus at 23° 17', then Venus is the winner of the war. Benefics who have lost a planetary war with a malefic may be rendered very weak, whereas benefics who have won a war with a malefic become much stronger. The rules of planetary war do not apply in the case of the Sun or Moon.

SEPARATIVE PLANETS

The Sun, Saturn, Rahu, Ketu, and the ruler of the twelfth house from the Ascendant are separative planets. To this some Vedic astrologers also add the planet Mars, whose effect is mainly destructive, or all the malefic planets. They serve to separate or remove us from the things in life that they influence.

If these separative planets aspect the factors representing the marriage partner; the seventh house, its ruler, and the significator of the partner (Venus for the male, Jupiter for the female), then separation is likely to occur. Divorce will happen easily and lasting relationships will prove difficult.

If they aspect the tenth house and its ruler, there may be loss of one's job or an inability to hold steady employment. If they aspect the second house and its ruler, along with Mercury, one will live away from one's parents as a child. If they aspect the fourth house, its lord, the Moon and Mercury, one may be in danger of being separated from one's mind (going crazy). If they aspect the fifth house, its lord and Jupiter, we may be separated from our children or, more likely, we may be unable to have them in the first place or, for women in particular, surgery on the reproductive organs may be possible. We can be separated or removed from the qualities of each house in this way, according to its nature. The results are more likely to occur if the same houses from the Moon sign are similarly affected.

The Sun creates independence or burns things up. Saturn creates loss, alienation or detachment. Rahu is dispersing in its action and gives an attraction to what is foreign or distant. Ketu makes us contract and causes negativity. The ruler of the twelfth house creates loss and retreat, which is the nature of that house.

RETROGRADE MOTION

Planets can appear to go retrograde, or backward in the zodiac, because of their different orbits than the Earth. Western astrology usually regards retrograde planets as causing difficulty, delays or obstacles. A retrograde Mercury, for example, is considered to cause problems in communication.

Retrogradation is a matter of some difference of opinion. Generally, retrograde benefics lose some of their benefic power and become unpredictable. For example, a retrograde Ascendant lord is said to weaken the health. Retrograde malefics remain harmful and can become more powerful. Retrogradation is sometimes considered to reverse the energy of the planets. Some say that retrograde planets lose strength when exalted, but gain strength when debilitated.

Retrogradation has an internalizing effect on a planet's energy. If Mercury is retrograde, the intellect will be more introverted. The individual may be more interested in history or occult pursuits. When afflicted, this may cause nervousness or speech difficulties, or just hesitancy in communication.

Retrograde planets indicate a karmic result and show an influence from the past. They may be functioning to fulfill some karmic debt or promise or for clearing up affairs from the past. The individual will not go forward with the influences of the planet but must take them backwards or inwards to consolidate or limit them.

PLANETARY YOGAS

More important than aspects in Vedic astrology are planetary yogas. These are planetary combinations that encompass many factors, including sign, house and aspect. Yoga itself means "a combination." Yogas may be simple or complex. Complex yogas may involve many factors and be hard to calculate or to recognize.

Most yogas are defined in terms of houses, noting the good and bad houses and house lords from the Ascendant. Hindu astrology books contain long lists of them, which astrologers memorize. Yet even when they exist in a chart, they require supporting factors to be really effective. It is more important to understand the principle behind yogas than to memorize all the possible yogas.

All chart interpretation, which must involve synthesizing or correlating indications in the chart, is a kind of building up of yogas. The more the same result is indicated by different factors in a chart, the more likely it is to occur. It is this principle of "yogic thinking" that we must grasp, the capacity to draw connections. Some very powerful charts may not have obvious classical yogas, but will have other combinations that make for great strength. The simpler yogas are not always as powerful as more complex formations that integrate the energy of many planets.

HEMMING IN OF PLANETS

If the Moon is in Libra, with Saturn in Scorpio and Mars in Virgo, then it has malefic planets around it on both adjacent sides. In this instance it is "hemmed in by malefics," which weaken and harm it. This is called *Papakartari Yoga* in Sanskrit. While this is not technically an aspect, it has a strong effect like a major aspect. The Moon will be strongly under the influence of these two planets and weakened by their malefic nature. Planets hemmed in by malefics can counter this to a great extent by receiving the aspect of a benefic.

If the planets involved are Jupiter and Venus, then the Moon would be "hemmed in between benefics," which protect it and strengthen it. This is called *Shubhakartari Yoga* in Sanskrit. Such formations must be considered in determining planetary influences and they may constitute various planetary yogas.

When all the planets are placed between Rahu and Ketu, another kind of negative hemming in of planets occurs. This is called *Kalasarpa Yoga*, the combination of the "serpent of time." It causes unpredictability, unexpected difficulties, strange events, and psychic gifts for good or ill. However, it does not weigh too heavily in itself and can be overpowered by other factors.

RAJA YOGAS

We have already discussed how certain planets by themselves can create Raja Yoga for different Ascendants. The same thing can occur when different planets combine. Combinations of planets ruling angles and trines also create Raja Yoga, whatever their nature may be. The strength of the yoga will be diminished, however, if the planets involved rule other, more difficult houses or have other afflictions. The yoga is usually strongest if the planets exchange signs, like the lord of the ninth being located in the tenth and the lord of the tenth in the ninth. Rahu can also create Raja Yoga. If Rahu is in an angle while the planet ruling it is located in a trine, this constitutes a type of Raja Yoga. By some accounts it also occurs if Rahu is located in a trine and its lord is in an angle.

REVERSE RAJA YOGAS

Yogas are formed not only by positive indications but also by a combination of negative influences that neutralize each other. Houses 6, 8 and 12 are also houses of difficulties. When their lords combine or exchange, difficulties increase. However, an exception occurs as reverse (Viprita) Raja Yogas. If all three of the lords of houses 6, 8 and 12 from the Ascendant and the Moon combine in one of these difficult houses (6, 8, 12), then great good fortune occurs because the three difficult house lords and all the problems that they signify get neutralized.

DHANA YOGAS: COMBINATIONS FOR WEALTH

Dhana yogas depend upon the ruler of the second, as the second mainly determines wealth. The eleventh as the house of income, the fifth as giving gains through speculation and the ninth as giving luck and unexpected windfalls are also to be considered. Sometimes the fourth as the indicator of property and vehicles comes into play. As with Raja Yogas, a combination of such house rulers creates this yoga, like the lord of the second in the eleventh and the lord of the eleventh in the second.

DARIDRYA YOGAS: COMBINATIONS FOR POVERTY

These typically exist by the combination of houses of wealth with those of houses of loss, like association of the second and eleventh with the twelfth. For example, if the lord of the second house of income is located in the twelfth house of loss and the lord of the twelfth house of loss is located in the second house of income, this is a yoga for poverty. Malefics in houses of wealth can also bring it about, like the lord of the sixth in the fifth, or the lord of the eighth in the ninth.

ARISTHA YOGAS: COMBINATIONS FOR DIFFICULTY

Arishta yogas are difficult combinations that bring about various calamities in life, particularly disease. They consist primarily of exchanges between the Ascendant lord, the indicator of the body, and lords of the difficult houses 6, 8 and 12. Combinations of the sixth, eighth and twelfth lords with one another can also create it. The Moon located in these houses has the same problem and can cause ill health in infancy (this can be cancelled if the Moon is waxing during a day birth or waning during a night birth).

SANNYASA YOGAS: COMBINATIONS FOR RENUNCIATION AND SPIRITUALITY

Various planetary combinations, including certain afflictions, help bring about spirituality in the chart. For example, a simple *Sannyasa Yoga*, a combination for renunciation and spirituality occurs when four or more planets, including the tenth lord, are located together in a single sign.

The Moon in a sign of Saturn aspected by Mars or the Moon in a sign of Mars aspected by Saturn is another such yoga. Afflictions to the Moon help to create detachment and remove the individual from any personal life. In fact, any Mars-Saturn aspects on the Moon can aid in this. However, the same combination can cause emotional unhappiness as well, if not supported by other spiritual factors. Afflictions to the second, fourth and twelfth houses, which are houses of enjoyment, also can aid in spirituality.

YOGAS INVOLVING THE MOON

Many planetary yogas exist involving the Moon. The Moon is a sensitive, gregarious and motherly planet. She does not like to be alone or to function on her own. An unassociated Moon is generally inauspicious, often even if she is otherwise well-placed. For example, the Moon in Cancer or Taurus may not be good if she has no benefic planets around her or influencing her.

The Moon does well in conjunction with benefic planets or with benefics in adjacent signs. It does better if Jupiter is located in an angle from her (called

Gaja Kesari Yoga). Aspected or hemmed in by malefics, particularly Saturn and Rahu, she suffers, and our mind and emotions may suffer with her. Many of the same issues occur if the Ascendant is similarly influenced. This is another instance of *Papakartari Yoga*, the "hemming in" influence that we have already mentioned. Similarly the Moon surrounded by benefics improves all the indications that she represents.

MAHAPURUSHA YOGAS

Among the most common and most useful of the yogas are the *Mahapurusha Yogas*, planetary combinations that create great people. These occur when planets are located in their own sign or exalted and at the same time in an angle from the Ascendant or the Moon. Only the five major planets are considered, not the Sun or the Moon, but these also benefit from such positions. Such positions serve to magnify the qualities of the planet involved and stamp the chart with its nature, character and force. They may make the person of the type belonging to the planet. People with such charts often have the physical characteristics of the planet.

MARS—RUCHAKA YOGA

The Mahapurusha Yoga for Mars is called *Ruchaka Yoga*, the radiant combination. It endows a person with strong Martian qualities like courage, determination, and independence, and gives a good power of action and achievement. Naturally, it is common in the charts of Mars type people: military leaders, politicians, lawyers, scientists, and business executives. It gives much success, but the tamasic qualities of Mars may come out, including tendencies towards domination and violence, so that it is not always spiritually beneficial.

MERCURY—BHADRA YOGA

The Mahapurusha Yoga for Mercury is called *Bhadra Yoga*, the auspicious combination. It gives strong mercurial qualities like good powers of speech, intellect, wit, humor, humanism and a balanced psychology. It is common in the charts of intellectuals, teachers, writers, and businessmen. It gives many talents to the mind but may augment the rajasic, agitated or commercial side of Mercury: the acquisitive mind and its seeking to grasp life in terms of names, forms and quantities.

JUPITER—HAMSA YOGA

The Mahapurusha Yoga for Jupiter is called *Hamsa Yoga,* the swan combination, the swan being the bird of spiritual knowledge. It gives strong Jupiterian qualities, an ethical, philosophical or religious nature, optimism, creativity, health, faith, prosperity and affluence. It is common in the charts of religious people, teachers, liberal social and business leaders, sometimes entertainers. It gives joy and compassion and can give spirituality but may just serve to make us self-promoting, Jupiterian on a superficial level.

VENUS—MALAVYA YOGA

The Mahapurusha Yoga for Venus is called *Malavya Yoga.* It gives strong Venusian qualities like comfort and prosperity in life, command of vehicles and material resources, beauty, charm, grace, and artistic talents. It is common in the charts of artists, beautiful women, those possessing wealth or social influence, sometimes even politicians. Again it can give lower or higher Venus effects depending upon its placement. On a higher level, it gives powers of devotion.

SATURN—SHASHA YOGA

The Mahapurusha Yoga for Saturn is called *Shasha Yoga.* It gives strong Saturnian qualities like power over people, positions of authority, control of material resources, with a strong work and achievement capacity. It is common in the charts of political and business leaders. As Saturn is a cruel planet, unless the Moon or Jupiter are strong the individual may be selfish, ruthless or destructive (Saturn in an angle is usually looked on with some suspicion). Benefically placed it gives detachment and spiritual insight, the capacity for silence.

Mahapurusha Yogas are prominent in the charts of famous people. However, they are not uncommon; many charts have at least one of them. To really work, they must be well-placed. Such yogas are stronger when the planet is in the tenth, the best angle, or if the yoga occurs with respect to both the Ascendant and the Moon. It also helps if the planet involved is the final dispositor in the chart or rules over many of the other planets. Additional strength can be gained if such planets combine with friendly planets or planets of like nature, like Mars with the Sun or Jupiter with the Moon. It is better if the planet in the yoga governs good houses from the Ascendant.

While giving strength and power in the outer world, these

combinations do not always give spiritual knowledge and can make a person prone to pride. Strong malefics in Mahapurusha Yogas, like the Mars and Saturn, can create tyrants (see the chart of Hitler for such a yoga for Mars). On the other hand, debilitated planets, though giving outer difficulties, can make us more humble. Many spiritual people, for example, have a debilitated Jupiter in Capricorn for this reason.

KUJA DOSHA

Mars in certain houses creates difficulties in marriage and relationship. This is called *Kuja Dosha* or the blemish of Mars. The relevant houses are the first, fourth, seventh, eighth and twelfth. Exceptions are for the first house if the sign is Aries, the fourth house if it is Scorpio, for the seventh if it is Capricorn or Pisces, for the eighth if it is Cancer, and for the twelfth if it is Sagittarius. These positions may be counted from the Moon as well.

Such a placement of Mars shows potential conflict in relationship or difficulties in the life of the spouse. A person with this planetary placement should generally only marry another person with a similar one. Mars in the seventh appears to be the most difficult of these (though it often gives success in the social world) and Mars in the first or eighth is often difficult as well.

Mars in the first can make us aggressive or contentious in our behavior. In the seventh it can cause conflict in relationship and the urge to dominate. Mars in the eighth may give a strong sexual drive or indicate the early death of the partner. In the fourth it may show an aggressive emotional nature or unhappiness in the home. Mars in the twelfth may indicate hidden passion or the wasting away of our vital energies.

Such placements should not be interpreted simplistically, since many charts have them. They should be reinforced by other negative influences to the seventh house, its lord and the marriage significator. Moreover, they reflect a more passive role for women in society and may not be so applicable in the modern world where the woman has to work and may therefore need a stronger Mars, which most of these positions give. In this regard, Kuja Dosha for a woman may only require that she has an independent type marriage.

If the factors representing relationship are afflicted by other malefics (like the Sun, Saturn, Rahu and Ketu), a person may have difficulties in relationship even without Kuja Dosha. In fact these positions may be worse, like the Sun in the seventh house, which usually denies marriage or makes it unhappy.

SHADBALA/ PLANETARY POWER RATIOS

Shadbala is an elaborate system of computation which aids in determining planetary strengths and weaknesses. It is perhaps the most sophisticated and detailed of such astrological systems and probably the most reliable. While Shadbala is not necessary to give an accurate astrological reading, it provides helpful information. As the calculations are very complex and require much skill and time to do, a computer program for them is essential. For reason of its complexity, we will only outline it here.

A planet strong in Shadbala will have power in the chart, but for good or ill depending upon its nature. One weak in Shadbala will be able to do little and may cause disease or difficulties. Along with Shadbala, signs, houses, aspects and yogas must still be considered. Shadbala is an enhancement but not a substitute for the comprehensive examination of a chart. Shadbala tells us if a planet is likely to have enough strength to fulfill its role in the chart. The chart tells us what that role may be and if it is likely to be ordinary or extraordinary. A planet strong in Shadbala will still not do well, for example, if it is under malefic influences by aspect or association. A planet strong in Shadbala may in fact make a person a bit one-sided in character. For example, I have seen charts in which the Sun had a very high Shadbala, but the person involved was a strong egotist!

FACTORS OF SHADBALA

Shadbala means six factors of strength, which are:

1. Positional Strength — Sthana Bala
2. Directional Strength — Dig Bala
3. Temporal Strength — Kala Bala
4. Motional Strength — Chesta Bala
5. Natural Strength — Naisargika Bala
6. Aspectual Strength — Drik Bala

1. Positional Strength

This consists of five factors.

1. Exaltation Strength (Uccha Bala): how close a planet is from its point of exaltation.
2. Divisional Strength (Saptavargaja Bala): its residential strength in the seven divisional charts.
3. Odd-Even Sign Strength (Ojayugmarasyamsa Bala).
4. Angular Strength (Kendra Bala): its strength in terms of house position.
5. Decanate Strength (Drekkana Bala): its strength in terms of decanate location.

2. Directional Strength

This is one of the main factors of planetary strength and weakness and helps us understand the power of the planets in the houses. The same planets become weak in the opposite house or direction.

Directional Strength

East	First house	Mercury, Jupiter
South	Tenth house	Sun, Mars
North	Fourth house	Moon, Venus
West	Seventh house	Saturn

3. Temporal Strength

This is a combination of nine factors based upon the time of birth in hours, days, months, and years, the strength of planets at these times or as ruling them.

1.	Day-Night Strength	Nathonnatha Bala
2.	Monthly Strength	Paksha Bala
3.	Four Hour Strength	Tribanga Bala
4.	Lord of the Year Strength	Abdadhipati Bala
5.	Lord of the Month Strength	Masadhipati Bala
6.	Lord the Day Strength	Varadhipati Bala
7.	Lord of the Hour Strength	Hora Bala
8.	Declinational Strength	Ayana Bala
9.	Planetary War Strength	Yuddha Bala

4. Motional Strength

This is the most complicated factor of Shadbala and relates to the motion of the planets around the Sun, including retrogression.

5. Natural Strength

This is the same for all charts. The Sun is the strongest planet, then the Moon, Venus, Jupiter, Mercury, Mars, Saturn, in accordance with their apparent brightness as seen from the Earth.

6. Aspectual Strength

This is according to the arc of aspect relative to the extended rules of determining aspects. It is not meant to substitute for calculating aspects in the chart.

10

Divisional Charts

FINE TUNING THE BIRTH CHART

In Vedic astrology a minimum of two charts are calculated, the basic birth chart (rashi chakra) and the ninth divisional chart (navamsha). Frequently six, and as many as sixteen, such charts may be considered. Divisional charts provide detail and specificity in the delineation of planetary influences. The Vedic system considers divisional placement by sign only, but some computer programs calculate them by degrees as well. As the calculation of these charts is time consuming, it is best to do them by computer. The following are the general rules on how they are determined.

Hora Chart or Second Divisional

The *hora* is the most basic divisional chart. The first half of odd signs like Aries is ruled by the Sun, the second half by the Moon. The first half of even signs like Taurus is ruled by the Moon, the second half by the Sun.

For example, if Mars is at 20° 15' Virgo, in the second half of an even sign, it would be in the hora of the Sun. The hora chart only gives solar or lunar status of planets and does not place them in signs like other divisional charts.

Drekkana or Decanate, Third Divisional

The decanate, *drekkana* in Sanskrit, is an important divisional chart. The first third or ten degrees, 00 00 – 10 00, of any sign is ruled by the sign itself. The middle third, 10 00 – 20 00, is ruled by the subsequent sign of the same element. The last third, 20 00 – 30 00, is ruled by the final sign of the same element.

For example, the first third of Sagittarius is in the drekkana of Sagittarius, the second third in Aries drekkana, and the last third in Leo drekkana. If Saturn is located in a birth chart at 15° 20' Sagittarius, it would be in the Aries drekkana.

Chaturtamsha, Fourth Divisional

Each sign is divided into four equal parts. The first fourth, 00 00 – 07 30, is the same as the sign itself. The second fourth, 07 30 – 15 00, is under the next sign of the same quality (cardinal, fixed or mutable). The third fourth, 15 00 – 22 30, follows the following sign of the same quality. The last fourth, 22 30 – 30 00, is of the final sign of the same quality.

For example, the first fourth of Aries is Aries, the second is Cancer, the third is Libra, and the last is Capricorn. If Venus is located at 20° 15' Aries, it would be in the third portion of the chaturtamsha, that of Libra, the third cardinal sign from Aries.

Saptamsha, Seventh Divisional

Each sign is divided into seven equal parts of 04° 17' 09". The first seventh of odd signs is governed by the sign itself with the rest following the signs in order through the zodiac. For even signs, the first seventh corresponds to the sign seventh from it, and the rest follow in order from that.

The first seventh of Aries, an odd sign, is Aries, the second seventh is Taurus, the third Gemini, and so on to Libra. The first seventh of Taurus, an even sign, would be Scorpio, the sign seventh from it. The second seventh division would be Sagittarius, the third Capricorn and so on to Taurus as its last seventh. In this way we are merely going through the signs in order. The following are the saptamsha divisions of the sign.

1. 00 00 00 – 04 17 09	2. 04 17 09 – 08 34 17
3. 08 34 17 – 12 51 26	4. 12 51 26 – 17 08 34
5. 17 08 34 – 21 25 43	6. 21 25 43 – 25 42 52
7. 25 42 52 – 30 00 00	

If the Moon is located at 25° 10' Taurus it would be in the sixth division, which would be Aries saptamsha (sixth from Scorpio).

Navamsha, Ninth Divisional

Each sign is divided into nine equal parts of 03° 20'. The first ninth of a sign is governed by the cardinal sign of the same element, followed by the rest of the signs from it in order through the zodiac.

The first ninth of Gemini (mutable air) is Libra (cardinal air), the second ninth is Scorpio, the third is Sagittarius, and so on all the way to Gemini at the end as the last ninth of its own sign.

1. 00 00 – 03 20	2. 03 20 – 06 40	3. 06 40 – 00 00
4. 10 00 – 13 20	5. 13 20 – 16 40	6. 16 40 – 20 00
7. 20 00 – 23 20	8. 23 20 – 26 40	9. 26 40 – 30 00

If Jupiter is at 22° 40' Scorpio, it is in the seventh navamsha. As Scorpio is a fixed water sign, its first ninth would be cardinal water or Cancer and its seventh would be Capricorn. This places Jupiter in Capricorn in the navamsha.

Dashamsha, Tenth Divisional

Each sign is divided into ten equal portions of 3° each. The rule is that the first tenth of odd signs is itself. The first tenth of even signs is of the sign ninth from them. Again we are just counting the signs off in order from the first tenth of Aries as Aries.

The first tenth or dashamsha of Aries is Aries; the first dashamsha of Taurus is Capricorn. The first dashamsha of Gemini is Gemini; that of Cancer is Pisces. The first dashamsha of Leo is Leo; that of Virgo is Taurus. The first dashamsha of Libra is Libra; that of Scorpio is Cancer. The first dashamsha of Sagittarius is Sagittarius; that of Capricorn is Virgo. The first dashamsha of Aquarius is Aquarius; and that of Pisces is Scorpio.

1. 00 00 – 03 00	2. 03 00 – 06 00	3. 06 00 – 09 00
4. 09 00 – 12 00	5. 12 00 – 15 00	6. 15 00 – 18 00
7. 18 00 – 21 00	8. 21 00 – 24 00	9. 24 00 – 27 00
10. 27 00 – 30 00		

If the Sun is in 08° 30' Gemini, for example, it would be in the third dashamsha, which would be Leo.

DWADASHAMSHA, TWELFTH DIVISIONAL

Each sign is divided into equal sections of 02° 30'. The first twelfth of each sign is the same as the sign itself with the rest counted off in order through the zodiac.

1. 00 00 – 02 30	2. 02 30 – 05 00	3. 05 00 – 07 30
4. 07 30 – 10 00	5. 10 00 – 12 30	6. 12 30 – 15 00
7. 15 00 – 17 30	8. 17 30 – 20 00	9. 20 00 – 22 30
10. 22 30 – 25 00	11. 25 00 – 27 30	12. 27 30 – 30 00

If Mercury is in 09° 35' of Virgo, it would be in the fourth dwadashamsha or Sagittarius.

Shodashamsha, Sixteenth Divisional

Each sign is divided into sixteen equal parts of 01° 52' 30" each. The first sixteenth of all cardinal signs begins with Aries, that of all fixed signs begins with Leo, that of all mutable signs with Sagittarius, and the rest are counted off in order from these.

Vimshamsha, Twentieth Divisional

Each sign is divided into twenty equal parts of 01° 30'. The first twentieth of all cardinal signs begins with Aries, of all fixed signs with Sagittarius, of all mutable signs with Leo, and the rest are counted off in order from these.

Siddhamsha, Twenty-fourth Divisional

Each sign is divided off into twenty-four equal parts of 01° 15'. All odd signs begin with Leo and all even signs with Cancer, with the rest counted off from these.

Bhamsha, Twenty-seventh Divisional

Each sign is divided into twenty-seven equal parts of 01° 06' 40". All fiery signs begin with Aries, all earthy signs with Cancer, all airy signs with Libra, and all watery signs with Capricorn. The rest are counted off in order from these.

Trimshamsha, Thirtieth Divisional

This chart is done in a peculiar way. There are no trimshamsha positions in Cancer or Leo.

Odd Signs	Even Signs
00 00 – 05 00 Aries	00 00 – 05 00 Taurus
05 00 – 10 00 Aquarius	05 00 – 12 00 Virgo
10 00 – 18 00 Sagittarius	12 00 – 20 00 Pisces
18 00 – 25 00 Gemini	20 00 – 25 00 Capricorn
25 00 – 30 00 Libra	25 00 – 30 00 Scorpio

Khavedamsha, Fortieth Divisional

Each sign is divided into forty equal parts of 45' each. All odd signs begin with Aries and all even signs with Libra, with the rest counted off in order from these.

Aksha Vedamsha, Forty-fifth Divisional

Each sign is divided into forty-five equal parts of 40' each. All cardinal signs begin with Aries; all fixed signs with Leo; and all mutable signs with Sagittarius, with the rest counted off in order from these.

Shastyamsha, Sixtieth Divisional

Each sign is divided into sixty equal parts of 30' each. Each sign starts with itself and the other divisions are counted off in order of the zodiac.

These sixteen divisional charts (which includes the birth chart or rashi chakra) are called *shodashavarga*, the group of sixteen. *Shadvarga*, the group of six, consists of the birth chart along with the second, third, ninth, twelfth and thirtieth divisional charts. When the seventh is added it becomes *saptavarga* or group of seven. Adding the tenth, sixteenth and sixtieth divisional charts, we get *dashavarga*, the group of ten.

Of the divisional charts the first, second, third, fourth, seventh, tenth, twelfth and thirtieth (rashi, hora, drekkana, chaturtamsha, saptamsha, dashamsha, dwadashamsha and trimshamsha) are the main ones used. The divisional charts also have their own special deities that are used in more esoteric readings.

USAGE OF DIVISIONAL CHARTS

Divisional charts are used to fine-tune the meaning of the rashi or birth chart. They are specially used for determining planetary strengths. Planets gain strength as they are located in the signs of their exaltation, own signs, or signs of friends, and lose strength in the signs of their enemies, or fall.

We can examine the signs in which each planet is located in each divisional chart. We judge these by the same rules of planetary friendship and enmity as used in the basic birth chart. In addition, each divisional chart has specific usages and focuses on particular areas of life.

The position of the Ascendant in these charts is the most specific factor, but unless the birth time is accurate it cannot be relied upon in the subtle subdivisions (particularly those beyond the twelfth divisional or dwadashamsha). An error of five minutes in the time of birth would change the Ascendant in all divisional charts more subtle than the twelfth. For this reason we often rely more upon the position of the Moon and the atmakaraka in these subtle charts. These are turned into the Ascendant and houses are read from their placement.

As the distant planets move slowly, their subtle subdivisions can be accurately calculated. They are often more revealing than their sign placements in the birth chart. The positions of Jupiter and Saturn in the subtler divisions is important for indicating general fortune.

Rashi Chart

This is the basic birth chart, relative to which all the divisional charts are judged. What is present in the birth chart may be heightened or diminished by the influence of the divisional charts but cannot be overridden by them. Divisional charts serve to fine tune the meanings in the birth chart but do not serve to radically change them. The birth chart always determines the field in which they operate and should be visualized behind them. Divisional charts are like a series of concentric circles with the birth chart as the outside circle. The subtler charts are contained within the fields of the larger.

Hora

As indicating the Sun and Moon, the hora chart shows the nature of the planets relative to solar and lunar, yang and yin, active and passive, male and female, individual and social, mental or emotional energies.

Masculine planets like the Sun, Mars and Jupiter are stronger in the hora of the Sun. Those of feminine nature like the Moon, Venus and Saturn are stronger in the hora of the Moon. Mutable Mercury does well either way, but which is better depends upon the planets whose influence it is under.

Solar division planets give more reliance on one's inner power and give initiative. Lunar division planets give more reliance on social influences, family, the past. Not enough planets in solar divisions will make us unable to gain recognition for what they do. Not enough in lunar divisions will create a lack of understanding and taking undeserved recognition.

The hora chart is often given a second house influence and thought to relate to wealth. When the ruler of the second is in its appropriate hora, it gives better results for the affairs of the second house. Hora means "hour." As each sign governs two hours of the day, that being the time it takes to cross the Ascendant, each hora governs about one hour.

Drekkana

The third divisional chart or decanate corresponds in meaning to the third house, relating to brothers, sisters, friends and alliances. It shows our capacity to work in a group or in association to achieve a particular goal. It indicates our energy, curiosity, courage, and prowess.

The position of the lord of the third house in the birth chart should be examined in the drekkana, as well as Mars, the natural indicator of the third house. Similarly, the position of the lord of the drekkana Ascendant should be examined in the birth chart. This is important for determining the affairs of siblings.

The drekkana is also useful for fine tuning Sun, Moon and Ascendant positions. For example, if Aquarius is the Ascendant but Gemini the decanate, the communicative and intellectual power of Gemini will come out in the humanitarian influence of Aquarius. When an individual has many planets located in the same sign, we can discriminate their action by their decanate positions. Special decanate symbols are important in horary astrology and as general interpretative tools.

Chaturtamsha

The harmonic fourth, like the fourth house, is traditionally said to deal with general well-being, emotion, home and happiness. If benefic planets like Jupiter and Venus or the rulers of benefic houses are strong in this chart, then well-being is enhanced.

The positions of the Moon, Mercury and the lord of the fourth house should be examined relative to this chart and can be taken as an indication of our emotional contentment and psychological happiness. This divisional chart is also used for purchase of homes and vehicles.

Saptamsha

The seventh divisional relates to children and grandchildren. Again, this is not to be taken literally. It refers to the creative projections of the individual in general, which, for the majority of us, relates to procreation. In this chart we see our creative capacities and the extent to which they can be concretely realized or recognized.

The position of the fifth lord from the birth chart in the saptamsha is important for showing the affairs of children. Similarly the position of the saptamsha lord (lord of the saptamsha Ascendant) in the birth chart must be considered as well

Navamsha

The navamsha is the main divisional chart and like the birth chart is examined for all the domains of life. For example, if we are looking into the affairs of children we should look at the fifth house in the navamsha as well as the birth chart. Or, if we are looking at the affairs of career, we should look at the tenth house in the navamsha as well as the birth chart.

The navamsha shows us the interrelationship between the birth chart and the nakshatras. Each navamsha sign corresponds to one quarter (03° 20') of the nakshatra. Twelve times nine navamshas equals twenty seven times four nakshatra quarters (108). This is perhaps why the navamsha is so important.

The navamsha traditionally refers to marriage and to the partner. It deals with relationship in general, and what we need to complement ourselves. Mainly, it refers to our ability to share our inner or spiritual values in relationship. In comparing the navamsha charts of couples we get an idea as to their spiritual or dharmic compatibility.

The indications of the navamsha are like that of the ninth house. It shows our dharma, the spiritual or religious motivation that we have. It reflects the nature of our soul and its aspirations, as the birth chart reflects the nature of our particular incarnation and the ego. As showing the forces that move us on an inner level it is a good index of our future life or the evolution of our soul. The navamsha is often more reflective than the birth chart of who we really are and what our soul is aiming to achieve.

A strong navamsha but a weak birth chart may show a person who has a limited potential but is able to manifest it well. A weak navamsha but a strong birth chart shows a strong potential but difficulty in manifesting it. The positions of Jupiter, the lord of the ninth house, and the atmakaraka or significator of the self in the navamsha are of particular importance in the navamsha. All the Jaimini planetary significators can be judged from this chart and are most specific to it.

If a planet is strong in both the birth chart and the navamsha, it will give very good results. A planet in its own sign or exalted in the birth chart but in its fall in the navamsha is weakened but still generally strong. A planet in the same sign in both the birth chart and navamsha is regarded as strong. It is called *vargottama*, which literally means "in the best subdivision."

Dashamsha

The tenth divisional chart is much like the tenth house in meaning. It shows the impact of the individual upon the world at large and his or her karmic impact upon life. It is important in the delineation of vocation and career, indicating power, position, and achievement. The dashamsha should be examined along with the tenth house in the birth chart and its lord, the Sun, Mercury, Jupiter, and other factors for career. If the lord of the tenth from the birth chart is strong in the dashamsha, it indicates that the individual will accomplish great actions or achieve his goals

Dwadashamsha

This is the chart of fate or destiny, of past karma. It traditionally indicates the parents but stands for past conditioning generally, including hereditary factors and past life influences. It can be used as an index of the last life or even something like the birth chart of the last incarnation. It indicates what the soul brings with it into this birth. It often shows the karmic reason for our particular character and destiny in life.

We can use the birth chart for the present life, the ninth for future life and the twelfth for the past life. In this way we can read the evolution of the soul. We can examine the father by looking to the ninth house in the dwadashamsha and the mother by the fourth house and compare these to the ninth and fourth houses in the birth chart.

Shodashamsha

Sixteen is four times four, so this chart refers to the affairs of the fourth house: happiness, home, property, and the acquisition of vehicles. It is used like the fourth divisional chart. If the fourth house lord is strong in this chart, then the affairs of the fourth house will be strengthened. This chart is also important in psychology, as relating to mental stability and emotional contentment.

Vimshamsha

This is said traditionally to be the chart of *upasana* or devotional meditation. It indicates the religious development of the soul and our capacity for the yoga of devotion (*bhakti yoga*). It shows our religious tendencies from past lives. It shows the *shakti* or goddess energy at work in our lives, and indicates our capacity to surrender to the Divine will. It helps indicate the form of the Divine that we are inclined to worship. It can also show creative and artistic capacity.

Twenty is five times four. The meanings of this house are like the fifth house, and therefore the factors pertaining to the fifth house, its lord and Jupiter should be examined here. It shows the joy, love and creativity of the soul.

Siddhamsha

This is traditionally said to be the chart of mental or meditative achievements, including the *siddhis* or psychic powers. In a higher sense, it is the chart of spiritual knowledge and shows the spiritual development of the soul. It shows our capacity for the yoga of knowledge (*jnana yoga*). Strong planets here enhance psychic and spiritual capacities for greater perception, skill and awareness.

On a general level, this chart indicates the educational career of the individual. Whether the knowledge gained will be spiritual or material depends upon the nature of the character from the birth chart.

The positions of the ninth lord, Mercury and Jupiter are important here, as well as the atmakaraka. Between the twentieth and twenty-fourth divisional charts we can understand many of the secrets of our spiritual unfoldment.

Bhamsha

This chart measures the strength or weakness of the planets relative to the nakshatras in which they dwell. It is a further fine-tuning of the navamsha chart (which itself measures 1/4 of the nakshatra). This chart indicates particular strengths and weaknesses of the Moon. It is also important for planetary significators.

Trimshamsha

This is the traditional chart of misfortune, enmity and disease. It is an important harmonic chart for discovering the dangers that we need to avoid in life. Major health difficulties or potential injuries can be seen in malefic placement of planets here.

The power of the lords of the third, sixth, eighth and eleventh houses can be gauged here. Also any planets located in the sixth, eighth or twelfth houses in the birth chart should be examined here. If they are poorly placed in this chart, they are much more likely to cause problems.

Khavedamsha

This chart deals with special auspicious and inauspicious effects of planets, sometimes said to be good and bad habits, particularly the proclivities of the emotional and psychological nature. As four times ten, it relates to the affairs of the fourth house.

Aksha Vedamsha

This helps fine tune all general indications, though it is often said to relate to the moral or ethical nature of the individual. As nine times five, it has fifth and ninth house indications of good or bad karma. It indicates which of the three major Hindu deities — Brahma the creator, Vishnu the preserver, or Shiva the destroyer — that the individual most reflects.

Shastyamsha

This is the subtlest of the divisional charts and is often used in the case of twins. It affords the subtlest fine-tuning of planetary effects and has special deities for indicating these.

Jupiter

Dressed in yellow, with a yellow body, who has four arms, the teacher of the Gods, peaceful in nature, whose vehicle is an elephant, who carries a rosary, a water pot and a staff in his hands, with a sapphire crest jewel on his head, making the gesture that grants boons — may Divine Jupiter ever grant us his grace.

11

Planetary Periods:

PLANETARY INFLUENCES THROUGH TIME

The planetary periods of Vedic astrology provide an easy and comprehensive system for judging the effects of planets throughout the development of our lives. They can be used in place of more cumbersome systems of progressions and transits, or these can be added to them for fine-tuning. The planetary periods are perhaps the most accurate system for showing how the planets distribute their effects through time and the different stages of our lives. It is worth having a Vedic chart done for the planetary periods alone, and a reading is not complete without them. We should all know the periods we are in, and contemplate the course of our lives according to how our periods change.

Vedic astrology always considers planetary periods in any reading. It does not require an additional chart or even transits to see this, but is in evidence in the birth chart itself and the positions within it. The Vedic chart gives us a list of planetary periods that provides an overview of the development of planetary forces through our entire life. These periods are very helpful for examining our life and for planning long term goals. They can show us major transitions in our life and character. Most of us undergo major changes periodically. Some of us change personalities in a dramatic way at certain times. The planetary periods provide the key to these events. Some periods may be so different from each other that the whole nature of the destiny, health or personality may change with them.

A few different systems are used for determining the planetary periods. The most common is the *Vimshottari Dasha* or 120 year cycle, which will be examined here. Other important dasha sequences are *Yogini Dasha* and *Jaimini Chara Dasha*, but up to a dozen such dasha systems are still used by various Vedic astrologers. Most Vedic astrologers use more than one dasha sequence, but the Vimshottari remains the most important. In Vimshottari Dasha each of the nine planets is given a period ranging from 6 to 20 years. The order is the same as that of the rulership of the lunar constellations (nakshatras), as the periods are based upon them.

Vimshottari Dasha

Sun — 6 years	Moon — 10 years	Mars — 7 years
Rahu — 18 years	Jupiter — 16 years	Saturn — 19 years
Mercury — 17 years	Ketu —7 years	Venus —20 years

No specific rationale is given for these amounts. We notice that the period of Rahu, a shadow planet, is much longer than that of major planets like the Sun and Moon. Still, even though we can't quite make sense of it, the system works quite well.

HOW TO DETERMINE THE PLANETARY PERIOD

The easiest way to calculate the planetary periods is with a computer program. The following shows a simple way to do it by hand. First we must determine the major planetary period (*maha dasha*) we are in, and then the minor period (*bhukti dasha*) within it. We can divide the minor period into smaller increments if we wish.

Find the nakshatra (see table) in which the Moon was located at birth. For example, if the Moon is located at 12° 26' Virgo, then its nakshatra will be Hasta. Look to the table and see what planet rules it. This is the Moon. Hence the major planetary period at birth would be that of the Moon.

Then determine how many more degrees and minutes the Moon has to travel to complete the course of the nakshatra. Each nakshatra is 13° 20' or 800' in length. In this case, Hasta begins at 10° 00' Virgo. Therefore, the Moon has already traveled through 02° 26' and 10° 54' remain (654'). Divide this remainder by 800 and this will show you what percentage of the period remains to be traversed (in this case .8175).

Next look to the table and note the duration of the period of the ruling planet. In our example, the Moon, whose period is 10 years, rules Hasta. Multiply the duration of the planetary period by the percentage of the constellation yet to be traveled (10 years by .8175 or 8.175 years).

Multiply the remainder minus the years times twelve to get the months (175 x 12 or 2.1 months). Finally, multiply the month remainder by 30 for the days (1 x 30 or 3 days). This gives the total yet to be transpired in the planetary period from the moment of birth (8 years, 2 months, 3 days). If the date of birth is Oct. 10, 1952, for example, we add the remainder of 8 years 2 months and 3 days to it. The Moon's period would begin at birth and end on Dec. 13, 1960.

All the other major planetary periods will begin on the same month and day that the first planetary period ends. In our case, the seven-year period of Mars would begin Dec. 13, 1960. Rahu would follow it on Dec. 13, 1967, and so on throughout the cycle of planetary periods.

Some Vedic astrologers employ a 360-day year for dasha purposes. This makes the dashas come progressively earlier, until by middle age they may begin several months earlier than they would for a 365-day year dasha.

Table of Planetary Periods
Major and Minor (dashas and bhuktis)

1. Sun Dasha 6 years

Sun	0	3	18
Moon	0	6	0
Mars	0	4	6
Rahu	0	10	24
Jupiter	0	9	18
Saturn	0	11	12
Mercury	0	10	6
Ketu	0	4	6
Venus	1	0	0

2. Moon Dasha 10 years

Moon	0	10	0
Mars	0	7	0
Rahu	1	6	0
Jupiter	1	4	0
Saturn	1	7	0
Mercury	1	5	0
Ketu	0	7	0
Venus	1	8	0
Sun	0	6	0

3. Mars Dasha 7 years

Mars	0	4	27
Rahu	1	0	18
Jupiter	0	11	6
Saturn	1	1	9
Mercury	0	11	27
Ketu	0	4	27
Venus	1	2	0
Sun	0	4	6
Moon	0	7	0

4. Rahu Dasha 18 years

Rahu	2	8	12
Jupiter	2	4	24
Saturn	2	10	6
Mercury	2	6	18
Ketu	1	0	18
Venus	3	0	0
Sun	0	10	24
Moon	1	6	0
Mars	1	0	18

5. Jupiter Dasha 16 years

Jupiter	2	1	18
Saturn	2	6	12
Mercury	2	3	6
Ketu	0	11	6
Venus	2	8	0

6. Saturn Dasha 19 years

Saturn	3	0	3
Mercury	2	8	9
Ketu	1	9	9
Venus	3	2	0
Sun	0	11	12

5. Jupiter Dasha 16 years (cont.)

Sun	0	9	18
Moon	1	4	0
Mars	0	11	6
Rahu	2	4	24

6. Saturn Dasha 19 years (cont.)

Moon	1	7	0
Mars	1	1	9
Rahu	2	10	6
Jupiter	2	6	12

7. Mercury Dasha 17 years

Mercury	2	4	27
Ketu	0	11	27
Venus	2	10	0
Sun	0	10	6
Moon	1	5	0
Mars	0	11	27
Rahu	2	6	18
Jupiter	2	3	6
Saturn	2	8	9

8. Ketu Dasha 7 years

Ketu	0	4	27
Venus	1	2	0
Sun	0	4	6
Moon	0	7	0
Mars	0	4	27
Rahu	1	0	18
Jupiter	0	11	6
Saturn	1	1	9
Mercury	0	11	27

9. Venus Dasha 20 years

Venus	3	4	0
Sun	1	0	0
Moon	1	8	0
Mars	1	2	0
Rahu	3	0	0
Jupiter	2	8	0
Saturn	3	2	0
Mercury	2	10	0
Ketu	1	2	0

Smaller periods can be calculated based upon the same ratios, but unless the birth time is very accurate, they may not be exact. Moreover, the timing of dashas differs based upon the ayanamsha used. A difference of one degree in the ayanamsha will change the dashas for a period of a year or so. For this reason, dashas are one of the best testing grounds for the different ayanamshas.

USE OF DASHAS

The planet ruling the major period will give the results of the houses it rules and the planets and houses that it aspects. *To use the planetary periods correctly, one must firmly understand the principles of house rulership and the temporal status of planets, which is specific for interpreting their results.* The dasha lord is considered to be casting an aspect on all the planets and houses but doubly so upon those it already aspects in the birth chart.

Most important is the relationship between the major and minor period lords. Whatever relationship is present between them in the birth chart will be magnified. Generally, the minor lord will be considered to be casting an aspect on the major lord, modifying the nature of its results.

If no direct aspect exists in the birth chart, their influences will still be combined. For example, if Jupiter and Venus have no aspect in the birth chart, the effects of a Jupiter-Venus aspect will still be in evidence during Jupiter-Venus periods, though not as strongly as if an aspect existed between them in the birth chart.

Besides aspects, note house relationships. Planets in inauspicious houses from each other, like the sixth, eighth or twelfth, will not tend to work well together. Those in auspicious house relationships, like trines or angles, will have positive effects even without aspects between them.

Also, note planetary friendship and enmity. Friendly planets will give better results as major and minor period lords. Inimical planets will cause some difficulties, even if they both have some auspicious nature relative to the birth chart as a whole. These different factors should be weighed and synthesized and used to adjust the effects of the periods.

A special tool is to turn the dasha lord into the Ascendant and to read houses from it during its period. For example, if a person is in a Jupiter period with Jupiter in the ninth house and Venus in the third, one could expect a relationship to occur in Jupiter's dasha, particularly during its Venus minor period, because Venus is located in the seventh house from Jupiter.

The general rule is that the most favorable times are when there is a combination of different benefic lords: when major, minor and subminor lords are all benefic in nature. Similar is a condition in which all period lords rule the same domain of life. A time in which the lords of the ninth, eleventh, second, or fifth houses combine will naturally be very good for business and income. On the other hand, when the lords of the sixth, eighth, twelfth, third, or eleventh combine, disease or difficulties will be more likely.

The beginning of a major benefic planetary period is particularly auspicious. This is a good time for projecting the goals or actions to be achieved within the period as a whole. However, a good planetary period does not always give its results immediately. In the beginning the seeds of its positive developments will come forth, but not necessarily the fruit. When minor periods begin, this is also a favorable time for the affairs of the minor lord that are in harmony with the major lord.

The beginning of planetary periods is a good time for remedial measures such as gems, mantras, or rituals to counter the possible negative influences of the period lords. If the period lord is benefic but weak, we can strengthen its influence through its gem. If it is malefic, we can propitiate it through mantra, ritual or worship. For example, if a negative Saturn minor period is starting within a positive Jupiter major period, one can either propitiate Saturn or strengthen Jupiter.

Of these period rulers, the major lord is the most important for determining the nature of the time, then the minor lord. For example, if the major lord rules the second, a house of livelihood, the minor lord rules the eleventh, a house of income, and the subminor lord rules the ninth, a house of fortune, material gain is likely. On the other hand, if the major lord rules the ninth, a house of religion, the minor lord the fifth, a house of intelligence and the subminor lord the second, a house of intellect, it would be favorable for communication of spiritual, religious or legal principles. Of course, the natural status of the planets must be considered as well. The period of a malefic like Saturn located in the sixth or eleventh house is likely to be good because of its favorable house placement.

TRANSITS (GOCHARA)

We should always consider the transits (current positions) of planets relative to the planetary periods. The transits of the strongest planet or the lord of the Ascendant in the birth chart are always important. We should give special notice to the transits of the planets ruling the major and minor periods, the dasha and bhukti lords. Transits have about 1/3 value in judging the effects of the periods. The rest is determined by the relationships between these planets in the birth chart. Strong transits are of particular importance when they occur at the juncture between planetary periods.

For minor planetary periods we note transits of the distant planets, Jupiter, Saturn, as well as the lunar nodes, as these have an effect for a period of up to one year. For subminor periods we examine the transits of the closer planets, Mars, Sun, Venus and Mercury, as their influence tends to dispense itself during a shorter period.

ASHTAKAVARGA

Ashtakavarga is a special Vedic system for judging benefic points for planets and houses. It is particularly important for transits. Planets transiting houses that are high in points (*bindus*) can expect good results, while houses with low point counts cause difficulties. Planets transiting portions of signs in which they have contributed positive points also give good results. Ashtakavarga is an entire system in its own right.

PLANETARY RETURNS AND THE ANNUAL CHART

Returns of planets to their natal positions are considered with transits. They are the most important transits. Monthly lunar returns, yearly solar returns, 12 year Jupiter returns, 19 year nodal returns and 29 year Saturn returns are particularly important. It is most important to note the returns of major and minor period lords.

The time of the solar return is particularly important and is the basis of the annual chart or *Varshaphal.* It is best to have a reading done every year relative to the annual chart as marking the main transits for the year, and to interpret it relative to the dashas. Because of its sidereal nature, the solar return will not occur at the exact time as one's birth time and requires a special calculation to figure out.

MUHURTA

Muhurta means "a moment" and refers to the branch of Vedic astrology concerned with determining favorable times for action. In the West, this branch is called electional astrology, though its rules are very different than in the Vedic system. Important events in life, like marriage or starting a business, do better if timed properly.

Many rules for forming muhurtas exist, and this is a whole science in itself. Five main factors are considered, which make up the *Panchanga* or five-limbed Hindu calendar. All Vedic astrologers should have a Panchanga and learn how to use it.

1. Day, *vara*
2. Nakshatra
3. *Tithi* or lunar day
4. *Karana* or half of lunar day
5. *Yoga* or Sun-Moon connection

When three or more factors are good, then an action is generally auspicious. When all five are good, then the timing of an action is excellent. However, even a good muhurta will fail if the dasha for the person is adverse. Only if the dasha is good should one look for an appropriate muhurta. If the dasha and muhurta are favorable one can go another step further and choose a favorable Ascendant as well. Special books on muhurta exist and can be studied for more information on the topic.

The Vedic calendar also uses special nakshatra months in which the tithis are calculated. These are the basis for the holidays of the Hindu calendar. Special days like the beginning of the astronomical year (the new Moon at the end of Pisces called *Chaitra Shukla Pratipad*) are regarded as excellent for all auspicious actions. The Vedic calendar tells us what each day is good for astrologically.

PRASHNA, HORARY ASTROLOGY

Astrological charts can be done to answer any question. This branch of Vedic astrology is called *Prashna*, which means "a question." In the West it is called *horary* astrology and the chart is called a horary chart. A chart can be drawn for any moment, and this will plot the course of events decided at that moment. Astrologers may do a chart for a client based upon the moment he or she comes to see them. This is helpful for predicting various aspects of the client's life, particularly the specific issues he wants to deal with in the reading.

In horary astrology, clients generally come with a particular question, like how their health will proceed. The moment they put the question to the astrologer becomes the time for erecting the chart. It is then interpreted for finding out how this issue will develop.

Prashna charts are interpreted similarly to birth charts but have their special rules as well. In Prashna aspects, like those of Western astrology, trines, squares and sextiles are used. In fact, it is relative to Prashna and Varshaphal (the annual chart) that there is the greatest connection between Vedic and Western astrology. Most traditional Vedic astrologers do more Prashna than natal astrology. After all, most people come to an astrologer with questions to be answered. A Prashna chart can deal with these questions specifically and without the possible inaccuracies of a wrong birth time. Vedic astrology has many classical texts on Prashna, particularly from the state of Kerala.

Part III

Astrology, Healing and Transformation

Venus

Clothed in white, white in luster, who has four arms, the teacher of the demons, whose nature is peaceful, whose vehicle is a white horse, who carries a rosary, waterpot and staff in his hands, with a diamond crest jewel on his head, making the gesture that grants boons — may Divine Venus ever grant us his grace.

12

Ayurveda and Medical Astrology

Ayurveda is the classical medical tradition of India, its natural healing system. As its name Veda suggests, Ayurveda has a close relationship with Vedic astrology. Its vast scope contains all forms of healing, from herbs to surgery and psychology. Ayurveda is a comprehensive health care system, aiming not only at the elimination of disease but also at the rejuvenation of body and mind. At its foundation lies a system for determining one's individual constitution, showing us how to ascertain the unique nature and health needs of each person. Ayurveda provides treatment methods that enable each individual to take responsibility for their own health, offering many forms of self-care.

Ayurveda and Vedic astrology are closely related aspects of Vedic science. Many astrologers in India have practiced Ayurveda and many vaidyas, Ayurvedic doctors, have been astrologers. Even when not trained in Ayurveda, astrologers still consider disease and its treatment. Even when not trained in astrology, Ayurvedic doctors refer to astrology and astrological treatment methods.

Both systems work well to supplement each other. Astrology provides a broad understanding of our energy patterns throughout the whole of life and all aspects of our nature. It is a much subtler healing science than any form of physical medicine. Ayurveda aids astrology by providing an applicable energetic system of medicine for the astrological model, which in origin and methodology is in harmony with it.

Anyone practicing medical astrology should have some training in a medical system like Ayurveda. Astrology reads our nature in such a broad and general way that daily or monthly fluctuations in health problems are hard to discern through it. Nor does the study of astrology alone give us the understanding of the appropriate tools of treatment, like diet and herbs.

Vedic astrologers can determine the physical constitution and appearance of the individual from the birth chart. They can figure out basic health, longevity and disease tendencies. They can see which planets have the power to cause disease, what kinds of diseases are likely to occur, what parts of the body are likely to be affected, and when these problems are likely to occur.

As health and longevity are primary concerns for everyone, they are often the first things examined in a chart reading.

MEDICAL ASTROLOGY

Medical astrology is one of the main branches of astrology. As it includes remedial measures for harmonizing planetary influences, it is perhaps the most practical branch as well. It includes the entire astrology of healing. Not only is astrology helpful for ordinary disease conditions, it also has means of diagnosis and treatment for diseases that are not curable by usual medical methods. It provides a better picture and methodology for dealing with diseases that come from internal causes.

Diseases, like all disharmonies in life, are associated with negative planetary influences. Several methods exist through which planetary influences can be harmonized. The foremost of these is gem therapy, which is based on color therapy. The gems corresponding to the planets redirect their influences in a positive way.

Mantras (words of power), yantras (power diagrams), special rituals (pujas and homas) and other yogic methods are also important. These work more on the level of the mind. They are particularly effective for mental disorders, including psychic imbalances (on which most mental disorders are based). They strengthen the aura and immune system, clearing out negative occult influences, which include negative karmas of past lives, negative thoughts of others, and subtle environmental pollutants such as low level radiation.

The planets represent the basic energies operating in the cosmos, the prime forces that operate in all life. As such, our life can be arranged to counteract the negative planetary influences in our chart. The right diet, right herbs, right location in which to live, right livelihood, and right spiritual practices can all be used to balance planetary forces. For example, Mars is a hot planet and, if it is too strong, it can cause heat disorders like fever, inflammation, and infection, as well as traumas and injury. Its influence can be countered by cooling food, cooling herbs, a cool climate, and cool colors, as well as by special gems and mantras.

THE THREE DOSHAS

Ayurveda classifies individuals according to the three biological humors or doshas. These correspond to the predominant elements in the individual. Three main types exist, namely Vata, which is dominated by air,

Pitta dominated by fire, and Kapha dominated by water. Ether is generally in the field of Vata and earth in the field of Kapha. Ayurvedic books can be consulted for more information on the doshas. I myself am planning a book on medical astrology dealing more specifically with this issue. Vedic astrology contains a classification of planets by the doshas:

Planets and Doshas

Vata	Saturn, Rahu, Mercury
Pitta	Sun, Mars, Ketu
Kapha	Moon, Venus, Jupiter

Saturn and Rahu are responsible for most Vata (nervous) disorders. Mars and Ketu are most responsible for most Pitta (inflammatory) disorders. The Moon and Jupiter cause more Kapha problems, problems of mucus and overweight.

Doshas and Signs

The twelve signs can be classified according to the doshas. Air, fire and water signs generally represent the air, fire and water humors, Vata, Pitta and Kapha.

Vata	Air Signs	Gemini, Libra and Aquarius
Pitta	Fire Signs	Aries, Leo and Sagittarius
Kapha	Water Signs	Cancer, Scorpio and Pisces

Earth signs can be divided up among the doshas. Fixed earth, Taurus, relates more to Kapha (the Moon, a watery planet, is exalted in this sign). Mutable earth, Virgo, is more commonly air, as air is mutable in quality (Mercury, an airy planet, is exalted in this sign). Cardinal earth, Capricorn, has some affinity to fire, as fire is cardinal in quality (Mars, a fiery planet is exalted in this sign). This gives us the following order:

Signs and Doshas

Vata	Gemini, Virgo, Libra, Aquarius
Pitta	Aries, Leo, Sagittarius, Capricorn
Kapha	Taurus, Cancer, Scorpio, Pisces

DOSHAS OF SIGNS BY RULING PLANET

As per the general rule, the planets are more important than the signs for determining the nature of things. The signs determine the field of action and are more indicative of the site of disease. The doshas of the signs also reflect their ruling planets.

Aries, Leo, and Scorpio tend to Pitta because fiery planets, Mars and the Sun, rule them. Taurus, Cancer, Libra, Sagittarius, and Pisces tend to *Kapha* because watery planets, Venus, Moon and Jupiter rule them. Gemini, Virgo, Capricorn, and Aquarius are prone to Vata because airy planets, Mercury and Saturn rule them.

HOW TO DETERMINE THE DOSHAS ASTROLOGICALLY

The most important factor for determining individual constitution is the Ascendant or first house, which governs the physical incarnation generally. Usually people follow the Ascendant in their physical type. Yet this is merely a general rule, and other factors have to be considered.

Planets located in the first house are important. Mars on the Ascendant, for example, often renders a person fiery, particularly if it also aspects the lord of the Ascendant. Along with the Ascendant, the influences upon it and upon its lord must be considered. Generally, a planet that aspects the Ascendant and its lord will have a very strong, if not determining, impact upon the constitution.

The Sun has to be considered as significator of the first house. It is good to examine the Sun for men and the Moon for women as indicating the physical type. However, when the Moon is stronger than the Ascendant it may determine the physical type even for men. Conjunctions of planets with the Sun or Moon are quite significant. Mars in conjunction with the Sun generally makes a person Pitta, for example, unless combust, in which case it often loses its power.

Planets in the sixth house or aspecting it and its lord also affect the physical constitution by creating our disease tendency and general digestive power. Planets impacting the eighth house are important for severe diseases.

The main rule is that the planet that has the greatest strength of influence on the various factors representing the body — the first and sixth houses, their lords, the Sun and Moon and their rulers — will generally determine the physical type. If two planets of the same dosha (like the Moon and Jupiter, which are both Kapha) affect these factors, then the judgment is more assured.

Ayurvedic constitution usually follows the nature of the strongest planet in the chart or the planetary type that the person represents. However, like all astrological determinations, it has its intricacy and variability and requires some study and experience for accuracy.

DISEASE-CAUSING PLANETS

Malefic planets, either natural or temporal, promote disease. Natural malefics are Rahu, Saturn, Ketu, Mars and the Sun in order of their power to cause disease. Temporal malefics are the lords of the sixth, eighth, eleventh, third and twelfth houses. Planets when weak also cause disease or become the sites of disease, benefics as well as malefics.

Planets cause disease by occupying malefic houses. Mainly, these are the eighth, sixth, and twelfth houses, but also the third and eleventh. Malefics are strong in the sixth house. Yet their strength is mainly in terms of power, prestige and wealth. They can still cause disease, particularly if under negative aspects, though without affliction they do promote good health and give a strong immune system.

Malefic planetary lords also cause disease. The lord of the sixth house causes injury, accidents, acute diseases, low vitality, poor digestion, and poor resistance to disease. The lord of the eighth causes poor vitality, chronic and wasting diseases, including premature death. The lord of the eleventh functions like that of the sixth but with less power. The lord of the third functions like that of the eighth but with less power.

The lord of the eighth house, the house of death, is particularly strong to cause disease, injury or degenerative disorders. The lord of the twelfth causes sorrow and shows confinement to a bed or hospital, a chronically sick person.

Signs, Houses and the Body

Aries	First House	Head
Taurus	Second House	Neck
Gemini	Third House	Upper Chest
Cancer	Fourth House	Breast
Leo	Fifth House	Solar Plexus
Virgo	Sixth House	Navel Region
Libra	Seventh House	Lower Abdomen
Scorpio	Eighth House	Pubic Region
Sagittarius	Ninth House	Thighs
Capricorn	Tenth House	Knees
Aquarius	Eleventh House	Calves
Pisces	Twelfth House	Feet

The signs and houses correspond to certain parts of the body. If both the sign and house of the same number are afflict-ed, the particular bodily part that corresponds to them is likely to become afflicted. For example, if Saturn aspects the ninth sign, the ninth house and their rulers, arthritis or paralysis of the hip is likely. If Saturn aspects the fifth house, the fifth house from the Moon and their rulers, there is apt to be infertility in women, with possible surgery or hysterectomy.

The sixth house and sixth sign, Virgo, which govern the digestive nerves, are particularly important in determining disease potential. The Sun in Virgo with the sixth house afflicted gives chronic poor digestion. The Sun in the sixth, aspected by malefics, similarly gives digestive problems, as will any poorly placed planet in the sixth. The Moon in the sixth gives emotional upset or depression that weakens the health through the digestive system.

The sixth house and sign represent our basic health and purity. Afflicted, they show disease and the accumulation of waste materials. They indicate how we are connected to our bodies and the way we take care of them. Afflicted, they show devitalization, which usually occurs through wrong habits, like bad diet, insufficient rest or excessive sexual indulgence.

Virgo governs Vata, the biological air humor in the body. As most diseases occur through Vata and through weak digestion, planets in this sign tend to cause disease. On the other hand, planets in this sign can make one a healer if they are benefically disposed. Sometimes our own diseases make us turn to healing. Virgo shows service to the physical body, either our own or that of others.

13

Astrology and Psychology

Vedic astrology follows the system of yoga in its understanding of the mind. Its definition of the mind is thus quite different than what we find in modern psychology. Vedic astrology recognizes the existence and influence of collective, cosmic and spiritual levels of consciousness which lie beyond our surface and personal mind and which modern psychology is only beginning to explore. Its concern is not just with bringing happiness or harmony to the outer layers of the mind, but with bringing the deeper layers of the mind into function by awakening our spiritual aspiration. This may be experienced by the surface mind as a kind of shock, negation, or at least a reorientation that challenges our idea of who we are.

On one level we could say that Vedic astrology, like yoga, has no psychology. It is not concerned with personal and emotional fulfillment as the real aim of our lives. It does not see our personal identity as our true self and cannot equate its happiness with our true welfare. It sees our outer nature as a particular formation of the cosmic energy and our inner nature as an aspect of cosmic consciousness. It regards our present mind and personality as a temporary veil or covering over the deeper and broader truth of who we are and our greater oneness with life.

Vedic astrology does not emphasize the limitations or sufferings of this life. It teaches us that we are Divine souls with infinite potentials that we can access if we give them our attention and work on them regularly. It tells us that we can achieve anything we want if we put our will to it. From its perspective, our personal and emotional problems come from not directing our life energy in a positive way. Its solution to emotional problems is to direct us toward some practical action to improve our condition in life, not to become entangled in trying to figure out their details.

On the other hand, we could say that Vedic astrology has a real science of psychology because it treats the real psyche or soul, not just the outer mind. Whereas modern psychology is concerned with the mind, the conditioned entity of memory, Vedic psychology is concerned with the soul, the unconditioned entity of pure consciousness. Whereas modern psychological methods aim at understanding and healing the conditioned mind, yogic psychology aims at going beyond the mind. Vedic astrology's concern is not with the personal traumas of this life as an issue in themselves, but with the ongoing evolution of the soul.

The law of karma tells us that we are responsible for our state in life, even the circumstances of our birth and childhood. We have created these situations and we can transcend them as well. It is not necessary to look back upon them. We should rather act in the present in such a way as to create an improved condition for ourselves for the future.

According to Vedic psychology, psychological disorders are caused by a disruption in our connection with our true soul. This is reflected in a lack of integration of our planets, particularly afflictions to the Moon, Mercury, the Ascendant, the fourth houses and their lords. Such psychological problems can be treated by spiritual and occult methods, including mantras, gems, colors, herbs and diet. Mere analysis is not enough, and drugs have long term side effects.

In the yogic view, true knowledge is only achieved when the mind is silent, when it is emptied of its burden of emotion and thought. This requires emptying the mind of its contents, not sorting them out or categorizing them. The practice of yoga itself is traditionally defined (*Yoga Sutras* I.2) as "the negation of the thought patterns of the mindstuff." According to yoga, the intellect can never give us perception of truth. Intellectual understanding has no real value to change our lives, though it can make us function more smoothly or efficiently. Yoga emphasizes not intellectual knowledge but consciousness, moment by moment awareness, as the factor of true understanding. Vedic astrology is not concerned with intellectual knowledge about the stars so much as reestablishing our connection with the Divine and cosmic forces working through them.

Nor does yoga consider that emotion can bring us to truth. It regards emotion, like intellectual thought, as a reaction of the surface mind, which must be stilled for the perception of truth to emerge. The feeling of oneness should guide us, not emotional needs and compulsions.

Vedic psychology is thus impersonal. It aims at the non-ego. It tells us that we are all different combinations of the same cosmic forces coming through the planets and stars. The ego, our sense of personal identity, is a fiction, an illusion that does not really exist. We all have the same basic nature, both superficial and deep, and must all go through the same basic life experiences, good and bad, for the growth of our consciousness. No soul gets any special treatment. Our differences come from being at different stages of this process, not because we are really different or separate, better or worse than one another.

As souls, we all have the same potential and the same basic problems to work out in our destiny. The spiritual goal is to go beyond the need to be somebody in the external world. In this regard our birth chart is the picture of our ignorance, the pattern of desire and karma in which we are caught. The purpose of astrology is not just to tell us what this pattern is but to show us the way out of it. As souls, we are not limited to the birth chart, though it represents the present phase of our manifestation. It is a structure that we have created, though not entirely in this life, and one that we can change in time by changing our daily action.

Vedic psychology has a spiritual orientation and a focus on the destiny of the soul, its movement from the ignorance to the knowledge, from bondage to the cycle of rebirth to liberation into the Divine. In this respect astrology has its limit, because the soul is our eternal being, beyond the influence of the stars. Astrology is an aspect of the real science of life that is yoga and meditation. If it caters too much to the outer goals of life, it defeats its real purpose and value.

This lack of spiritual knowledge in astrology has caused many practitioners of yoga and meditation to dismiss it as being of no value. Certainly much of astrology can be viewed this way, particularly the popular personality-oriented astrology; yet it is not astrology that is at fault or limited but our superficial way of applying it.

The essence of Vedic psychology lies in directing us to the spiritual life. This means we must first become conscious of the soul within us. This means awakening to our inner Sun, the light of truth within us which is the real light of the world. It is to see the universe within us. This is to longer look to the outer world for our definition of who we are but to go back to our internal light, our eternal nature. It is to question our identification with the body, senses and mind and to find our true nature as a conscious being, not an object or persona in the world.

From this basic insight into our true nature we must reorient our faculties and the domains of our life as represented by the planets. We need to make them orbit the inner Sun of truth perception. This is the yoga or the way of spiritual reintegration inherent in astrology and its symbolism. We can practice this even if we do not use astrology or know our birth chart. It is a universal symbolism for the development of consciousness. We can meditate upon the qualities and meanings of the planets within us and reintegrate their forces in our own minds.

First we must harmonize the Moon, the indicator of our receptivity in life, to this inner Sun. We must make ourselves become receptive to the Sun of truth and become detached from the influences of the outer world. To do this we must become conscious of our dependence upon the Divine or cosmic intelligence as the source of our being. We must learn to surrender to the Divine and to the presence of truth. We must realize the limitations of the mind and not take its fluctuations for our true awareness.

Then we must harmonize our Mars, our energy and motivation in life. This is to direct our will to spiritual practices, like service, yoga, mantra and meditation. It does not mean neglecting our duties in life but using them to develop skill in action. It is to no longer seek power and achievement outwardly but to open up to the flow of grace. This requires seeing through the manipulative structure of society and our own ego. It means doing our work in the best way but not seeking any results, becoming one with the process rather than calculating what we are going to get out of it.

Then we must bring into play our Mercury, our rational process, on a higher level. We must reorient our intelligence toward inner truth rather than outer information. To do this we must no longer believe in the reality of the known, the measurable and the quantifiable. We must see through the glamour of names and forms and the fiction of numbers. We must be sensitive to the unique being in things which reflects the eternal. We must look to the unknown, the immeasurable, the quality of beauty and presence that is Divine.

Then we must employ our Jupiter, our will to truth and growth This is to seek expansion in the realm of consciousness, to unite our life energy with the cosmic life around us. It is to exist as a source of grace, beneficence and good will. It requires no longer seeing our true good as developing outwardly, but surrendering and growing inwardly. Through this we must become conscious of the good of all and of our role in life to guide and help others along the path of light.

Then we must harmonize our Venus, our devotion and affection. This is to direct our love and creativity to the unfoldment of the cosmic wonder and joy. It is to see that the joy and beauty comes from the Divine or from consciousness, from our own deepest Self. Joy does not belong to outer objects but is merely reflected upon them. This is to reclaim our own joy and contentment in life through being and consciousness. For this, life must become a form of worship, and all beauty must be recognized as an expression of the spiritual heart.

Then we must seal the process with our Saturn, give it a firm form and structure in our own daily activity. We need the consistency, concentration and seriousness to bring things to conclusion. This requires dedication, calm, coolness and the willingness to persist in the face of adversity, to even greet suffering or opposition as a friend. It requires detachment, the capacity to be alone, and the ability to abide in stillness. This is a moment by moment awareness that does not overlook anything but remains at the essence.

On this basis we must confront again the hidden side of life and the psyche. It is not enough to clear things up on the outer layers. We must eradicate the seeds of falsehood from the deepest recesses of the mind. We must deal with the illusory power of the mind, the power of secret or hidden desires that come through Rahu. We must face the ghosts and demons of our subconscious, including the elemental fears and desires upon which this world of ignorance is built. We must understand all the habits, addictions and dependencies upon which our attachment to the world of appearances is based.

Finally we must deal with Ketu, our capacity to negate ourselves. We must be careful not to sabotage ourselves in the process or to turn back at the moment of victory. We must learn to negate ourselves into the Divine, not into the undivine. We need the utmost refinement of insight to pierce through the veil of time and illusion and come to rest into the eternal light. We must follow the process of negation to the ultimate point of pure affirmation, seeing our Self in all beings and all beings in our Self.

In this way we return to the Sun of truth with the full manifestation of its powers, the integration of all its rays. While we can look at this process as an unfoldment in time, it is more an unfoldment of related qualities and will not follow the same line of development in each individual. It is like the tracing of a lotus from the central point. While this is largely a process of yoga and meditation, the remedial measures of astrology can be helpful tools to facilitate it.

PSYCHOLOGICAL INDICATIONS OF THE PLANETS

Sun ☉

The Sun in its higher level represents the true or Divine Self (atman), just as on the lower level it represents the ego or self-image.

The main solar issue is identity. Our true identity is in consciousness as consciousness, not in any other thing with which we may be identified. Whatever we are identified with is a form of darkness. Our true nature lies in the capacity to illumine things, not in the things that our mind illumines.

Our true being is in the light. It is the light. It is by going within that we find the true light. Any external light we reflect, however great, creates darkness within us.

Moon ☾

The Moon represents the mind or consciousness generally (manas), our general feeling potential.

The main lunar issue is peace and receptivity of the mind. This is achieved by surrender of the mind to the Divine, not by any mental activity nor by following any personal or social force. Our feeling sensitivity does not have to be denied or controlled. It needs to be directed in the right way, which is to be open to the presence, the Divine significance of each thing and each moment.

Mars ♂

Mars represents the need of energy to transform itself. All energy seeks a result. All life requires a direction and a goal.

The issue of Mars lies in directing our energy toward real transformation, the change of our own consciousness. We should not direct our energy toward a goal that is momentary. Yet as long as we pursue the outer goals of life, such as pleasure, wealth and status, that is what we are doing. The real transformative result is the ability to draw our consciousness into the realm of oneness, not to gain some specific limited goal.

Mercury ☿

Mercury represents the power of judgment (buddhi). It can create a net of information and speculation that traps the soul in the realm of the senses, or it can create a ladder of values and principles through which the soul can ascend.

The main issue of Mercury is right discrimination; whether we direct our reason toward organizing the impressions gathered from the senses or toward discriminating truth from falsehood. The latter changes Mercury into the god of wisdom.

Jupiter ♃

Jupiter represents the law of our nature, our creative intelligence, where we find our grace and beneficence in life.

The main issue of Jupiter lies in aligning ourselves with the flow of Divine grace, the inner good rather than the outer social good. This requires projecting a spiritual creativity that raises the world, not just a material creativity that merely furthers the outer powers and structures. We must learn to be beneficent in the presence of the Divine, not merely to be good to gain the admiration of others. It requires an optimism based on the knowledge of the eternal.

Venus ♀

Venus represents our capacity to project love and beauty. Life comes from bliss and expresses bliss. We all want eternal happiness.

The issue of Venus lies in how we define our happiness. We can define it outwardly as pleasure or inwardly as joy. We can seek it in transient things and thereby lose it, or we can seek it in the eternal and truly find it. True joy, however, only comes through suffering, while mere pleasure usually results in suffering. Because we hold to the immediate and do not see the end result, we remain trapped in the illusion of outer happiness. The higher Venus energy arises through devotion, defining our object of love as consciousness itself.

Saturn ♄

Saturn represents the power of our actions. If we do something regularly, it sets a certain force in motion. This power of our action goes with us from life to life. Our destiny is mirrored in our daily activity.

The issue of Saturn is to create an ongoing conscious action toward improving our condition, expanding the powers of truth and peace in life. It is to really put into practice what we have learned, not just to acknowledge it mentally. It is to have the patience and attention to bring things to conclusion and perfection.

Rahu ☊

Rahu represents the illusory power of our unfulfilled desires. These operate at a subconscious level to distort our perception. This projection force of the mind is a powerful creative force that can also be used for meditation, once we have gained control of it. Rahu represents the challenge to master our secret wishes and to accept what is, the present, as the truth.

Ketu ☋

Ketu represents the illusory power of our fears and our attachment to what we have accomplished. These prevent us from positive action and change. It shows the death from which we are in flight during life. The death we fear is not really physical death, but the death of the ego. It is only when we embrace death as a creative force, a power of renewal and transformation, that we can go beyond its shadow.

PSYCHOLOGICAL IMPACT OF THE HOUSES

The first house as the house of the self is also the house of the ego. Afflictions to the first house, its ruler and significator (the Sun) show ego problems.

The fourth house is the house of the emotional mind. Afflictions to it, its ruler and significator (the Moon) show emotional problems. Mars afflictions cause anger. Saturn afflictions give grief and depression. Rahu afflictions give confusion and psychic imbalance.

The fifth house is the house of intellect and intelligence. Afflictions to it, its ruler and significator (Jupiter) show power judgement, lack of discrimination or wrong values. Mars afflictions makes us rash and critical. Saturn gives dullness and darkness to the mind. Rahu gives confusion and wrong perception.

The ninth house is the house of the higher Self or Atman. When it is strong, we are deeply connected to our higher nature and in contact with the benefic forces of the universe and the cosmic mind.

Saturn

Dressed in blue, dark blue in color, who has four arms, the son of the Sun, who appears fearful, whose nature is peaceful, whose vehicle is an ox, who moves slowly, who carries a trident, bow and mace in his hands, with a sapphire crest jewel on his head, making the gesture that grants boons — may Divine Saturn ever grant us his grace.

14

Remedial Measures

HOW TO BALANCE THE INFLUENCES OF THE STARS

Like any other science, astrology has its technology. The purpose of astrology is not just to give us a broader knowledge of ourselves; it is also to provide us with tools to access the deeper aspects of our nature and to better deal with the forces of our subtle environment. This astrological technology consists of methods to harness our energies to improve our relationship with the cosmos. It employs various factors from nature, like gems, but according to a spiritual and occult view.

Western astrology has been more concerned with theory than with practice. It lacks a consistently defined technique for balancing planetary influences. It had such methods during the Middle Ages with the uses of gems, metals, herbs and incantations, but these were largely lost during the development of modern science. Such methods were better preserved in India. In Vedic astrology the use of gems, mantras, deities, and rituals have always been part of astrology.

Today most Western astrologers use the tools of modern psychoanalysis to deal with their clients, derived mainly from Jungian psychology, as Jung himself accepted and used astrology. They explore the personal, emotional and sexual issues of their clients using the birth chart as a key to the unconscious. They help clients arrive at a greater clarity about their needs and their actions.

Some Western astrologers are reintroducing occult methods, like the use of gems. Yet even with these there is much variation on how they are interpreted and applied. Some use spiritual methods like trying to attune to various masters or to the seven rays, or opening up past life influences. These derive mainly from Theosophy or Alice Bailey, who based their work mainly on Hindu and Buddhist teachings, modifying and modernizing them. Other astrologers apply modern nutrition, Western herbalism or macrobiotics to the birth chart for medical treatment. While it is a highly creative field, many of these approaches may not stand the test of time, though they may work for one practitioner or another.

Yet a typical modern astrological reading may not give the client anything to do about their planetary influences other than tell them to be aware of them and try to understand them in terms of their personal life experience. A client may leave feeling helpless before the forces of fate, warned as to an imminent danger but not given any practical means of averting it. A Vedic astrologer, on the other hand, is as much concerned with helping clients balance their planetary influences as with informing them what these influences may be. Vedic astrologers help us to better relate with and transform our karma. Vedic astrology is not a science of fate or doom but a system for alleviating suffering and warding off negative influences.

Vedic astrology helps us implement a life regimen in harmony with the stars. From its point of view we cannot live in harmony with the cosmos by maintaining our usual life style or enhancing it with mere theoretical knowledge. We need a practical means of attunement with the cosmos and its influences. Such methods are not only astrological but spiritual. They entail using the subtle forces around us, like gems and colors, as well as internal methods of ritual, mantra and meditation. If we are not doing such things on a daily basis, our knowledge of astrology may not be able to change our lives.

WHICH PLANETS TO STRENGTHEN

The main issue in applying astrological remedial measures is determining which planet to strengthen in the chart. There are several ways of doing this that can be complex. However, the first basic principle is simple. *A planet should generally be strengthened if it is a good planet and weak in the chart.* The caution is that we should be careful in strengthening natural malefic planets like Saturn and Mars even when they are weak, particularly with methods like gemstones, which can increase their power. Benefics, when weak are usually safe to strengthen.

To determine what planet to strengthen, we should gauge the status of planets both naturally and temporally, as per the rules of malefic and benefic planets and house rulership. We can strengthen weak natural malefics if they are also temporal benefics, like Saturn for Libra Ascendant or Mars for Cancer and Leo Ascendants.

Besides strengthening weak planets, it can be helpful to strengthen the planets that rule the Ascendant or the ninth house, even when these are not weak. These increase the positive energy in a chart. A planet that is well placed and benefic can be strengthened, but this may not be as helpful as to strengthen benefics that are weak or ill placed. Some astrologers strengthen both the weakest and the strongest planet in the chart, as long as neither one is malefic. Different Vedic astrologers have variant opinions on these issues. As usual, there is no one way to look at things, and we should try to get as broad a perspective as we can.

The following astrological remedial measures outline typical ways to strengthen weak planets. We should exercise some scrutiny in using these astrological treatment methods. For example, the indications of a weak Sun and a weak Mars are similar, as they both indicate low fire and a weak will. The difference is that a weak Sun gives a poor self-image, while a weak Mars creates lack of motivation and poor work ability. Hence a Vedic astrological reading is generally necessary for determining which remedial measures are most appropriate.

In this regard, the use of substances like gems or herbs can be more dangerous than mantra or meditation. We can use mantra and meditation to ward off negative planetary influences that may be afflicting us, like an overly strong Saturn, Rahu or Mars. Yet we would not strengthen these planets with gems or herbs under such conditions. We should acknowledge and propitiate all the planets occasionally through mantra, meditation or ritual, as we all have to work through their forces.

Yantras (inscribed geometrical designs) for the planets are useful in the same way as gems but don't have the side-effects; like mantras, they are of a propitiatory nature. They can be used by everyone, though it is more helpful to use the yantras of the planets that are afflicting us or those whose properties we wish to strengthen. (see section on Planetary Deities)

In the use of gems, the quality of the gem is one factor; the other factor is how we purify and energize it. Gems should be of good quality and without major flaws. Note that natural gemstones, particularly emeralds, will commonly have some minor flaws. This is not a problem if the flaws are minor or do not disturb the diffraction of the gem.

Gems can function to strengthen either the higher or lower influences of the planets, depending upon how we use them. A gem for Venus, for example, may serve to increase attachment or give us more pleasure or wealth in life, if we use it on a lower level. For it to increase love and creativity, the higher powers of Venus, we must energize it with a spiritual intention or ourselves have a highly spiritual nature to begin with. Merely to use astrological gems does not guarantee that they will improve our condition spiritually. Used wrongly, they can confuse or disturb us on a subtle astral level. For this reason, gems should be cleared and empowered with mantras or other spiritual influences and intentions.

Fingers and the Planets

Index finger	Ether	Jupiter
Middle finger	Air	Saturn
Ring finger	Fire, Water	Sun, Moon
Little finger	Earth	Mercury

Gems are usually worn on the finger belonging to the planet, which also relate to the respective element. The gems for the other planets can be worn on the fingers of planets with whom they are friends. Venus stones can go on Saturn or Mercury fingers. Moon and Mars stones can be worn on Sun or Jupiter fingers. *Gems should be set so as to touch the skin (open at the bottom) for maximum effect.* This is a very important point. Otherwise they may have little influence.

Please note that planets may not be weak in all aspects of their influence. A person may have a weak Sun in terms of career, shown through a failure to achieve any recognition, but he may not necessarily have a weak Sun in terms of health (i.e. he may not have a weak heart). I have combined these indications together below, but this does not mean that they always occur together.

Natural malefics like Saturn, Mars, Rahu and Ketu create difficulties both when they are too strong and when they are too weak. When they are too strong they weaken other planets, and under such a condition it is the other planets that we must strengthen. Yet malefics may spoil other planets even when they are weak, owing to the aspects that they cast. So we must be careful even in strengthening weak malefics if they are afflicting benefic planets. Generally, when we strengthen a weak malefic we should strengthen a friendly benefic as well. If we strengthen Saturn, for example, it is good to strengthen Venus or Mercury. This helps bring out the positive side of the naturally malefic planet.

SUN

Indications of a Weak Sun

The main factors are a lack of self-confidence, poor self-esteem or self-respect. The person will have low self-worth and a poor self-image and gain little success or recognition. He or she will be weak in will and courage and be prone to fear and uncertainty. He will lack drive and motivation and depend on others emotionally and materially. He will look to others, usually family and friends, for a sense of identity and will find it difficult to do things on his own. The father of the person usually does not have a good fate in life.

On the physical level, the individual will suffer from low energy, pallor, anemia, cold extremities, weak digestion, and poor appetite. She or he may have a weak or slow pulse, weak heart and poor circulation. There may be edema, accumulation of water and phlegm and general hypofunction of the organs and nervous system. The eyesight may be poor. There may be arthritis and weakness of the bones. Their resistance will be low, particularly to cold and damp conditions.

Astrological Factors

A weak Sun is evidenced by the Sun in its debility in Libra, in inimical signs (like those of Saturn), in difficult houses like the eighth and twelfth, or through malefic aspects to the Sun like those of Saturn, Mars, Rahu or Ketu. Ketu's close conjunction is particularly difficult.

The Sun is a benefic planet for Aries, Leo, Scorpio, and Sagittarius Ascendants. For them, the positive qualities of the Sun like leadership, independence, intelligence and insight can be enhanced by remedial measures, even if the Sun is not weak.

Gemstones

The main gemstone for the Sun is a ruby. It should be a minimum of two carats in size, set in gold of fourteen carats or more and worn on the ring finger of the right hand. It should be of good quality, without flaws and transparent.

As a substitute, a good quality garnet can be used, but it should be of at least three carats in size, preferably five. A large garnet pendant or strand of garnet can be worn around the neck.

These gems should first be worn on a Sunday, preferably at the rising of the Sun, particularly when the Sun is strong, as when in its own sign or exalted (Sagittarius is also good). An astrologer can recommend a special time or muhurta for this.

When to be Careful Wearing a Gemstone for the Sun

Gems for the Sun should usually not be worn if the individual suffers from fever, bleeding, ulcers, hypertension, or infectious diseases (high Pitta).

Psychological indications are excess ambition, seeking of power, a dominating nature, a strong ego, pride or vanity.

Astrological factors are when the Sun is the lord of malefic houses like the third, sixth and eleventh. We should be careful wearing gems for the Sun when benefic planets in the chart, like the Moon, Venus, Mercury or Jupiter are combust or in opposition to it. One should remember that the Sun, as a malefic planet, tends to spoil the indications of the houses that it occupies. Wearing a gem for the Sun can harm the house in which it is located, particularly trines and angles; the exceptions are houses three, six, ten and eleven, where it does well.

Colors

One should meditate on the red or golden solar orb as residing in the heart. One should use bright, clear, transparent, warm colors; generally, red, yellow, gold and orange, avoiding dark colors, places and environments, particularly cloudy colors, grays and blacks.

Herbs and Aromas

Solar energy is increased by taking spicy and fiery herbs like cayenne, black pepper, dry ginger, pippali, saffron, calamus, bayberry and cinnamon (specifically the Ayurvedic formula Trikatu). Calamus is best for the sattvic side of solar energy in the mind.

Aromatic oils and fragrances for the Sun are camphor, cinnamon, eucalyptus, and saffron.

Mantras

There are many mantras for the many names of the Sun, like Surya, Savitar, Aditya, Ravi, Mitra, Varuna, Aryaman, Pushan, Indra, and Agni.

- The main name mantra is Om Suryaya Namah!
- The main bija (seed) mantra is Om Sum! (pronounced soom)

Another good seed mantra for the Sun is *Ram* (pronounced rahm), the name of the avatar Rama. This increases our connection with the Divine light. *Om* can also be used, as it is said to be the sound of the Sun. The Sun is the essence of all vowels. Another good mantra is *Hrim* (hreem), which projects the golden light of the heart. These mantras should be chanted preferably on a Sunday during the day (at dawn, noon or sunset).

Deities

The Sun relates to the Divine Father, which in the Hindu religion is Shiva Mahadeva, the great God. Yet the Sun represents the Divine generally, and whatever form of God we worship can be used for this purpose. Vishnu is worshiped as the Sun, representing the more immanent or benefic side of solar energy.

The Sun is also the Divine Son. The great avatars are sons of the Sun. Christ follows in this line as well, with his birth at the winter solstice (the Sun reborn), as do Rama, Krishna and Buddha.

Yoga

Usually the individual will do well in practicing meditation and the yoga of knowledge to connect with the higher Self. The main thing is to establish a sense of self-identity according to our inner nature as pure consciousness. We must learn to discriminate between the lower self and the higher self. We should trace the origin of the I-thought to the Divine light within the heart.

Lifestyle

The individual should cultivate independence and courage, challenging his or her fears. He should bring the light into all the dark corners of his mind. He should learn to appear in public alone and become able to spend time alone. He should take more initiative and play a leadership role in life.

The person should spend time outdoors in the Sun, along with sunbathing twenty minutes or so a day. He should rise early in the morning and greet the Sun, preferably with a prayer or chant to the Divine at dawn, noon and sunset. The yogic "Sun salutation," *Surya namaskara*, should be done regularly.

MOON

Indications of a Weak Moon

A weak Moon appears in a person as ungroundedness, emotional instability, anxiety, fear of intimacy, lack of friendliness and weak emotions. The individual will lack contentment and find it difficult to stand the stress and strain of human contact. There will be moodiness, depression and negativity, along with possible neurosis and mental imbalance. The mind may be cloudy, dull or disturbed. The mother may also suffer or not prosper in life.

Physical factors of a weak Moon include anemia, low body fluids, possible dehydration, low body weight, dry skin, constipation, weak lungs and weak kidneys. There will be difficulty withstanding dryness and heat. For women there may be infertility and menstrual problems.

Astrological Factors

The Moon is weak when in its fall in Scorpio, when in inimical signs, when aspected by malefic planets like Saturn, Rahu, Ketu or Mars, or when placed in difficult houses like the sixth, eighth or twelfth. The aspects of Rahu and Saturn are the most difficult, particularly if not compensated by an aspect from Jupiter or Jupiter's location in an angle from the Moon. The Moon is also particularly weak when close to the Sun or combust, as in the case of the new Moon. The Moon is also weak if it stands alone in the chart, with no benefics near it or aspecting it,.

The Moon is a benefic planet for Cancer, Scorpio and Pisces Ascendants. For these people, regimens for the Moon can increase its positive powers of emotional strength, friendliness and love. But as the Moon is an Ascendant in itself, there are many instances when the Moon can be strengthened just as the Ascendant lord can.

Gemstones

The best gem for the Moon is a natural ocean pearl. It should be at least two carats in size, set in silver or white gold, and worn on the ring finger. Cultured pearls can be used as substitutes, as can moonstone, but these should be larger in size, three or five carats, or worn as large pendants or strands.

Such gems should be put on first on a Monday when the Moon is waxing, in Taurus, Cancer, Pisces, or in friendly signs and not conjunct with or strongly aspected by malefics. Or a good muhurta should be chosen astrologically, particularly a good nakshatra like Rohini, Pushya, Punarvasu, Chitra, Hasta, or Shravana.

When to be Careful Wearing a Gemstone for the Moon

Gems for the Moon should not usually be worn when there is phlegm, edema, congestion, or overweight (high kapha). Psychological factors are strong emotions, sentimentality, greed or attachment, and excess involvement with family or society.

Astrological factors are the Moon as a malefic lord (lord of houses like the third, sixth and eighth). When it is such a malefic lord, the Moon can cause problems even when full.

Colors

The best color for the Moon is white. White shades of colors like blue, green or pink can be helpful, but the shades should also be bright. Dark and cloudy colors should be avoided, particularly gray and black, as well as too much red or too many fiery colors. Very transparent colors should not be used.

Herbs and Aromas

Good herbs for the Moon are demulcent and tonic herbs like marshmallow, slippery elm, comfrey root, solomon's seal, shatavari, white musali, bala, and rehmannia, particularly taken in milk decoctions.

Fragrances of white flowers like jasmine, gardenia, lotus and lily are good, as is sandalwood oil. These can be applied to the region of the heart or the third eye.

Mantras

- The main name mantra for the Moon is *Om Chandraya Namah!*
- The seed mantra is *Cham* (pronounced chum) and also Som.

Also useful is *Om Somaya Namah!* as a name mantra and *Shrim* (shreem), perhaps the main mantra of the Goddess, as a seed mantra. These mantras should be repeated on Mondays or in the evening, particularly just before the time of the full Moon. The time of the half Moon is also good.

Deities

The Moon relates to the Goddess or the cosmic feminine generally, the Divine Mother. She is the great Goddess Mahadevi, the consort of Shiva as Mahashakti. She has many forms in different spiritual traditions like Parvati, Lakshmi, Tara, Kwan Yin, Isis, or the Virgin Mary. We should meditate upon the Goddess as dwelling in our hearts, as residing in the lunar orb or wearing the crescent Moon on her head, particularly on the day of the full Moon.

Yoga

Lunar energy is usually increased by devotional practices (Bhakti Yoga), particularly when directed to the Goddess or Divine Mother. We should strive to develop peace, faith, receptivity, and surrender to the Divine.

Lunar energy usually requires that we ally with a spiritual tradition, but we should apply our faith with openness to truth rather than with emotional attachment.

Lifestyle

An atmosphere of faith, devotion, and caring increases lunar energy. The individual should seek a maternal or supportive environment of family and friends. She should also consider how she can help others in a nurturing way, as in some service work. She should mingle with others and open her heart to a community.

MARS

Indications of a Weak Mars

A weak Mars is evidenced by lack of energy, low motivation, and inability to do work consistently. The individual will find it difficult to stand on his own and defend himself, being fearful and easily dominated by others. One may not know how to express anger or see through the manipulations of other people. The person will be overly passive and easily controlled and may have been abused, even physically.

Physically, the immune system will be weak, with low appetite, poor absorption, low body weight, weak muscles, weak liver and small intestine. There will be a tendency to bleeding or to injuries, with slow healing of wounds or sores and possible anemia. Men may experience a lack of sexual vitality or positive drive in life. Women may suffer through their partners, who themselves may be weak characters.

Astrological Factors

Mars is weak when in its fall in Cancer, when aspected by malefics like Saturn and Rahu, when combust, and when in difficult houses like the eighth and twelfth.

Mars is a benefic planet for Cancer, Leo, Sagittarius and Pisces Ascendants and is usually good for Aries and Scorpio as well. Here its positive qualities, like energy and insight ,can be improved even if it is not weak.

Gemstones

The main gem for Mars is a red coral. It should be at least three carats in size, set in white gold or silver and worn on the index or ring finger of the right hand. As red coral is a common and not too expensive gemstone, no substitutes are required, though carnelian can be used (generally as a large pendant). Pink coral has a more balancing but less strengthening effect on Mars energy than the red.

Such gems should be put on first on a Tuesday, preferably when Mars is in its own sign or exalted. Friendly signs, particularly those of Jupiter are also good. It is best if a good muhurta is chosen astrologically.

When to be Careful Wearing a Gemstone for Mars

Gems for Mars should not be worn when there is fever, infection, bleeding, ulcers, or excess sexual drive (high pitta). Psychological factors include too willful or impulsive a character, or an aggressive, wrathful or martial disposition.

Astrological factors are Mars as a malefic lord (particularly for Gemini and Virgo Ascendants), or Mars in conjunction with benefics like the Moon, Mercury, and Venus. Generally we should avoid gems for Mars if it is in the seventh house or strongly disposed in angles or trines. Mars usually spoils the houses it occupies, except houses three, six, ten and eleven.

Colors

Mars energy is increased by the use of the color red and by fiery colors generally, but in darker hues or opaque tones. Cool colors, blues and greens, and very transparent bright colors like yellow should be avoided. Mars types like military colors.

Herbs and Aromas

Most of the spices that are good for the Sun work for Mars, like cinnamon, saffron, turmeric, cayenne or black pepper, but combined with tonics like ginseng, astragalus, and ashwagandha. When Mars is strong, however, we need bitter herbs like aloe, gentian, golden seal and echinacea to cool down its energy.

Mantras

- The name mantra for Mars is *Om Kujaya Namah!*
- The seed mantra for Mars is *Om Kum!* (with the u-vowel pronounced as in put)

Mars has other names like Angaraka and Mangala. Also useful is the mantra for fire, *Om Ram!* (pronounced like rum, different than the solar mantra). We should meditate upon this mantra in the solar plexus or navel chakra. Mars mantras should be chanted especially on Tuesdays.

Deities

Mars relates to the war God or Divine Warrior who is called Skanda, Karttikeya, or Subrahmanya, the second son of Shiva and Parvati. He is the leader of the heavenly army. Any warrior God or Goddess can be helpful for developing Mars energy.

Yoga

Mars is increased by the yogas of knowledge and technique, particularly by practices that aim at the development of energy and insight. Mars types like to work on themselves in a practical way, through physical practices or mental methods like visualization and ritual. On a lower level, martial arts can be used to strengthen Mars energy. Yet such methods may also cater to a negative Mars influence and bring about a seeking of power or prestige for the ego.

Lifestyle

To increase Mars energy, one should learn to be more aggressive, daring, active, expressive and energetic. Usually some form of physical activity should be taken up and the body should be strengthened. There should be a definite discipline in life physically, emotionally and spiritually. Yet it should not be applied harshly, but with intelligence and adaptability.

MERCURY

Indications of a Weak Mercury

A weak Mercury manifests as low intelligence, poor communication skills, speech defects, weak memory, and an inability to calculate. The character exhibits immaturity, childishness, foolishness, lack of self-control, addictions and dependencies. The individual may be slow, dull, daydreaming or irrational. The mind will be weak or confused, with poor powers of expression.

Physical factors are weakness of the nervous system, nerve pain, tremors, anxiety, insomnia, and palpitations. There will be dry or itchy skin, hypersensitivity of the senses, nervous indigestion, and allergies. The lungs and heart may be weak. Generally the person will have poor health in childhood.

Astrological Factors

Mercury is weak when aspected by malefics like Saturn, Rahu, Ketu, the Sun and Mars, when in its fall in Pisces or when in inimical signs, and by residency in difficult houses (the sixth, eighth, and twelfth). Mercury-Moon aspects and conjunctions can also disturb it.

Mercury is a benefic planet for Taurus, Gemini, Virgo, Libra, Capricorn, and Aquarius Ascendants. For such charts we can apply the remedies for Mercury to increase higher Mercury qualities like discrimination, intelligence and power of communication.

Gemstones

The main gem for Mercury is an emerald. It should be at least one and half carats in size, set in gold and worn on the middle or ring finger of the right or left hands, or on the little finger, the finger of Mercury.

Substitutes are peridot, jade, green zircon or green tourmaline. Such gems can also be worn as pendants or strands, hanging down to the region of the neck. As rings they should be at least three carats in size, as pendants five.

They should be put on first on a Wednesday when the Moon is waxing and preferably when Mercury is strong, in friendly signs, its own signs or exalted. A good muhurta can also be chosen.

When Not to Wear a Gemstone for Mercury

Gemstones for Mercury are relatively safe, harmonious and balanced. They have the mutable nature of Mercury, however, and so we should be careful about wearing them with stones for malefics like Saturn, Mars or the Sun. We must be careful about what influences Mercury gems may pick up or may have had when we first got them.

Astrological factors are Mercury as a malefic lord (lord of houses like the sixth and eleventh, particularly for Aries or Scorpio Ascendants), or when it is aligned with Saturn or Rahu.

Colors

Mercury is increased by emerald or green color. Hence it is good to spend time in a lush natural environment of grass or forests. Sitting under a green light can be helpful.

Reds and oranges should be avoided, as well as very dark colors. Mercury likes neutral shades and not too strong colors; it prefers mild greens, blues, grays and browns, mainly earth tones.

Herbs and Aromas

Good herbs for Mercury are nervines like gotu kola, bhringaraj (eclipta), skullcap, passion flower, betony, jatamansi, zizyphus, camomile, and mint. Basil, particularly holy basil (tulsi) is specific for Mercury (Vishnu).

Good oils and aromas are mint, wintergreen, eucalyptus, cedar, thyme, and sage, which clear and open the mind. Yet they should be balanced with mind-calming oils like sandalwood, plumeria (frangipani) and lotus.

Mantras

- The name mantra for Mercury is *Om Budhaya Namah!*
- The seed mantra for Mercury is *Om Bum!* (with the "u" pronounced as in "put")

Important is the seed mantra *Aim* (aym), the mantra of the guru (the spiritual teacher) and of Saraswati the Goddess of Wisdom. Such mantras should be repeated on Wednesdays.

Deities

Mercury relates to Vishnu, the deity who pervades the universe and maintains it as the indwelling cosmic intelligence.

Mercury is the Divine teacher or God of wisdom, such as Hermes or Thoth. In this regard, he is also the Buddha, the enlightened one, the avatar of knowledge, meditation and compassion. He is also the Divine child, the baby Christ or baby Krishna.

Yoga

Mercury energy is increased by the yoga of knowledge, particularly by spiritual teachings that emphasize reason, discrimination, clear expression and objective perception. It often gives us the role of a teacher. The practice of mantra is helpful, as is the study of spiritual philosophies like Vedanta and the learning of Sanskrit or other sacred languages.

Lifestyle

The individual should do more reading, studying, writing and thinking. Mathematical and philosophical studies are good, including taking courses, seminars or going to school. One should cultivate a greater awareness of the world generally, and strive to increase one's powers of communication, perhaps studying a new language.

Yet time for silence of mind and relaxation in nature should always be preserved. The highest quality of the intellect is not its ability to organize our cognition of the outer world, but of the inner world. This involves not accepting the view of the senses as real, but looking for the light of truth in the indwelling consciousness.

JUPITER

Indications of a Weak Jupiter

When Jupiter energy is low we suffer from lack of joy and enthusiasm, weak will, and lack of faith. We feel narrow, contracted and devoid of meaning. There will be pessimism, depression, anxiety, melancholy, moodiness, or self-pity. We lack compassion, friendliness and congeniality. Material and financial difficulties are likely. Our creative energy will be low. Children may be denied or may cause suffering. For women, the husband may be a cause of sorrow or hardship.

Physically, there will be poor vitality, weak immune function, low fat or body weight, poor liver and pancreas function, and weak absorption. Often there will be chronic disease and poor functioning of the nerves and glands. Positive health and vitality will be rare. (It should be noted that these are similar to the signs of too strong or malefic a Saturn influence, as these two planets usually operate in opposition to each other.)

Astrological Factors

Jupiter is weak when in its fall in Capricorn, when aspected by malefics like Saturn, Rahu, Ketu and Mars, and when in difficult houses like the sixth, eighth and twelfth.

Jupiter is a benefic planet for Aries, Cancer, Leo, Scorpio, Sagittarius, and Pisces Ascendants. For these signs, strengthening Jupiter will increase its positive qualities of joy, creativity and intelligence, even if they are not lacking in the person.

Gemstones

The main gem for Jupiter is a yellow sapphire. It should be set in gold and worn on the index finger of the right hand. It should be at least two carats in size.

Yellow topaz is a substitute of almost equal value. Citrine is weaker and should be worn as a large ring (five carats), a pendant or strand. Yellow zircon can also be used.

Such gems should be put on first on a Thursday, preferably when the Moon is waxing and when Jupiter is in its own sign, exalted or a friendly sign. It is best if Jupiter is conjunct or in an angle from the Moon. Or a good muhurta can be chosen.

When Not to Wear a Gemstone for Jupiter

Gems for Jupiter are generally the most safe and balanced of all stones, as Jupiter is the best benefic. Astrological factors that may cause us not to use them are mainly Jupiter as lord of malefic houses (like for Taurus or Libra Ascendants).

Colors

Jupiter energy is increased by the use of yellow, orange and gold — clear, bright and transparent colors generally. Dark colors should be avoided, as well as strong shades like red, blue, violet or purple.

Herbs and Aromas

Jupiter energy is increased by tonic herbs like ashwagandha, bala, licorice, ginseng, and astragalus, particularly taken in milk decoctions, with ghee or as herbal jellies. Rich foods may also be necessary, nuts like almonds, walnuts, cashews, sesame seeds and oils like ghee, sesame and almond.

Mantra

- The name mantra for Jupiter is *Om Brihaspataye Namah!*
- The seed mantra for Jupiter is *Om Brahm!* (bruhm)

Other benefic mantras are good for Jupiter like *Shrim* (shreem). This increases prosperity generally. *Om* itself is quite good as it connects us with the expansive Divine energy. These mantras should be chanted on Thursdays.

Deities

Jupiter relates to Brihaspati, the priest of the Gods. He also relates to Ganesh or Ganapati, the elephant faced God, the first son of Shiva and Parvati. Ganesh mantras can be used for Jupiter like *Om Gam Ganeshaya Namah!*

Jupiter is also the king of the Gods and the wielder of the thunderbolt as Zeus, Thor or Indra ,and Indra's mantra is *Om Indraya Namah!*

Yoga

Jupiter directs us to the spiritual life generally and gives us the propensity for a broad and integral path, combining knowledge, devotion, practices and service, as in the path of Raja Yoga. Its basic impulse is toward devotion (faith), but from that it develops knowledge. Strengthening Jupiter requires some religious or spiritual activity, usually done in a formal manner.

Lifestyle

Jupiter energy is increased by being more optimistic, having more faith, by the performance of rituals and doing of good deeds. The individual should be more friendly, sociable, and communicative, but according to his or her higher principles. One should seek to align oneself with the forces of goodness. Any type of action to render help to others or raise the consciousness in the world can be useful.

VENUS

Indications of a Weak Venus

A weak Venus appears as a lack of beauty, charm, or grace, as well as a lack of taste or refinement. The individual may be coarse, aggressive, unrefined or vulgar. She may have difficulties in her romantic life and lack in love or affection. For women, feminine qualities will be low or feminine happiness may be denied. For men, relationships with women may be difficult or the wife may suffer. There will be difficulty in expressing feelings.

Physically, there will be weakness of the kidneys and the reproductive system, with infertility or impotence. There may be weakness of the bones, low energy, or poor immune function, with a tendency towards bleeding.

Astrological Factors

Venus is weak when in its fall in Virgo or when in inimical signs, when aspected by malefics like the Sun, Mars, Saturn, Rahu and Ketu, and when in difficult houses like the sixth and eighth.

Venus is a benefic planet for Taurus, Gemini, Virgo, Libra, Capricorn and Aquarius Ascendants, particularly for Capricorn and Aquarius. For these Ascendants remedial measures for Venus can increase her higher powers of devotion, joy and creativity.

Gemstones

The main gem for Venus is a diamond. It should be at least one carat in size and set in gold or white gold and worn on the middle or little finger.

Substitutes are a white sapphire, clear zircon (at least three carats) or quartz crystal. The latter is better used as a pendant (at least five carats in size, preferably ten) or in strands.

Such gems should be put on first on a Friday, preferably when Venus is exalted, in its own signs or friendly signs (like those of Mercury and Saturn) and not too close to the Sun. Or a good muhurta can be chosen.

When Not to Wear a Gemstone for Venus

Gems for Venus as a benefic are relatively safe. However, they can increase sexuality, attachment and power of the ego or the senses if we are caught in the lower aspects of Venus energy. Hence we should strive towards the higher Venus energy of devotion and surrender. We should not use gems for Venus if we have a high sex drive or a strong need for comfort and luxury.

Astrological factors are Venus as a lord of malefic houses (like for Sagittarius and Pisces Ascendants), or a strongly sensual Venus (Venus in fixed signs or aspected by Mars in houses like the fifth, seventh or twelfth).

Colors

Venus likes all colors, particularly a rainbow-like effect. She prefers pastels, light blues, and pinks. Dark and heavy colors are not good, nor are colors that are too bright or penetrating. Light, flowery variegated colors are best.

Herbs and Aromas

Venus likes all flowers and sweet fragrances like rose, saffron, jasmine, lotus, lily, and iris. These are great for improving her energy and disposition. Tonic herbs for the reproductive system are also good like shatavari, white musali, amalaki, aloe gel, rehmannia, dang gui, and red raspberry.

Mantras

- The name mantra for Venus is *Om Shukraya Namah!*
- The seed mantra is *Om Shum!* (with the u pronounced as in put)

The general mantra for the Goddess, *Shrim* (shreem), is also good for Venus. Another useful mantra is the Goddess mantra *Hrim* (hreem), the mantra of love, beauty, modesty and opening of the heart. These mantras should be chanted on Fridays.

Deities

Venus is the beautiful, youthful and often erotic form of the Goddess as Lakshmi, Lalita, Tripurasundari, Venus, Aphrodite, or Astarte. She should be worshiped on a Friday with flowers, particularly by lakes, streams or by the sea. Art, beauty and grace are essential to her worship.

Yoga

Venus relates mainly to Bhakti Yoga or the yoga of devotion. It makes us receptive to divine love, joy and beauty, as found in the stories of Radha and Krishna or in Sufi love poetry. It inclines us to chanting, rituals, dance, devotional singing and visualizations. Generally it causes us to approach the divine in the form of a particular deity or teacher, a beloved that we serve and adore, particularly the Goddess.

Venus can also give occult knowledge and powers, like the ability to see visions or travel astrally, but it can get us caught in the glamour and illusion of the astral plane. It is good for Tantra and also for astrology.

Lifestyle

Venus energy is increased by cultivating refinement and sensitivity, by taking a more appreciative or affectionate mode in life. We should become more creative and artistic, and strive to improve our expression in life. It is helpful to have more beauty and color around oneself. One should increase one's feminine attributes if one is a woman. For a man it helps to give more regard to the women in one's life, particularly the relationship partner, the muse on the intellectual plane, or the Goddess as a form of devotion.

SATURN

Indications of a Weak Saturn

Saturn's weakness causes agitation, tremors, inability to handle stress, insomnia, and general ungroundedness. The individual will be easily intimidated by people or by circumstances. There will be a lack of practicality and a poor perception of reality. The individual may suffer from the government or organized institutions and have difficulty making money. There will be lack of consistency, poor endurance and inability to face difficulties. The person will quit easily and have no long term drive or planning.

Physically, there will be weakness of the bones and nerves, poor vitality, and weak longevity. There will be constipation, holding in of waste materials and possible decay of body tissues. Healing will be slow and resistance to infectious diseases will not be good. In extreme cases, diseases like epilepsy, paralysis, or cancer are possible.

Astrological Indications

Saturn is weak when in its fall in Aries, when in inimical signs, when aspected by malefics like the Sun, Mars, Rahu and Ketu, and when in difficult houses like the eighth and twelfth.

Saturn is a benefic planet for Taurus, Libra, Capricorn and Aquarius Ascendants, particularly Taurus and Libra. For these, gems for Saturn will increase its better qualities of objectivity, detachment, independence and authority, even when Saturn is not weak in the chart, but they should be used with care or balanced by a gem for friendly benefics like Venus and Mercury.

Gemstones

The main gem for Saturn is a blue sapphire. It should be at least two carats in size, set in gold and worn on the middle finger.

Substitutes are lapis lazuli, malachite or amethyst, which should be used in larger size (three to five carats) in rings or as pendants or strands.

Saturn gems should be put on first on a Saturday, when Saturn is well placed in the chart, preferably aspected by Jupiter. It is often good to wear an additional gem for a friendly benefic like Venus, Jupiter or Mercury.

When Not to Wear Gemstones for Saturn

Gems for Saturn should always be worn with care, as Saturn is a great malefic. Often it is best to give them a trial run, even if all factors appear good. They should not be used when there is selfishness, inertia, possessiveness, coldness or calculation in the nature; or when the individual is proud or manipulative.

Astrological factors are when Saturn is the lord of difficult houses (for Aries, Cancer, Leo, Scorpio, Sagittarius and Pisces Ascendants), or when it is conjunct or strongly aspecting benefics like the Moon, Venus, Jupiter, or Mercury. Saturn tends to spoil the indications of good houses (trines and angles), so we should be careful wearing its gems when it is located in them.

Colors

Best to strengthen Saturn are dark blue tones. Browns, grays and blacks are good, but in excess may strengthen the negative side of Saturn. Generally Saturn does not like much color, and to strengthen it we should avoid bright colors and too much of any color.

Herbs and Aromas

Good herbs for a weak Saturn are myrrh, frankincense, guggul, ashwagandha, shilajit, haritaki, and comfrey root: herbs to strengthen overall vitality and promote healing. The Ayurvedic formula Triphala is specific for Saturn, as it both cleanses all waste materials and also the deeper tissues.

Good aromas for Saturn are sandalwood, frankincense, cedar and juniper, which promote healing much like the herbs.

Mantras

- The name mantra for Saturn is *Om Shanaye Namah!*
- The seed mantra for Saturn is *Om Sham!* (pronounced shum)

The Vedic chant for peace, *Om Shanti, Shanti, Shanti,* is good for Saturn. Also helpful is the Kali mantra *Krim* (kreem). These mantras should be chanted on Saturdays.

Deities

Saturn relates to the deity of time as Shiva (Kala) or his consort (Kali). We can worship Shiva in his dark blue form and chant his name *Om Namah Shivaya!* Or we can worship Kali. As a dark planet, Saturn's worship often relates to the dark or terrible forms of the Divine.

Saturn is the grandfather spirit, and can be propitiated by the worship of our ancestors or by the Divine Father or Grandfather.

Yoga

Saturn requires self-discipline, renunciation, surrender, and detachment as well as the doing of good karma: the yogas of knowledge and service. He is more concerned with practice than with theory. In his higher form he is the silent sage. He requires inaction and letting go on our part.

To cleanse the influence of a negative Saturn, some form of karmic expiation may be required like prayer, atonement, pilgrimages or giving of charity.

Lifestyle

When Saturn is weak one needs to cultivate peace, calm, detachment, equanimity. There should be a strict routine in life, following an authority or tradition. Travel should be reduced, and stimulation of the nerves and senses should be avoided. Strong emotional expression should be avoided, as well as situations of stress and strain. Time should be spent in nature and in solitude. Slowing down, quiet and retreat are helpful.

RAHU

Signs of a Weak or Afflicted Rahu

Rahu's weakness displays itself through hypersensitivity, agitation, fear, and anxiety. There may be hallucinations, the taking of drugs, moodiness, strange fantasies and imaginations. These people may not know who they really are and may be taken over by any influence or suggestion, the more unrealistic the better. They are often unpopular, out of touch with the times and have few friends. They like to debase themselves or their nerves in unwholesome pursuits. They tend to dissipate themselves in useless activities.

Physical factors are weak immune function, easy contraction of contagious diseases, nervousness, tremors, insomnia, pallor, and nervous indigestion. The connection with the physical body will be low, with possible loss of control of body functions. This may develop into nervous and mental disorders of various types.

Astrological Factors

Rahu suffers in difficult houses, particularly the eighth, and by malefic aspects like those Saturn, Mars and the Sun. The planet ruling Rahu should also be weak, in its fall, combust, or poorly aspected.

When Rahu is in strong houses like the tenth and its lord is benefic and strong, it can be good to wear gems for Rahu to increase its positive powers like the capacity to influence society in a benefic manner.

Gemstones

The main gem for Rahu is a hessonite garnet (gomedha). There are two main varieties, one cinnamon in color, the other golden. Other golden or cinnamon colored grossularite garnets can be used as substitutes. They should be at least three carats in size, set in gold or silver and worn on the middle finger of the right or left hand. Darker red or opaque garnets should not be used, as these increase the negative (eclipse-causing) power of Rahu.

Such gems should be put on first on a Saturday or the day of the planet that rules it in the chart. Rahu should be in favorable signs or those favorable to the planet that rules it. Or a good muhurta should be chosen.

When Not to Wear a Gemstone for Rahu

Gems for Rahu are relatively safe (except the darker ones). Rahu is the predominant influence in the materialistic age (the force of Maya) and the brighter gems for it help remove its darkening effect upon us. When Rahu is in a trine or afflicting benefics in the chart, it is better not to use its gemstones.

Colors

Colors for Rahu are much like those for Jupiter; bright, yellow, and gold but also like those for the Sun: red and orange and transparent. These serve to counter the negative effect of Rahu to cause eclipses and increase its positive effect to transmit positive energies.

Herbs and Aromas

Rahu is a very subtle force and cannot be dealt with on a simple outer level with herbs. Aromas for clearing the psychic air can be helpful, like camphor, bayberry, sage, eucalyptus or wintergreen, as can calming fragrances like sandalwood, lotus and frankincense. Calamus is the best herb for Rahu, but other nervines are helpful.

Mantras

- The name mantra for Rahu is *Om Rahave Namah!*
- The seed mantra is Om Ram! (pronounced rahm)

The mantra for Shiva, *Hum* (hoom), is also good as it destroys illusions and clears our psychic field of negative influences and suggestions, as is the Durga mantra, *Dum* (doom). These mantras should be chanted on Saturdays or on the day of the planet in whose sign Rahu is located in the chart

Deities

The best deity for Rahu is Durga, the Goddess as the demon slayer. Also useful is the avatar Rama, the Divine hero. Durga is the Goddess form that clears our minds of illusions and negativity; Rama is the form of the Goddess who destroys the demons of the subconscious (lower astral). Whenever Rahu's influence is high, we need to take refuge in the Divine, in whatever form is closest to our heart.

Yoga

People with a weak Rahu should avoid yogic practices that open up to the astral plane, including visualization, hypnosis and modern high tech yogas (using tapes and videos). Bhakti Yoga or devotion is best, as Rahu's influence makes discernment and meditation difficult. Some form of psychic clearing, expiation or exorcism in extreme cases may be helpful. One should be allied with a clear tradition and consistent discipline and avoid wishful thinking, the seeking of experiences, or the development of occult powers.

Lifestyle

When Rahu is weak one should avoid exposure to powerful sensations, mass media or high tech influences, drugs, too much sex, excess talking, or too much imagination. Everything artificial should be avoided, from junk food to artificial environments. Peace, quiet and rest should be cultivated, as well as opening up to Jupiterian influences (love, faith and compassion). We need a protective and nurturing environment to strengthen physical and psychic immunity.

KETU

Indications of a Weak or Afflicted Ketu

Typical signs of a weak Ketu are lack of insight, poor discrimination, lack of confidence, self-doubt, and inability to concentrate. Perception will be poor or disturbed and the vision may be weak. There may be self-destructive tendencies and the individual will be prone to violence or injury as under Mars, but of a collective nature (Ketu when weak makes us susceptible to being hurt in wars or mass calamities). The person may feel constricted, contracted and lacking in freedom. He or she may be attached to the past or to lost causes.

Physically, there is weak digestion, poor circulation, ulcers, anemia, and chronic bleeding disorders. There may be muscular problems or nervous system disorders, with possibly difficult or mysterious diseases like cancer or MS, as under Rahu.

Astrological Factors

Ketu is weak in difficult houses, particularly the eighth, when aspected by malefics like Saturn and Mars, or when the planet that rules the sign that Ketu is located in happens to be weak.

When Ketu is strong, when it is with a benefic planet in its own sign or exalted, or when it is in the twelfth house and not aspected by malefics, gems for Ketu can be worn to increase its higher qualities of knowledge, insight and concentration.

Gemstones

The gem for Ketu is a cat's eye (chrysoberyl family). It should be at least two carats in size and is preferably set in gold. It should be worn on the middle finger of the right hand generally. Other forms of cat's eye can be used as substitutes.

These gems should be put on first on a Saturday, or on the day of the planet which rules Ketu. Ketu should be in favorable signs or those favorable to the planet that rules it. Or a good muhurta should be chosen.

When Not to Wear a Gem for Ketu

Those suffering from bleeding, fever, infections, ulcers, or pain in the eyes (high pitta conditions) should not wear Ketu gems.

Astrological factors are when Ketu is in conjunction with benefic planets (unless they are exalted or in their own signs), or when its ruler also rules malefic houses like the sixth and eleventh. Gems for Ketu should be worn with care and are perhaps the least commonly prescribed of all astrological gems.

Colors

Colors for increasing Ketu are like those of the Sun: bright, fiery, penetrating, transparent, red, orange, and yellow. Opaque or whitish tinged colors should be avoided, as well as all dark or cloudy colors.

Herbs and Aromas

Ketu, like Rahu, is subtle. Herbs to increase perception like sage, calamus, bayberry, wild ginger, and juniper may be useful.

Penetrating aromatic oils like camphor, cedar, myrrh and frankincense are good. Afflictions of a strong Ketu, however, require cooling nervines like gotu kola, bhringaraj, skullcap and passion flower.

Mantras

- The name mantra for Ketu is *Om Ketave Namah*!
- The seed mantra is *Om Kem!* (pronounced like came)

These mantras increase our powers of perception. They should be chanted on Saturdays or Tuesdays or the day of the planet in whose sign Ketu is located in the chart.

Deities

Ketu relates to Rudra, the terrible form of Shiva as the God of death and transformation. He relates to Chitragupta, the god of death and karma, who keeps track of our misdeeds. In this regard he resembles Pluto, the Roman God of the dead. The worship of the terrible forms of the Divine can help overcome the negative influence of Ketu.

Ketu also relates to Brahma, the God of knowledge, once we have seen through his lower terror (our fear of death). He is also connected to Ganesha as the lord of secret knowledge and power.

Yoga

Ketu is increased by the yoga of knowledge, the capacity for self-inquiry, much as with the Sun. Ketu shows the state in which we "have no head" or have gone beyond the mind. It causes us to seek to transcend time and the senses. Meditation on death is also helpful for developing the higher yogic powers of Ketu.

Lifestyle

The individual should have more confidence in his or her thoughts and perceptions. Spiritual and occult studies can be helpful, or any kind of focused research, learning to control and direct the power of insight. It is often good to study astrology. It is best to follow a teacher or tradition, however. At least there should be some discipline in the life and development of will and energy but along with compassion and freedom.

Rahu

Dressed in black, black in color, who has four arms, who is fearful to behold, a head without a body, whose body is a serpent, whose vehicle is a lion, who carries a sword, trident and discus in his hands, with a hessonite crest jewel on his head, making the gesture that grants boons — may Divine Rahu ever grant us his grace.

15

Worship of the Planets

Devotional worship of the planets is an important method for balancing the planetary influences in the chart or for just attuning ourselves with the cosmos. Done regularly and with conviction, it is stronger than wearing gemstones. Such devotional practices involve mantras, symbols, rituals, visualizations and meditations of various types.

Each planet has its representative deity with its specific form. Each planetary deity has a certain appearance, implements and ornaments, and a particular vehicle (the animal it rides, signifying its underlying power).

The planetary deities, even those of female planets like Venus and the Moon, are portrayed as male, while the signs and nakshatras are regarded as female. The planets are the forces (male) that work in the fields of the signs (female). The planetary deities also have their ruling deities (adhidevata) and their over-rulers (pratyadhidevata). These may be male or female according to the nature of the planets.

The standard scheme is as follows:

Planet	Deity	Over-ruler
SUN	*Agni* Fire God	*Shiva* Great God
MOON	*Apas* Water Goddess	*Parvati* Great Goddess
MARS	*Bhumi* Earth Goddess	*Skanda* War God
MERCURY	*Vishnu* Maintainer	*Narayana* Cosmic Person
JUPITER	*Indra* King of Gods	*Brahma* Creator
VENUS	*Indrani* Queen of Gods	*Indra* King of Gods
SATURN	*Yama* God of Death	*Prajapati* Creator
RAHU	*Durga* Goddess of Power	Serpent God
KETU	*Chitragupta* God of Karma	*Brahma*, God of Knowledge

Animals for the Planetary Gods

Sun —	Seven-headed Horse	Moon —	Deer
Mars —	Goat	Mercury —	Lion
Jupiter —	Elephant	Venus —	Horse
Saturn —	Ox	Rahu —	Lion
Ketu —	Serpent		

OTHER PLANETARY SYMBOLS

Grains for the Planets

Sun —	Wheat	Moon —	Basmati Rice
Mars —	Red Dhal	Mercury —	Mung Dhal
Jupiter —	Chick Peas	Venus —	Lima Beans
Saturn —	Sesame Seeds	Rahu —	Black Gram
Ketu —	Horsegram		

Each planet corresponds to a particular form of grain or legume used for the worship of the planets. Each planet can be represented by a small bowl of its symbolic grain, which can be placed on an altar. Generally, these are good foods to take when their respective planet is weak in the chart. Each planet has its own symbol used in its worship or in its meditation.

Symbols for the Planets

Sun —	eight-pointed star	Moon —	crescent moon
Mars —	triangle	Mercury —	arrow
Jupiter —	square	Venus —	five pointed star
Saturn —	bow	Rahu —	magnet
Ketu —	flag		

Directions of the Planets

Each planet relates to a specific direction from which its influence comes.

SE —	Venus	E —	Sun	NE —	Jupiter
S —	Mars			N —	Mercury
SW —	Rahu	W —	Saturn	NW —	Moon

When making the planets into symbols or yantras, or when placing them in a pattern on an altar, their directions are, with the Sun in the center:

SE —	Moon	E —	Venus	NE —	Mercury
S —	Mars	C —	Sun	N —	Jupiter
SW —	Rahu	W —	Saturn	NW —	Ketu

YANTRAS

Just as each planet has a mantra, a special sound energy, so too it possesses a yantra, a special energy pattern. The yantra is the visible form or energy body of the mantra or of the planet to which it corresponds.

Two general types of yantras exist. First there are the numerical yantras, wherein numbers are inscribed. Second there are the geometric mantras based on certain designs. The most common geometrical yantra is that for the Sun, the Surya yantra. The most common planetary yantras are the numeri-cal types. They are all based on a certain sequence.

Numerical Yantras

The numerical yantras follow the same sequence, which is based on the magic square of the number five. This is a mathematical design with the number five in the center that, whichever way we add the numbers, horizontally, vertically or diagonally, comes up with the number fifteen. The number for each respective planet occurs in the upper center, starting with the Sun as one. The solar yantra shows the basic form of this pattern.

Sun Yantra

6	1	8
7	5	3
2	9	4

This shows the manifestation of solar energy. Five is the root number of manifestation. We have five elements, five sense organs, and five limbs (two arms, two legs and head). The total of the sides and diagonals is 15. The total of all the numbers is 45, or 9 x 5, and shows the full development of the fivefold solar force.

This same numerical sequence, called the Writing from the Lo River or the Book of Lo, is the basis for the I Ching, which in turn is the basis of Chinese Astrology. We see therefore in these numbers the key to all Oriental astrology.

Moon Yantra

8	2	9
8	6	4
3	10	5

The Moon yantra is based on the number two. As the number one is increased to two for this yantra, so are all the other numbers increased by one: the total is18, which is the number that completes the lunar manifestation. The total for the lunar yantra is 54.

Mars Yantra

8	3	10
9	7	5
4	11	6

The Mars yantra is based on the number three. The numbers add up to 21 for each column or 63 for the total.

Mercury Yantra

9	4	11
10	8	6
5	12	7

The Mercury yantra is based on the number four. The numbers add up to 24 for each column and 72 for the total.

Jupiter Yantra

10	5	12
11	9	7
6	13	8

The Jupiter yantra is based on the number five. The numbers add up to 27 for each column and 81 for the total.

Venus Yantra

11	6	13
12	10	8
7	14	9

The Venus yantra is based on the number six. Each column equals 30 and the total equals 90.

Saturn Yantra

12	7	14
13	11	9
8	15	10

The Saturn yantra is based on the number seven. Each column equals 33 and the total equals 99.

Rahu Yantra

13	8	15
14	12	10
9	16	11

The Rahu yantra is based on the number eight. Each column equals 36 and the total equals 108.

Ketu Yantra

14	9	16
15	13	11
10	17	12

The Ketu yantra is based on the number nine. Each column equals 39 and the total equals 117.

Special yantras inscribed with mantras or names of the planets also exist. Common is a triangular yantra with the names of Mars. Special yantras exist for Saturn made out of five metals and inscribed with the names of Saturn.

MANTRA YANTRA

A simple yantra for the planets can be made with the solar yantra and the bija (seed) mantras for each planet.

Mantra Yantra

Shum	Sum	Ram
Sham	Gum	Am
Cham	Kem	Bum

All the a-vowels should be pronounced with a short a-vowel sound as in our word the. The u-vowels are also short as in our word put. The e-vowel is like our long a-vowel as in came.

OTHER PLANETARY YANTRAS

Yantras for the deities corresponding to the planets can be used for balancing planetary influences as well. Sri Yantra is best for all general purposes. Yantras should be used along with their mantras and meditation on their deities. Some typical ones are as follows.

Sun	Surya Yantra, Gayatri Yantra, Vishnu Yantra
Moon	Sri Yantra, Lakshmi Yantra
Jupiter	Ganesh Yantra
Mercury	Vishnu Yantra
Venus	Sri Yantra, Lakshmi Yantra
Rahu	Kali Yantra, Durga Yantra
Ketu	Mahamrit-yunjaya Yantra

USE OF YANTRAS

Copper yantras can be used for purifying water or for energizing medicines. They can be placed on altars, meditation seats, meditation or treatment rooms, or in other important places. Small yantras can be worn like gemstones in pendants or rings. Yantras for the planets should be frequently energized with the appropriate mantras.

Silver or gold yantras have more power. Copper is the most commonly used substance and is not too expensive. Those on steel, silk or the bark or wood of sacred trees (like sandalwood) have less power. Copper tends to tarnish and has to be cleaned periodically. Chemical copper cleaners may be toxic, so should be removed completely before using the yantras to purify water or using purified water to make or take medicines. Yantras may be written on paper or inscribed on more durable substances. However, it is important to meditate upon the meaning of the numbers and designs. Yantras are less expensive than gemstones. They can be as effective as gems if used with mantras. Unlike gems, they possess no side effects.

Part IV.

Sample Charts and Appendices

Ketu

Dressed in gray, of the color of smoke, who has two arms, whose head is cut off, who has a serpent's head, whose vehicle is a serpent, who carries a mace in his hand, with a cat's eye crest jewel on his head, making the gesture that grants boons —may Divine Ketu ever grant us his grace.

16

Vedic Astrology in Practice

The following charts demonstrate major principles in Vedic astrological interpretation. They show how the factors given in the book apply on a practical level. We cannot learn astrology merely theoretically; we must examine as many charts as we can. While the rules of astrology do work, they do not do so in a rigid or mechanical way. To see both their relevance and the fluidity of their application, we must look to actual charts. The real art in astrology is to find the factors that are predominant, which outweigh the others and determine the overall effect of the chart.

The charts are mainly those of famous people or people of some notoriety. They are dramatic and we do not always find charts to be so clear and easy to read. I have included a number of charts of spiritual teachers, to show the astrological factors that may be helpful for the development of higher consciousness. I have also shown charts of some rather evil individuals to demonstrate the opposite poles of human nature.

Both the basic birth (rashi) and navamsha charts are presented as well as the major planetary periods (Maha Dashas). To understand these charts, please examine the major aspects that exist between the planets according to the rules of Vedic astrology. Also note the houses the planets rule in each chart and their meanings. If necessary, go back to the pages in the book that present this material. Consider dispositorship as well, as planets project the influences of the planets located in their signs.

Note how frequently planets will be found in their own signs, exalted or debilitated and prominent in angles according to the Vedic house and sign system.

The navamsha charts will vary according to the ayanamsha used, as will the planetary periods. Here I have used the standard Lahiri ayanamsha because it is the most commonly used today. One can read the charts from the self-indicator (*atmakaraka*) or the Moon in the navamsha, as the birth times may not be accurate enough to guarantee the accuracy of the Ascendant in this subtle chart. Another very helpful method is to use the birth chart Ascendant as the Ascendant in the navamsha as well. These examinations are merely introductory. For adept Vedic astrologers examining all factors in a chart, any chart can be the subject of many pages of interpretation!

CHART 1. MAHATMA GANDHI

Birth Chart

	Ju		
			Mo Ra
Ke			
	Sa	Me Ve Ma Asc	Su

Navamsha

Mo		Ke Ve Ma	Su
Me Sa			
Ju ASC	Ra		

October 2, 1869, 7:33 am LMT, 69E33, 21N44

Ascendant 09° 24' Libra	Sun 16° 54' Virgo
Moon 28° 09' Cancer	Mars 26° 22' Libra
Mercury 11° 44' Libra	Jupiter 28° 08' Aries Rx
Venus 24° 25' Libra	Saturn 20 °19' Scorpio
Rahu 13 °39' Cancer	Ketu 13° 39' Capricorn
Uranus 29 °39' Gemini Rx	Neptune 26° 22' Pisces Rx
Pluto 27 °41' Aries Rx	

Planetary Periods

Birth — Mercury/Saturn	Ketu — Feb. 10, 1872
Venus — Feb. 10, 1879	Sun — Feb. 10, 1889
Moon — Feb. 10, 1905	Jupiter — Feb. 11, 1940
Rahu — Feb. 11, 1922	Mars — Feb. 11, 1915
Death — Jupiter/Ketu	

Gandhi's chart shows the social impact of an idealistic Libra Ascendant seeking to reform the world according to spiritual values. Five strong angular planets in moveable signs dominate the chart, giving good power of political action. Yet on top of these, balancing their outgoing nature, Saturn in the second affords renunciation and control of the senses, typified by Gandhi's skill at fasting for long periods of time.

The Sun in the twelfth in Virgo makes for a self-abnegating and virtuous nature. Gandhi worked behind the scenes and never assumed any office himself. Jupiter in the seventh gives an expansive nature in relationship and an additional reformist zeal as lord of the third and sixth. The Moon in its own sign in the tenth house, with Rahu on the Midheaven, provides the capacity to influence the masses. Note that Rahu and the Moon are not too close, so that Rahu is not strongly afflicting the Moon.

The influences of Mercury, Venus and Jupiter overcome and transform Mars and turn it into a benefic force. Libra Ascendants love the truth when Mercury, Venus and Jupiter combine their influences. Gandhi typified this love of truth with his Satyagraha (those who hold to truth) movement. Yet Libra Ascendant also tends to extremism and Gandhi's critics accused him of fanaticism.

The positions from the Moon are also strong, with Jupiter in the tenth from the Moon and acting as the lord of the ninth or dharma house from it, creating a Raja Yoga. The several planets in Libra are in the fourth from the Moon and show an idealistic and passionate mind, with the fifth lord of intelligence, Mars, along with the fourth lord of emotion, Venus, and Mercury, the general significator of the mind.

The Moon as the self-indicator (*atmakaraka*) is located in Pisces navamsha, in an angle from Jupiter in its own sign in Sagittarius. This shows a sattvic and devoted nature, a Moon-Jupiter soul.

The major period of Rahu in the tenth house brought Gandhi into public prominence as the leader of India's independence movement. His death occurred in Jupiter-Ketu dasha, with Jupiter in the seventh in a maraka or death-giving house and Ketu acting as a planet of termination.

CHART 2. ADOLF HITLER

Birth Chart

	Su Ve Ma Me		Ra
			Sa
Mo Ju Ke		ASC	

Navamsha

	Ra	Me	Su
Sa			Mo Ju
	Ve Ma	Ke ASC	

April 20, 1889, 6:30 pm LMT, 13E03, 48N15

Ascendant 02° 44' Libra	Sun 08° 29' Aries
Moon 14° 14' Sagittarius	Mars 24° 04' Aries
Mercury 03° 20' Aries	Jupiter 15° 56' Sagittarius
Venus 24° 23' Aries Rx	Saturn 21° 09' Cancer
Rahu 22° 44' Gemini	Ketu 22° 44' Sagittarius
Uranus 27° 10' Virgo Rx	Neptune 08° 32' Taurus
Pluto 13° 52' Taurus	

Planetary Periods

Birth – Venus/Venus	Sun – Dec. 14, 1907
Moon – Dec. 14, 1913	Mars – Dec. 14, 1923
Rahu – Dec. 14, 1930	Death – Rahu/Venus

Hitler's chart also shows the power of the Libra Ascendant to influence the masses, though in this case through fanaticism and intolerance. It is not a self-proclaimed dark force that wreaks havoc in the world but a self-righteous and egoistic idealism. Hitler appealed to the idealism of the human mind but in a perverted way with his idea of the super-race, along with his misuse of the Hindu spiritual term Aryan and its symbol the swastika.

Hitler's chart shows Ruchaka Yoga, the Mahapurusha or "great person" yoga of Mars very strongly, with Mars in its own sign and in an angle from the Ascendant. Mars aspects both the Ascendant and its lord, Venus. It is the dispositor of Venus and also defeats Venus in a planetary war (being located before it in the same degree). Such a Mars confers upon the Libra field of action a martial nature and creates a pitta (fiery) type constitution.

The Sun exalted in the seventh house gives leadership ability and adds to the firepower of Mars. It is near its maximum degree of exaltation, making for a great general and leader. The Sun and Mars dominate Mercury and Venus and render them violent in their energy. Note how this compares with Gandhi's chart, where Mercury and Venus are stronger than Mars and bring out the higher side of the Libra energy. Hitler's seventh house, though good for political power, is not good for personal relationship, and shows a domineering and manipulative person who can have no real friends. It also shows powerful enemies.

The strength of Mars and Saturn make Hitler tamasic, a creature of darkness and delusion. Both these malefics aspect Venus, the lord of the Ascendant, and dominate the chart. Saturn in the tenth house confers Raja Yoga or gives great power and prestige for Libra Ascendant. Yet Saturn in the tenth, even for Libra, raises us up for a time only to bring us down.

Ketu along with Jupiter in the third house in its own sign, Sagittarius, boosts up Jupiter and the house, combining with its lord. The martial power and prowess associated with the third in Vedic astrology comes out here. The lord of the tenth, here the Moon, is not thought to do well in the third, a house of impulse. It is said to cause rash action leading to one's downfall in life.

Venus as the atmakaraka is located in the sign Scorpio in the navamsha, along with Mars. This further shows Hitler's vindictive nature on an inner level. Saturn also aspects the tenth in the navamsha.

Hitler's entire rise and fall occurred within the major period of Rahu, the planet of illusion and worldly power. As is not unusual, Rahu caused him to seek expansion until it brought about a collapse, as it makes us push our energies until we overextend ourselves. Hitler came to power in the early part of Rahu Dasha in 1933. He started World War II under Rahu-Mercury in 1939. His fortunes turned during the Rahu-Ketu period that began in June of 1941. The collapse of Germany occurred during the period of Rahu-Venus, when its negative influence reached the Ascendant lord. Rahu's perverted energy warped his power of military judgment and caused him to spread his military resources too thin by invading Russia and bringing America into the war.

A typical difference between the tropical and Vedic or sidereal placement of planets in signs comes out in this chart. In the tropical chart Hitler has a debilitated Mars in Taurus and Jupiter in its fall in Capricorn.

Tropical astrologers read these to show his evil and materialistic nature. In the Vedic system the planetary yogas are evident, planets in their own sign or exalted and at an angle from the Ascendant. The Vedic idea is that a strong Mars is necessary to give martial power, not a debilitated one. A strong Jupiter would also be helpful. The evil or tamasic nature is read through the strength of Mars and Saturn dominating the chart, not by their being weak or poorly placed. If they were weak he could not have been as successful as he was.

CHART 3. PARAMAHANSA YOGANANDA

Birth Chart

Ju Ma	Ra		
			Mo ASC
Su Me	Ve	Ke	Sa

Navamsha

	Me Mo	ASC	
Ve Ju			Sa Ra
Ke			
		Ma Su	

January 5, 1893, 8:38 pm LMT, 83E23, 26N47

Ascendant 06° 31' Leo	Sun 23° 12' Sagittarius
Moon 03° 14' Leo	Mars 13° 18' Pisces
Mercury 00° 55' Sagittarius	Jupiter 23° 51' Pisces
Venus 24° 44' Scorpio	Saturn 20° 13' Virgo
Rahu 12° 40' Aries	Ketu 12° 40' Libra
Uranus 17° 41' Libra	Neptune 16° 37' Taurus Rx
Pluto 17° 21' Taurus Rx	

Planetary Periods

Birth — Ketu/Sun	Venus — April 26, 1898
Sun — April 27, 1918	Moon — April 26, 1924
Mars — April 27, 1934	Rahu — April 27, 1941
Death — Rahu/Venus	

This is the chart of a great yogi, one of the first to bring the teachings of yoga to the West. While it is difficult to read enlightenment from a chart, we can find strong indications of spirituality if we examine the charts of realized souls.

As Yogananda was a monk, there are strong signs of renunciation. The Moon is rising as lord of the twelfth house of loss, showing the capacity for a noble self-negation. Saturn is in the second house, one of its best placements for renunciation because it detaches us not only from wealth and work (second house) but also, by aspect, from the home and emotions (fourth house). In Yogananda's chart it also aspects Venus, the planet of sexuality, located in the fourth house. Saturn in Virgo, a discriminating sign, is particularly good for self-control and asceticism.

Jupiter, the religious planet, is the final dispositor in the chart and resides in the profound and occult eighth house in its own sign, giving high intelligence and probing insight as well as good yogic powers. It dominates Mars and through this gives a strong will for spiritual work. Jupiter and Mars as fourth and fifth lords create a Raja Yoga relative to spiritual matters. The fourth lord of the mother, Mars, being located in the eighth house of death with the eighth lord Jupiter, caused Yogananda to lose his mother at a young age.

The Sun as Ascendant lord is located in the fifth house in the religious sign Sagittarius, showing good religious karma from past lives and a spiritual temperament, along with Mercury, the planet of the mind, giving good intelligence. Rahu in the ninth house brought him before the public and caused him to reside and teach in a foreign land.

Venus as the self-indicator (atmakaraka) is well placed in the navamsha in Aquarius, another mystical sign, along with Jupiter in the tenth house of work. This shows Yogananda's devotional nature and his public influence.

Yogananda came to the West during his Sun dasha and gained fame under the dasha of the Moon. His Mars dasha allowed him to accomplish much work and start several institutions. Under Rahu his work continued to expand dramatically, but Rahu as a malefic in his house of fortune weakened his health and helped bring about his early passing.

CHART 4. RAMAKRISHNA PARAMAHANSA

Birth Chart

Ve		Ra	Ju
Su Me Mo ASC			
Ma			
	Ke	Sa	

Navamsha

	Mo		
Ju Me Sa	ASC		Ke Ma
Ra			
Su		ASC	Ve

February 18, 1836, around sunrise, LMT, 87E58, 22N55

Ascendant 07° 04' Aquarius	Sun 08° 24' Aquarius
Moon 23° 39' Aquarius	Mars 23° 46' Capricorn
Mercury 16° 38' Aquarius Rx	Jupiter 16° 04' Gemini Rx
Venus 10° 35' Pisces	Saturn 15° 12' Libra
Rahu 04° 25' Taurus	Ketu 04° 25' Scorpio
Uranus 10° 17'Aquarius	Neptune 14° 17' Capricorn
Pluto 23° 12' Pisces	

Planetary Periods

Birth — Jupiter/Saturn	Saturn —Sept. 12, 1849
Mercury — Sept.12, 1868	Ketu — Sept. 13, 1885
Death — Ketu/Venus	

Ramakrishna was such a great mystic that he became honored as an avatar or Divine incarnation shortly after his death. This is obviously a highly spiritual chart. Aquarius itself is often a spiritual Ascendant, giving strong faith, power of worship and surrender. Here it contains both the Sun and Moon: a triple Aquarius, so that all planetary factors affect all three Ascendants (Ascendant, Sun and Moon). The lord of all three Ascendants, Saturn, is exalted in Libra, the ninth house of religion, bringing Divine grace and spiritual discipline to them all.

Jupiter in the fifth in an air sign, Gemini, grants high intelligence, good advice, and good religious karma, making Ramakrishna a great guru.

Mars exalted in the twelfth house gives the power of spiritual work, service and renunciation. Venus exalted in the second, as it is the dispositor of detachment-oriented Saturn and Rahu, gives devotion in the higher sense. It does not give lower Venus values such as a seeking of wealth and comfort, but a love of chanting and doing rituals to the deities, the higher power of Venus. Ketu in the tenth, with Mars as the tenth lord in the twelfth house of liberation, gave Ramakrishna the career of a temple priest.

Planets in air signs, giving an airy or vata constitution, dominate Ramakrishna's chart. Particularly important is Jupiter's influence from the fifth to Saturn and the Ascendant, countering the lower side of Saturn energy. Yet this also caused him to neglect his body and gave him a shorter life than was otherwise indicated.

Aquarius is also strong in the navamsha with Jupiter, Saturn, and Mercury located there in the fifth house, showing the religious bent of the mind on an inner level. Aquarius as a sign of Saturn, a dark planet, relates to Kali, the dark or black form of the Divine Mother worshiped by Ramakrishna.

CHART 5. ALBERT EINSTEIN

Birth Chart

Su Me Ve Sa			ASC
Ju			Ke
Ma Ra			
	Mo		

Navamsha

ASC	Ra		
Ve Me			Su
Mo			
	Ju	Sa Ma Ke	

March 14, 1879, 11:30 am LMT, 10E00, 48N30

Ascendant 19° 28' Gemini	Sun 01° 19' Pisces
Moon 22° 21' Scorpio	Mars 04° 44' Capricorn
Mercury 10° 58' Pisces	Jupiter 05° 18' Aquarius
Venus 24° 48' Pisces	Saturn 12° 00' Pisces
Rahu 10° 28' Capricorn	Ketu 10° 28' Cancer
Uranus 09° 06' Leo Rx	Neptune 15° 41' Aries
Pluto 04° 14' Taurus	

Planetary Periods

Birth — Mercury/Moon	Ketu — Dec. 13, 1888
Venus — Dec. 13, 1895	Sun — Dec. 13, 1915
Moon — Dec. 14, 1921	Mars — Dec. 15, 1931
Rahu — Dec. 14, 1938	Death — Rahu/Mars

Einstein's chart demonstrates a strong intellectual capacity, which we would expect from this "almost avatar" of science. Gemini itself is an intellectual Ascendant and most of the planets are in mutable signs, giving flexibility and curiosity of mind. Most notably Mercury, the ruler of the Ascendant, has its debility cancelled, as it is both in an angle from the Ascendant (in the tenth) and with an exalted Venus in Pisces. In this position, Mercury gives profound intelligence and functions even better than when exalted. It allowed Einstein to probe into the deeper levels of the mind in which the intellect opens up to cosmic intelligence, though it did give him troubles in school when young.

Venus is near its maximum degree of exaltation and, as ruler of the fifth house of creative intelligence, gives a love of knowledge, along with writing abilities. His four planets in the tenth made him very famous, a world-renowned figure or legend in his own time. The exchange of signs (mutual reception) between Saturn and Jupiter as the lords of the ninth and tenth is a powerful Raja Yoga that afforded him recognition and the respect of world leaders. Jupiter in Aquarius in the ninth house of religion gives an humanitarian disposition and a concern for social causes, which Einstein was well known for.

Mars exalted in the eighth house of profound insight, in an earthly sign, gives scientific and mathematical ability and inventiveness (usually ruled by the eighth in Vedic astrology). Its association with Rahu adds to its strength and influence. This Mars-Rahu conjunction in the eighth house of transformation shows Einstein's work with nuclear energy, which is a Mars-Rahu force, a secret power of fire.

The Moon also has its fall cancelled, owing to the exaltation of Mars, the ruler of Scorpio, in Capricorn. Such a Moon in the sixth house gives profound intelligence and a strong capacity for service. The Moon also benefits by being in an angle from Jupiter. Rahu's dasha, beginning in 1938, brought Einstein into the public eye for developing the atomic bomb.

CHART 6. WOODY ALLEN

Birth Chart

			Ke
Sa Mo			
Ma			ASC
Ra	Su Ju Me		Ve

Navamsha

	Ke		ASC
Ma Sa			
	Su	Ju Me Mo Ra	Ve

December 1, 1935, 10:55 pm EST, 74W00, 40N43

Ascendant 09° 12' Leo	Sun 16° 04' Scorpio
Moon 01° 08' Aquarius	Mars 03° 08' Capricorn
Mercury 11° 32' Scorpio	Jupiter 12° 09' Scorpio
Venus 29° 55' Virgo	Saturn 11° 03' Aquarius
Rahu 20° 19' Sagittarius	Ketu 20° 19' Gemini
Uranus 09° 13' Aries Rx	Neptune 23° 43' Leo
Pluto 05° 07' Cancer Rx	

Planetary Periods

Birth — Mars/Mercury	Rahu — Oct. 27, 1938
Jupiter — Oct. 2, 1956	Saturn— Oct. 27, 1972
Mercury — Oct. 28, 1991	Ketu — Oct. 27, 2008
Venus — Oct. 28, 2015	

Woody Allen's chart shows a dramatic and self-involved Leo Ascendant. Yet the chart is dominated by Saturn in the seventh house, which is not only located with the Moon but also aspects the Ascendant and its lord, the Sun. Saturn in its own sign in an angle from the Moon and Ascendant creates a Mahapurusha Yoga for Saturn. This gives Allen a vata or airy type temperament and a Saturnian bent of mind. Most of Allen's dramas, both on and off the screen, reflect around his failures in relationship, which such a Saturn clearly indicates. His doubly debilitated Venus (in both the rashi and navamsha) adds to his problems with the opposite sex.

The positions are similarly strong from the Moon with the Sun, Jupiter and Mercury occupying the tenth from it. The same planets aspect the tenth house of the birth chart from the fourth house. Such a strong tenth house gives great fame.

The Sun, Jupiter and Mercury in Scorpio in the fourth house of the emotional mind aspected by Saturn show his psychological self-involvement. Mars exalted in the sixth gives him a strong power of work and action to turn his psychodramas into commercial successes.

The navamsha shows an exchange between Mercury and Venus as fourth and fifth house lords, lords of the emotional and intellectual minds, affording him great artistic talent. He is a great director, writer and performer. Allen's Saturn dasha from 1972–1991 proved excellent for his career. His subsequent Mercury period has brought personal problems. Mercury afflicts Mars both in the birth chart and navamsha, making him prone to depression.

CHART 7. BILL GATES, COMPUTER MOGUL

Birth Chart

Mo		Ke	ASC
			Ju
	Ra	Su Sa Ve	Ma Me

Navamsha

	ASC	Ju	Ma Ve Sa
Ra			Me
Su			Ke

October 28, 1955, 9:45 pm PST, 47N36, 122W20

Ascendant 22° 58' Gemini	Sun 11° 45' Libra
Moon 14° 28' Pisces	Mars 16° 50í Virgo
Mercury 23° 19' Virgo	Jupiter 04° 32' Leo
Venus 26° 56' Libra	Saturn 28° 20' Libra
Rahu 24 °53' Scorpio	Ketu 24° 53' Taurus
Uranus 09° 02' Cancer	Neptune 04° 59' Libra
Pluto 05° 42' Leo	

Planetary Periods

Birth — Saturn/Rahu	Mercury — Dec.16, 1953
Ketu — Dec. 17, 1975	Venus — Dec. 17, 1982
Sun — Dec. 17, 2002	Moon — Dec. 16, 2008

The chart of someone as wealthy as Bill Gates should yield a number of Dhana Yogas or combinations for wealth. Gemini, a computer-oriented sign, rises. The Ascendant lord Mercury is exalted in the fourth house in its own sign Virgo, an earth sign good for bringing about material results. It is placed along with the eleventh lord Mars, which is good for income. The Moon, the lord of the second house of livelihood, is in the tenth house of fame, aspected by both wealth-giving Mars and Mercury. The fifth house of speculative gains has an exalted Saturn as ninth lord, Venus in its own sign, and the Sun with its debility cancelled. This gives good income through speculation and through the stock market. Such a strong and wealth-giving fifth house gives good business sense.

From the Moon a viprita or reverse Raja Yoga prevails with Saturn the twelfth lord, Venus the eighth lord, and the Sun as the sixth lord together in the eighth house from the Moon. When all lords of dushthanas are located together in a single dushthana, this causes destruction of all difficulties or, to put it another way, great good fortune.

Gates's favorable Venus dasha started in December 1982. The very favorable period of Venus-Saturn occurred between Oct. 17, 1995 — Dec. 17, 1998 in which his wealth gained global dominance. His Sun period commences in a few years and is bound to have something of a limiting effect, but probably not major, owing to its debility, which even if cancelled shows difficulties to be overcome.

CHART 8. RAMANA MAHARSHI

Birth Chart

Sa	Ma		Mo Ke
Ju			
Su Ra	Me Ve	ASC	

Navamsha

		Ke	Mo
Ju			Ve
Me			Su
Sa	Ra ASC	Ma	

December 30, 1879, 1:15 am LMT, 78E10, 09N55

Ascendant 04° 34' Libra	Sun 15° 36' Sagittarius
Moon 28° 31' Gemini	Mars 21° 58' Aries
Mercury 23° 07' Scorpio	Jupiter 16° 29' Aquarius
Venus 00° 29' Scorpio	Saturn 17° 03' Pisces
Rahu 23° 23' Sagittarius	Ketu 23° 23' Gemini
Uranus 16° 43' Leo Rx	Neptune 17° 12' Aries Rx
Pluto 05° 16' Taurus Rx	

Planetary Periods

Birth — Jupiter/Venus	Saturn — Oct. 4, 1885
Mercury — Oct. 5, 1904	Ketu — Oct. 5, 1921
Venus — Oct. 5, 1928	Sun — Oct. 5, 1948
Death — Sun/Rahu	

Ramana Maharshi is probably the most respected Self-realized sage of modern India, a great jnani or master of spiritual knowledge. He had a spontaneous realization at the age of seventeen when meditating upon death, and he never fell from that exalted state.

Jupiter, the indicator of spirituality, is strong in the fifth, the house of intelligence and past karma, in the spiritual sign Aquarius, aspecting both the Ascendant and the Moon. It is also in the ninth, the religious house, from the Moon. The Moon is strong, a day after full, in Gemini in the ninth house. As the lord of the tenth, the Moon gives fame and popularity as a teacher. Both the Moon and Jupiter are vargottama, in the same sign in both the birth chart and navamsha, giving them more power.

The Sun is strong in the third, a house of discipline, in Sagittarius, the religious sign of Jupiter. The lunar nodes augment the strength of the luminaries and give them powers of higher consciousness, Rahu elevating the Sun and Ketu deepening the Moon. This combination of the Sun and Moon with Rahu and Ketu in mutable signs and cadent houses shows self-knowledge and the illumination of the mind, as well as much time spent in meditation and seclusion. The nodes with the Sun and the Moon show the ability to go beyond ordinary consciousness for good or ill depending upon their placement.

Mars aspects the Ascendant and the second house, giving a high and piercing intelligence. Mars is particularly strong, being at an angle from the Ascendant and in its own sign (giving Ruchaka Yoga). Yet it was the acetic side of the Mars influence, not the military side, that came out for Ramana. This is owing to the strength of Jupiter and the ninth house. Ramana was considered to be an incarnation of Skanda or Muruga, the God of the planet Mars, who on an inner level represents knowledge and asceticism.

Saturn in the sixth gives asceticism and renunciation. Saturn and Jupiter exchange signs as lords of the ninth and tenth from the Moon, giving another Raja Yoga. The Moon as the self-indicator (atmakaraka) is well placed in Gemini (vargottama) in the navamsha and aspected by Jupiter and Saturn. So Ramana's spiritual abilities are quite evident with such a chart.

CHART 9. SRI AUROBINDO

Birth Chart

		Ra	
			Ju Ma ASC
			Me Ve Su
Sa Mo	Ke		

Navamsha

	Su	Mo	Ve Ra
Ju ASC			Ma
Ke	Sa Me		

August 15, 1872, 5:00 am LMT, 88E24, 22N36

Ascendant 21° 19' Cancer	Sun 00 °18' Leo
Moon 05° 30' Sagittarius	Mars 05 °22' Cancer
Mercury 23° 30' Leo	Jupiter 21° 34' Cancer
Venus 08° 30' Leo	Saturn 23 °30' Sag. Rx
Rahu 17° 45' Taurus	Ketu 17 °45' Scorpio
Uranus 10° 45' Cancer	Neptune 04° 11' Aries Rx
Pluto 00° 40' Taurus Rx	

Planetary Periods

Birth — Ketu/Mars	Venus — Sept. 22, 1876
Sun — Sept. 22, 1896	Moon — Sept. 24, 1902
Mars — Sept. 23, 1912	Rahu — Sept. 24, 1919
Jupiter — Sept. 24, 1937	Death — Jupiter/Mars

Sri Aurobindo was a major figure in the Indian independence movement before Gandhi, but renounced politics to become a great yogi. He was perhaps the greatest visionary of modern India, a seer and rishi of the highest order.

Mars and Jupiter rising in Cancer are a strong political combination and Raja Yoga (Jupiter as the lord of the ninth and Mars as lord of the tenth). Mars has cancellation of debility in two ways (being in the Ascendant and with an exalted Jupiter). Yet Aurobindo applied this world-changing energy to his yoga and became a revolutionary in that field, striving to bring a Divine grace into the physical body itself.

The Sun, Mercury and Venus in the second in Leo create a good combination for poetry, and Sri Aurobindo was a great poet, linguist and philologist, a prolific writer. He had a sun-like gift of speech and writing ability. These planets are also in the ninth house from the Moon, indicating the spiritual and philosophical nature of his writings. Saturn combined with the Moon gives detachment and spirituality in Sagittarius, a sign of Jupiter, and gives work and service (karma yoga) in the sixth house, a house of service. It also helped make him a great philosopher who examined the entire issue of human suffering.

The Sun and Moon are both exalted in the navamsha, adding to his strength of character. Both Jupiter and the Moon, the lords of the first and ninth house in the birth chart, are in mutual reception, creating an overall spiritual and religious nature. Sri Aurobindo's yoga looked to the transformation of the physical body. The Moon and Jupiter are also first and sixth house lords, showing his concern with the body in his yoga.

With all this Cancer influence, it is not surprising that Aurobindo was a great devotee of the Divine Mother and emphasized the descent of the Divine Shakti, not human effort, as the way of transformation. Sri Aurobindo is often contrasted with Mahatma Gandhi as being more the spiritual founder of modern India. His teachings have a powerful futuristic vision.

CHART 10. ANANDAMAYI MA, WOMAN SAINT

Birth Chart

Ve ASC	Su	Me	
Ma Ra			Ju
			Ke
	Mo	Sa	

Navamsha

Ve	Ma	Sa	Ke
ASC			
Me			
Mo Ra			Su Ju

April 30, 1896, 03:42 am IST, 91E13, 23N45

Ascendant 24° 24' Pisces	Sun 17° 38' Aries
Moon 19° 57' Scorpio	Mars 21° 09' Aquarius
Mercury 00° 44' Taurus	Jupiter 08° 37' Cancer
Venus 28° 43' Pisces	Saturn 23° 50' Libra Rx
Rahu 08° 36' Aquarius	Ketu 08° 36' Leo
Uranus 00° 36' Scorpio Rx	Neptune 23° 57' Taurus
Pluto 20° 30' Taurus	

Planetary Periods

Birth — Mercury/Venus	Ketu — Feb. 20, 1909
Venus — Feb. 20, 1916	Sun — Feb. 20, 1936
Moon — Feb. 20, 1942	Mars — Feb. 21, 1952
Rahu — Feb. 20, 1959	Jupiter — Feb. 20, 1977
Death — Jupiter/Mercury	

Anandamayi Ma is probably the most famous woman saint, yogi and seer of modern India, recognized throughout the world. She was connected with Swami Shivananda, Paramahansa Yogananda, and Sri Aurobindo among the other great teachers of the country. She was regarded as a veritable incarnation of the Divine Mother. Her joy and laughter gave her the name Anandamayi or "permeated with bliss."

Her extraordinary chart shows four exalted planets: Venus, Sun, Jupiter and Saturn. Exalted Venus is located on the Ascendant near its maximum degree of exaltation. It is exalted in the navamsha as well. As the eighth lord, Venus brings austerity and spiritual power to its position. Meanwhile Saturn is exalted in the eighth house, giving further spiritual power and knowledge. The strength of the eighth lord and eighth house also gave her a long life of over eighty-five years.

Jupiter, the tenth lord of public recognition, is exalted in the fifth house of devotion and good past life karma. Meanwhile the Moon as the fifth lord is in the ninth house of spirituality aspected by Jupiter, with its debility cancelled by the exaltations of both Mars (ruler of the Moon's sign) and Jupiter (located in Cancer ruled by the Moon). Such a Moon gave great spiritual achievement in the ninth house. The exalted Sun as sixth lord in the second house gave her good powers of work and communication. She traveled all over India and ashrams were established in her name throughout the country. She was famous for her devotional singing and chanting.

Mars along with Rahu in the twelfth in Aquarius gave her a selfless nature and a seeking of liberation. From the Moon, exalted Venus is in the fifth house, while Jupiter, the fifth lord, is exalted in the ninth house. Exalted Saturn is in the twelfth house of liberation. With such a strongly spiritual chart it is not surprising that Ma Anandamayi was in a high state of realization from birth.

CHART 11. THEODORE BUNDY, SERIAL KILLER

Birth Chart

		Ra	
			Sa
			ASC
	Mo Ma Ke Su Me	Ve Ju	

Navamsha

Ju	ASC		Ve Ra
Mo			Me
Ma			
Ke	Sa		Su

November 24, 1946, 10:35 pm EST, 73W12, 44N29

Ascendant 01° 56' Leo	Sun 09° 09' Scorpio
Moon 24° 34' Scorpio	Mars 20° 15' Scorpio
Mercury 01° 21' Scorpio Rx	Jupiter 19° 57' Libra
Venus 27° 31' Libra Rx	Saturn 15° 45' Cancer Rx
Uranus 27° 22' Taurus Rx	Neptune 17° 02' Virgo
Rahu 18° 37' Taurus	Ketu 18° 37' Scorpio
Pluto 20° 59' Cancer Rx	

Planetary Periods

Birth — Mercury/Rahu	Ketu — Oct. 23, 1953
Venus — Oct. 23, 1960	Sun — Oct. 23, 1980
Moon — Oct. 23, 1986	

As we have seen, a number of spiritual charts show illumination of the mind. Let us examine another chart that shows the forces of evil and ignorance. Ted Bundy was a mass murderer of young women who was eventually executed for his crimes. The chart is saturated with violence and sex and shows the darkest part of the Scorpio influence.

Five planets are in turbulent Scorpio in the fourth house of the emotional nature. Most noticeable is the debilitated Moon, which is close to the Sun, as it is just past new. Before it, in Scorpio, is a conjunction of the three fiery planets: Mars, Ketu and the Sun. Finally we have Mercury, which by its mutable nature takes on and magnifies the influence of Mars. The fourth house, the Moon, Mercury and the lord of the fourth house (Mars) are all severely afflicted, showing a deranged mind and emotional nature. The Moon brings with it the influence of Saturn in Cancer, which it rules. The Sun as the lord of the Ascendant is strongly afflicted. Here we see Mars energy at its worst, a mind and heart saturated with violence. This violence is directed against the Moon or women.

Jupiter and Venus are at the end of Libra in a cross sign conjunction with the planets in Scorpio. Such a close grouping of planets, particularly with strongly disposed malefics, is not good. The planetary rays get confused and murky (particularly in Scorpio). The benefic conjunction of Venus and Jupiter in Libra allowed Bundy to appear like a nice person and to attract women, as did the generally warm and expressive Leo Ascendant. Yet in the third, a martial house, Jupiter and Venus are an impulsive combination and kept him preoccupied with sex. Saturn in the twelfth shows his negative fate and time in prison.

Such people display a very dark but hidden character, which can appear outwardly friendly, helpful and affectionate. They thrive on the drama and the polarity generated by this deception. It was no doubt that inflated ego, the need for drama (Leo), and the love of deception (Scorpio) that motivated Ted Bundy. Quite often, behind the attempts to please others is the ego's need for power and drama, which can become violence when the darkness and ignorance behind it come out into the open.

All of his planets are between the tenth and the fourth houses, on the personal side of the chart, with nothing on the relationship side. They are between Rahu and Ketu, showing a Kalasarpa Yoga involving the emotional nature and the public.

CHART 12. NAPOLEON BONAPARTE

Birth Chart

			Ke Ve
			Sa Me
Mo			Su Ma
Ra		Ju ASC	

Navamsha

Mo	Ra Su	Ju	
Ve ASC			
			Sa
	Me	Ke Ma	

August 15, 1769, about noon LMT, 08E40, 41N55

Ascendant 14° 43' Libra	Sun 02° 06' Leo
Moon 08° 15' Capricorn	Mars 21° 24' Leo
Mercury 15° 30' Cancer	Jupiter 24° 22' Libra
Venus 16° 23' Gemini	Saturn 05° 15' Cancer
Rahu 01° 38' Sagittarius	Ketu 01° 38' Gemini
Uranus 20° 51' Aries	Neptune 18° 03' Leo
Pluto 27° 05' Sagittarius Rx	

Planetary Periods

Birth — Sun/Venus	Moon — May 29 1770
Mars — May 28, 1780	Rahu — May 29, 1787
Jupiter — May 30, 1805	Saturn — May 30, 1821

We can use Vedic astrology for chart rectification. The exact time of Napoleon's birth is not known but is presumed to be around noon. By the laws of Vedic astrology he should be a Libra Ascendant, because this Ascendant on that day shows the potential to create an emperor. It shows several Raja Yogas, or planetary combinations that can create kings.

For Libra Ascendant, according to the rules we have discussed, Saturn is the main planet that can create Raja Yoga, as it rules both a trine and an angular house (the fourth and fifth). Here it is in the tenth house, the best angle, giving it great power. The Moon as lord of the tenth also grants Raja Yoga. Both Saturn and the Moon are in mutual reception, bringing their influences together. This situation is stronger than if each were in its own sign, as the mutual aspect is reinforcing. To this is added Mercury, the lord of the ninth, the other great benefic and power-giving planet for Libra. It adds strength to Saturn and prevents the quick fall that would occur if Saturn were alone in the tenth.

Jupiter in the Ascendant gives an aggressive, expansive nature as lord of the third and sixth houses. The Sun and Mars in Leo in the eleventh show a dominating personality, power of leadership and generalship and the capacity to win kingdoms. Venus as lord of the Ascendant is well placed in the ninth, giving luck and fortune.

We see a charismatic leader, possessed of a great idealism that could influence the masses. It is true he fell from power after a time. This was mainly from the rash influence of Jupiter (who incidentally also stands for the British in his chart, as it is the ruler of the sixth house of enemies). We note in his planetary periods that Rahu raised him to power, while Jupiter caused his downfall. His downfall was mainly his own doing. His impulsive and unnecessary invasion of Russia overextended his resources. It was a product of the egoism that began in 1804 when he proclaimed himself emperor. Still, we see in his chart an idealistic and noble person, quite unlike the results of the negative Mars-Saturn combination in Hitler's chart.

CHART 13. H.P. BLAVATSKY, OCCULTIST

Birth Chart

			ASC
Ke			Su
Ju			Ma Sa Ra Me
			Mo Ve

Navamsha

Su	Ra Ve		Mo ASC
			Sa Ma
			Ju
		Ke	Me

August 21, 1831, 2:17 am LMT, 35E01, 48N27

Ascendant 28° 01' Gemini	Sun 26° 59' Cancer
Moon 18° 00' Virgo	Mars 11° 20' Leo
Mercury 17° 44' Leo	Jupiter 25° 44' Capricorn Rx
Venus 12° 02' Virgo	Saturn 11° 28' Leo
Rahu 00° 18' Leo	Ketu 00° 18' Aquarius
Uranus 20° 47' Capricorn Rx	Neptune 01° 25' Capricorn Rx
Pluto 21° 49' Pisces Rx	

Planetary Periods

Birth — Moon/Mercury	Mars — August 7, 1835
Rahu — August 7, 1842	Jupiter — August 7, 1860
Saturn — August 7, 1876	Mercury — August 8, 1895

Blavatsky was a great occultist and a prolific author, the founder of the modern Theosophical movement. Most of modern Western occultism, including the recent New Age movement, has its origins in her work and that of her followers, such as Annie Besant, Rudolf Steiner and Alice Bailey. The impact of her work was strongly felt in her lifetime in Europe, America and India.

The chart shows a strong Mercury influence. The Ascendant and Moon in both the birth chart and the navamsha are in signs of Mercury. Gemini, the most communicative and intellectual of the signs, is rising in both (vargottama).

The Moon with benefic Venus in the fourth house gives a creative, sensitive and spiritual mind and the capacity to write many books. Note that Venus is both lord of the ninth from the Moon and lord of the fifth house of creative intelligence from the Ascendant. The debility of Venus in Virgo is cancelled by angularity from both the Ascendant and the Moon and functions very well. Such a strong Venus dominates the chart and gave Blavatsky broad intellectual powers, occult perception and knowledge of the subtle worlds, as well as compassion.

Mercury has powerful conjunctions in both the birth and navamsha charts, being exalted in the latter. In the birth chart it is with Saturn, lord of the ninth house of dharma. Ketu in the ninth house gives insight and perception on a deep level. Yet Mercury is also afflicted by three malefics, which gave Blavatsky a mental state far removed from that of ordinary people. Her strong planets in the third house gave her much curiosity, a powerful will, a critical mind and a strong vital energy. The Sun in the second also gives strong powers of speech and communication.

Jupiter is doubly a significator of relationship for Gemini women, naturally indicating the husband and also representing him as lord of the seventh. Her Jupiter is poorly placed in the difficult eighth house and in its fall in Capricorn, showing the corrupt materialistic background of the upper class Russian men she had to deal with. This fallen Jupiter is also the lord of the seventh from the Moon, which itself is afflicted by Mars. Blavatsky had two very short and difficult marriages.

CHART 14. HILLARY CLINTON

Birth Chart

Mo		Ra	ASC
			Sa Ma
	Ju Ke	Me Ve Su	

Navamsha

Sa		Ve	Me
			Ke
Ma Ra			Mo
Su	ASC		Ju

October 26, 1947, 08:00 pm EST, 87W39, 41N51

Ascendant 04° 30' Gemini	Sun 09° 40' Libra
Moon 05° 59' Pisces	Mars 21° 08' Cancer
Mercury 28° 11' Libra Rx	Jupiter 07° 29' Scorpio
Venus 23° 43' Libra	Saturn 28° 13' Cancer
Rahu 00° 25' Taurus	Ketu 00° 25' Scorpio
Uranus 02° 47 'Gemini Rx	Neptune 18° 14' Virgo
Pluto 22° 27' Cancer	

Planetary Periods

Birth — Saturn/Mercury	Mercury — Jan. 15 1963
Ketu —Jan. 15, 1980	Venus — Jan. 15, 1987
Sun — Jan. 15, 2007	Moon — Jan. 15, 2013

Hillary Clinton shows a communicative Gemini Ascendant, with a strong Moon in the tenth house in Pisces, aspected by the tenth lord Jupiter. The Moon is also in the tenth house of the navamsha. This brings her before the public as a powerful social and political leader. Mars in the second house of speech, aspecting the fifth house and fifth ruler as well, gives her strong critical powers of speech and makes her a lawyer. The fifth house as a whole is strong with a Raja Yoga of Mercury and Venus as the fourth and fifth lords. This makes her an advisor to the most powerful political leader in the world, the president of the United States.

Jupiter, her seventh lord and the general indicator for the husband in a woman's chart, is afflicted by Ketu in the sixth house of enemies. This shows the intrigue around her marriage and the many enemies it causes both her and her husband. Saturn also afflicts the seventh from the Moon. The seventh house, however, is strong in the navamsha, with Venus in its own sign aspected by Jupiter, perhaps showing some inner compensation for her outer marital difficulties.

Her husband Bill Clinton was elected president in Nov. 1992 during her powerful Venus-Moon period. Venus is the strongest planet for Gemini Ascendant, and the Moon in the tenth house brings her before the public. The Venus-Mars period that began Jan. 1993 shows the conflict and controversy she became immediately involved in after her husband assumed office. Hillary's chart remains strong throughout her Venus period up to 2007 and again gains more strength during her Moon dasha after 2013. Her Moon dasha may be her best and shows that she will remain a dominant important political figure for the next several decades, achieving high offices of her own.

CHART 15. JACKIE KENNEDY ONASSIS

Birth Chart

	Ra Mo	Ve Ju	
			Su Me
			Ma
Sa		Ke ASC	

Navamsha

	Sa Mo	Ke	Ju ASC
	Ra	Ma Su	Me Ve

July 28, 1929, 02:39 pm EST, 72W23, 40N53

Ascendant 26° 51' Libra	Sun 12° 17' Cancer
Moon 02° 49' Aries	Mars 21° 57' Leo
Mercury 09° 32' Cancer	Jupiter 16° 42' Taurus
Venus 28° 54' Taurus	Saturn 01° 46' Sagittarius Rx
Rahu 24° 58' Aries	Ketu 23° 52' Libra
Uranus 18° 27' Pisces	Neptune 07° 16' Leo
Pluto 26° 28' Gemini	

Planetary Periods

Birth — Ketu/Venus	Venus — Feb. 4, 1935
Sun — Feb. 4, 1955	Moon — Feb. 3, 1961
Mars — Feb. 4, 1971	Rahu — Feb. 4, 1978
Death — Rahu/Moon	

Jackie Kennedy's relationship situation is mirrored with her Moon-Rahu combination in the seventh house, showing fame (Moon is tenth lord), scandal and tragedy (Rahu). The Rahu-Ketu axis is close the Ascendant-Descendant axis, which gives trouble, confusion and illusion in relationship. It was in her Moon-Rahu period that her husband, President Kennedy, was assassinated. It was in her Rahu-Moon period that she herself died. The Moon dasha as a whole gave her great fame.

Her relationships were prominent and public, but filled with deception and unhappiness. Mars as the lord of the seventh house is in the eleventh house of abundance, affording more than one marriage. Jupiter as the significator of marriage is in the eighth house of death. Venus in the eighth in its own sign is good for sex appeal but not for marital happiness.

Mercury as the ninth lord in the tenth house not only gave her prominence and publicity but also brought her an eventual career in the publishing business. The Sun as eleventh lord in the tenth is good for wealth as well as fame. Wealth is also indicated with Mars as the lord of the second house of livelihood located in the eleventh house of income. Saturn as a malefic and a Raja Yoga planet is strong in the third, an upachaya house.

Mars afflicts the fifth house from the Ascendant and the Moon, as well as the fifth in the navamsha, causing miscarriages. Saturn aspects the fifth house as the fifth lord, however, giving delays but eventually allowing her to have children.

Turning the birth chart Ascendant, Libra, into the navamsha Ascendant places Sun and Mars in the first with the Moon and Saturn in the seventh. This shows marital unhappiness and harm to the spouse as well.

CHART 16. INDIRA GANDHI, PRIME MINISTER

Birth Chart

		Ju	Ke
			Sa ASC
Mo			Ma
Ra Ve	Su Me		

Navamsha

ASC		Ju	Ra
Mo			
Sa			Su Ma
Ke		Me Ve	

November 19, 1917, 11:17 pm IST, 81E50, 24N27

Ascendant 29° 20' Cancer	Sun 04° 07' Scorpio
Moon 05° 40' Cancer	Mars 16° 22' Leo
Mercury 13° 14' Scorpio	Jupiter 15° 00' Taurus Rx
Venus 21° 00' Sagittarius	Saturn 21° 47' Cancer
Rahu 09° 18' Sagittarius	Ketu 09° 18' Gemini
Uranus 27° 15' Capricorn	Neptune 14° 22' Cancer Rx
Pluto 13° 37' Gemini Rx	

Planetary Periods

Birth — Sun/Mercury	Moon — Nov. 1, 1919
Mars — Oct. 31, 1929	Rahu — Oct. 31, 1936
Jupiter — Nov. 1, 1954	Saturn — Nov. 1, 1970
Death — Saturn/Mars	

Here, in the chart of a leader of one of the largest countries in the world, we see the political side of the Cancer Ascendant. The exchange of signs between the Moon and Saturn brings out the broader social and political side of the Cancer influence, with Saturn giving a detaching influence to the Moon. So it was a Saturnian political Moon that Mrs.

Gandhi had, not a domestic one.

The strongest political factor for this chart is the exchange of signs between Mars as lord of the fifth and tenth, the Raja Yoga planet for Cancer, and the Sun as lord of the second. This gives a sharp mind, strong speech, good powers of advising and directing people, and the ability to communicate with powerful individuals. This combination of Sun and Mars influences makes the nature fiery (pitta). Mercury with the Sun augments the combination and Jupiter's aspect as the ninth lord gives it yet more power and favor from those above (mainly from Mrs. Gandhi's powerful father, Jawaharlal Nehru, India's first prime minister).

The exchange between the lords of the first and seventh (the Moon and Saturn) gives the ability to relate to the public and adapt to social circumstances. Such factors make for a great diplomat, as well as a highly intelligent leader concerned with the cultural and spiritual, not just the economic and political, welfare of her country. Jupiter's influence on the Sun and the Moon aids in providing an interest in spiritual subjects. Indira Gandhi frequented many great gurus like Sri Anandamayi Ma, J. Krishnamurti and the Mother at the Sri Aurobindo Ashram.

The influence of Mars on the eighth house of death both from the Ascendant and the Moon was an important factor in her assassination. Mars itself is in the second, a maraka house or house of death. Jupiter's period raised her to power, particularly under Jupiter-Moon. At the beginning of her powerful Saturn dasha she won the Bangladesh war and was at the height of her career. Saturn's period eventually caused her to lose power, but she regained it again, only to be assassinated during Saturn-Mars, with Saturn also being the lord of the seventh, a maraka or death-giving house. Reflecting her Cancer Ascendant, the main criticism against her was that she promoted her children to power by any means possible and tried to create a dynasty, thus weakening the country she otherwise tried so hard to strengthen.

CHART 17. JIM JONES, CULT LEADER

Birth Chart

Ve Mo Ra	Su Me		Ju
			Ma
Sa			
ASC			Ke

Navamsha

Ve		Ju	
Ma			Ke Me ASC
Sa Mo Ra			
Su			

May 13, 1931, 10:00 pm CST, 84W56, 40N03

Ascendant 11° 24' Sagittarius	Sun 29° 30' Aries
Moon 20° 01' Pisces	Mars 23° 22' Cancer
Mercury 10° 41' Aries	Jupiter 24° 02' Gemini
Venus 28° 45' Pisces	Saturn 00° 17' Capricorn Rx
Rahu 21° 04' Pisces	Ketu 21° 04' Virgo
Uranus 24° 30' Pisces	Neptune 10° 05' Leo Rx
Pluto 27° 05 Gemini	

Planetary Periods

Birth, Mercury/Venus	Ketu — Feb. 1, 1944
Venus — Feb. 1, 1951	Sun Feb. — 1, 1971
Mars — Feb. 1, 1977	Death, Moon/ Rahu

Jim Jones was a disturbed religious-political leader who brought himself and his followers to a mass collective suicide in Guyana in November of 1978. First, the chart shows how Rahu can be a very disturbing planet. Note the position of the Moon. It is in Pisces, a sensitive or mutable sign, and waning in the fourth house that represents the emotional mind, within one degree of malefic Rahu. It is aspected by Saturn as well. It is the dispositor of a fallen Mars in the eighth house of death.

Though the Moon is with an exalted Venus, which gave him charisma and the power to move people emotionally, Venus was also the sixth lord, adding aggression to the mind. Such factors show an overly reactive and defensive mind and the use of drugs. The darkness, paranoia and self-destructiveness of the mind are thus evident, the potential for such extreme delusion that it could offer up hundreds in a ritual suicide.

The Moon-Rahu-Saturn conjunction in the navamsha, hemmed in between malefics, indicates a similar negative mental state in that chart. Mars, as might be expected in a chart like this, is in its fall in the eighth house of death. Its only aspect is from malefic Saturn. It is also in the eighth house of the navamsha. This shows a violent death.

The strong Jupiter, lord of the Ascendant, in the seventh in Gemini gave Jones a capacity to influence others, the status of a preacher and politician. His fifth house is also good, with Mercury and an exalted Sun, giving him intelligence and the capacity to advise others. Hence we see a misplaced idealism and self-righteousness, which is typically found behind most destructive action. No doubt his Jupiter energy confused the many who got caught in his Moon-Rahu paranoia.

His death occurred during his Moon-Rahu period in Nov. 1978. The Moon period itself began in Feb. 1977. With so many afflictions, it quickly led to a mental breakdown that had disastrous consequences on his many followers. The previous Mars dasha of seven years prepared the way by its eighth house location, indicating that he had probably already committed a number of crimes, if not murder.

CHART 18. SAM SHEPARD

Birth Chart

Ke			
Ve Me			Mo Ra
Su	Ju ASC	Ma Sa	

Navamsha

	Ve	Ma	
Me			Ra
Ke			Su
Sa	Mo Ju	ASC	

December 29, 1923, 5:30 pm EST, 81W42, 41N30

Ascendant 11° 53' Scorpio	Sun 13° 53' Sagittarius
Moon 25° 44' Leo	Mars 23° 28' Libra
Mercury 03° 29' Capricorn	Jupiter 14° 46' Scorpio
Venus 11° 03' Capricorn	Saturn 07° 55' Libra
Rahu 11° 05' Leo	Ketu 11° 05' Aquarius
Uranus 21° 22' Aquarius	Neptune 27° 14' Cancer Rx
Pluto 19° 42' Gemini Rx	

Planetary Periods

Birth — Venus/Mercury	Moon — May 20, 1931
Mars — May 20, 1941	Rahu — May 19, 1948
Jupiter — May 20, 1966	Death — Jupiter/Saturn

Sam Shepard was the basis of the "Fugitive" movies and TV series. A doctor accused of murdering his wife, he claimed innocence and said that a mysterious one-armed assailant had killed his wife. Looking at his chart through Vedic astrology, we see a person obsessed with sex and capable of violence.

The Moon is located in the tenth house along with Rahu, showing a disturbed emotional nature that gave him prominence. Mars, the lord of the Ascendant, is located in the difficult twelfth house, which is also the house of "bed pleasures" and a sign of Venus. Mars is located along with malefic Saturn, which is the lord of the fourth house of the emotions, creating a Mars-Saturn character, a hard-hearted and potentially violent person. Mars aspects Venus and Mercury, which are located in Capricorn, another sign ruled by Saturn. Mars also aspects the seventh house, Taurus, another Venus ruled sign. Venus is both the seventh lord as well as the general significator of the wife, so that the violence of the native through Mars affects the wife in all respects.

Ketu, another violent planet, is located in the fourth house of the mind as well. The Ascendant is hemmed in between malefics. Jupiter on the Ascendant gave Shepard a good expression and the help of his son (the fifth lord), but only served to mask his more violent traits. A strong Kalasarpa Yoga prevails, a malefic combination that happens when all the planets are located between Rahu and Ketu. Though not strong in itself, it is augmented by the other factors in the chart, and gives further deceptive powers.

In the navamsha, Venus, the Ascendant lord, is located in the seventh house, where it exchanges houses with the seventh lord Mars, which is in the eighth house of death. Again the factors of the first and seventh house are connected with sex and violence. The Moon is debilitated in Scorpio and Ketu again afflicts the fourth house of emotions.

The murder occurred during the malefic period of Rahu-Saturn. Shepard was released from prison when Jupiter's dasha began but did not long survive it. Given such a chart, it is difficult to exonerate Shepard, the movies notwithstanding. Shepard may not have acted alone, but he does not appear innocent either as to temperament, motive or timing.

Appendices

1 – GLOSSARY OF TERMS

—SANSKRIT—

Abhijit — nakshatra counted between the twenty-second and twenty-third, the star Vega

Agni — fire, the Sun, the deity of Krittika nakshatra

Agnihotra — daily sunrise and sunset fire offerings

Akshavedamsha — forty-fifth divisional chart

Amatya karaka — significator of friend or confidant

Amsha — division, relative to divisional charts

Angaraka — another name for Mars

Antar Dasha — subminor planetary period

Anuradha — seventeenth Nakshatra

Apachaya — houses 1, 2, 4, 7, 8

Apoklimas — cadent houses

Ardra — sixth nakshatra

Artha — wealth or material goals

Ashtakavarga — system of point calculation or bindus for planets and signs

Ashwini — first nakshatra

Ashlesha — ninth nakshatra

Asuras — demons

Atman — Divine Self or Soul

Atmakaraka — significator of inner Self or Atman

Ayanamsha — difference between sidereal and tropical zodiacs

Ayana bala — strength of planets relative to solstice points

Ayurveda — Vedic medicine, medicinal approach used with Vedic astrology

Bhadra Yoga — Mahapurusha Yoga of Mercury

Bhamsha — twenty-seventh divisional chart

Bharani — second nakshatra

Bhava — house

Bhava chakra — house chart

Bhava madhya — midpoint of house

Bhava sandhi — transitional point between houses

Bhava bala — strength of houses

Bhrigu — famous Vedic astrology family

Bhukti Dasha — minor planetary period

Bija mantra — seed syllables

Bindus — points in Ashtakavarga system

Brahma — cosmic creative force

Brahmins — spiritual class of people

Brihaspati — Jupiter

Buddhi — intelligence, reason

Budha — Mercury (not Buddha)

Chakra — horoscope wheel; force centers of the subtle body

Chandra — Moon

Chandra lagna — Moon as Ascendant

Chandra rashi — Moon Sign

Chara rashis — cardinal signs

Chaturtamsa — fourth divisional chart

Chaturvimshamsha — twenty-fourth divisional chart

Chesta bala — motional strength

Chitra — fourteenth nakshatra

Dara Karaka — significator of wife or marriage partner

Dasha — major planetary period

Dashamsha — tenth divisional chart

Devas — Gods

Dhanus — Sagittarius

Dharma — career, honor or status

Dig bala — directional strength of planets

Drig bala — aspectual strength of planets

Drishti — planetary aspect

Durga — Goddess as the demon-slayer; related to Rahu

Dushtanas — difficult houses, 6, 8 and 12

Dvadashamsha — twelfth divisional chart

Dvisvabhava Rashis — dual natured or mutable signs

Gaja Keshari Yoga — Yoga of Jupiter in an angle from Ascendant or Moon

Ganesh — the elephant faced God, related to Jupiter

Graha — planet, also demon

Guru — Jupiter, spiritual guide

Hamsa Yoga —Maha Purusha Yoga of Jupiter

Hasta — thirteenth nakshatra

Hora — Planetary hours, 1/2 division of sign, hour in general

Jaimini — author of another system of Hindu astrology

Janma Lagna — ascendant sign

Janma Rashi — birth sign, meaning Moon sign in birth chart

Janma Nakshatra — birth nakshatra of Moon

Jyeshta — eighteenth nakshatra

Jyotish — Vedic or Hindu astrology, science of light

Kala bala — temporal strength of planets

Kali — dark form of the Goddess; related to Saturn

Kali Yuga — dark or iron age

Kama — desire

Kanya — Virgo

Kapha — biological water humor

Karaka — significator

Karana — twofold division of Tithi

Karma — law of cause and effect

Kataka — Cancer

Kendra — angular house or quadrant

Ketu — south node of the Moon or dragon's tail

Khavedamsha — fortieth divisional chart

Krittika —third nakshatra

Krishna — great Hindu avatar

Kuja — Mars

Kuja Dosha — difficult placements of Mars for marriage

Kumbha —Aquarius

Kuta — point system, used in marriage compatibility

Lakshmi — Goddess of fortune and beauty; related to Venus

Lagna — Ascendant

Magha — tenth nakshatra

Maha dasha — major planetary period

Maha Purusha Yogas — planetary combinations that give strong personalities

Malavya Yoga — Maha Purusha Yoga of Venus

Mangala — another name for Mars

Mantras — sacred or empowered sounds

Matri karaka — significator of mother

Mesha — Aries

Mina — Pisces

Mithuna — Gemini
Moksha — liberation
Mrigashiras or *Mrigashirsha* — fifth nakshatra
Muhurta — electional astrology
Mula — nineteenth nakshatra
Mulatrikona — root trine, specially favorable sign positions for planets, nearly as good as exaltation
Naisargika bala — natural strength
Nakshatras — 27 lunar constellations or asterisms
Navamsha — ninth divisional chart

Pada — quarter, particularly of nakshatra (03° 20')
Paksha bala — strength of planets relative to phases of the moon
Pañchanga — astrological forecasting in Vedic astrology, based on the five factors of day, nakshatra, tithi, karana and yoga; name of sidereal yearly almanac
Panaparas — succedent houses
Panchanga — Hindu almanac
Parashara — father of Vedic astrology, author of main system used
Pitta — biological fire humor
Prashna — question, refers to horary astrology
Puja — Hindu rituals
Punarvasu — seventh nakshatra
Purvashadha — twentieth nakshatra
Purva Bhadrapada — twenty-fifth nakshatra
Purva Phalguni — eleventh nakshatra
Pushya or *Pushyami* — eighth nakshatra
Putra karaka — significator of son or children

Rahu — north node of Moon or dragon's head
Raja Yoga — combination of planetary influences or planet which gives great power
Rajasic — agitated in quality
Rama — seventh avatar of Vishnu, Divine warrior; related to the Sun
Rashi chakra — basic sign chart
Ravi — Sun
Revati — twenty-seventh nakshatra
Rohini — fourth nakshatra
Ruchaka Yoga — Mahapurusha Yoga of Mars
Rudra — fierce form of Shiva; related to Ketu
Sadesati — seven year period centered on Saturn's transit of the natal moon
Sambhanda — full relationship between planets
Saptamsha — seventh divisional chart
Sapta varga — seven vargas or harmonic charts
Sattvic — spiritual in effect
Satya Yuga — age of truth or golden age
Shadbala — system of determining planetary strengths and weakness
Shadvargas — six main divisional charts
Shani or *Shanaishcharya* — Saturn
Shasha Yoga — Mahapurusha Yoga of Saturn
Shastyamsha — sixtieth divisional chart
Shatabhishak — twenty-fourth nakshatra
Shiva — God of the Hindu trinity who destroys the creation and takes us back to the transcendent
Shodashamsha — sixteenth divisional chart
Shravana — twenty-second nakshatra
Shravishta — twenty-third nakshatra
Shukra — Venus
Siddhamsha — twenty-fourth divisional chart, same as Chaturvimshamsha
Simha — Leo
Skanda — War God; related to Mars
Soma — Moon
Sthira rashis — fixed signs

Surya — Sun
Swati or *Svati* — fifteenth nakshatra

Tajika — annual chart or solar return and system of its interpretation
Tamasic — dark in quality
Thula — Libra
Tithi — thirty-fold division of lunar month
Treta Yuga — third or silver age
Trikonas — trine houses
Trimshamsha — thirtieth divisional chart

Upachaya — houses 3, 6, 10, 11
Uttarashada — twenty-first nakshatra
Uttara Bhadrapada — twenty-sixth nakshatra
Uttara Phalguni — twelfth nakshatra, also called Uttara

Vakra — retrograde
Vara — day
Varadhipati — ruler of the day
Varshaphal — solar return or annual chart
Vata — biological air humor
Varga — divisional or harmonic charts
Vargottama — in the same sign in both the birth chart and navamsha
Vedanta — Vedic philosophy of Self-realization
Vedas — Vedic scriptures
Vimshamsha — twentieth divisional chart
Vimshopak — varga calculation of planetary strength and weakness
Vishakha — sixteenth nakshatra
Vishnu — God of the Vedic trinity who preserves and maintains the creation and the cosmic order
Vrishchika — Scorpio
Vrishabha — Taurus

Yajña — rituals to propitiate the planets, often using sacred fires, pronounced Yagya
Yantras — mystic diagrams, used to harmonize planetary influences
Yoga — combination of planetary influences; Sun-moon relationships in Panchanga or astrological forecasting; spiritual practice
Yuddha — planetary war
Yugas — world ages

—ENGLISH—

Angular — houses 1, 4, 7 and 10
Ascendant — first house or rising sign
Aspects — relationship between planets according to angle between their positions
Astral plane — subtle or dream plane

Benefics — planets with facilitating or strengthening effect

Cadent — houses 3, 6, 9, 12
Cardinal signs — Aries, Cancer, Libra, Capricorn
Causal plane — plane of cosmic law and cosmic intelligence
Combust — close conjunction of planets with the Sun
Conjunction — location of planets in close proximity to each other
Cusp — central point of a house

Decanate — threefold division of signs
Descendant — lowest point in chart or nadir, cusp of fourth house
Dispositorship — rulership of planets over other planets located in its signs
Divisional charts — subdivisions of birth chart

Electional astrology — astrological science of determining favorable times for action

Exaltation — best sign placement for a planet

Fall — same as debility, most difficult sign placement for a planet

Fixed signs —Taurus, Leo, Scorpio, Aquarius

Harmonic charts — subdivisions of the birth chart

Horary astrology — astrology directed towards specific issues

Horary chart — chart based on a question

Houses — twelvefold division of zodiac according to degree rising on eastern horizon

House significators —planets generally controlling the affairs of specific houses

Malefics — planets of difficult or damaging effect

Midheaven — highest point in the chart, cusp of the tenth house

Mutable signs — Gemini, Virgo, Sagittarius, Pisces

Mutual receptivity — exchange of signs between planets

Natal — relative to the birth chart, as natal moon

Natal chart — birth chart

Planetary war — condition caused by conjunction of planets to within one degree

Retrograde — backward movement of planets in zodiac

Sidereal zodiac — zodiac of fixed stars

Solar returns — returns of the Sun to its place in the birth chart

Succedent — houses 2, 5, 8, 11

Transits — current planetary positions relative to birth positions

Trine houses — houses 1, 5 and 9

Tropical zodiac — zodiac defined by the equinoctical points

2 – BIBLIOGRAPHY

Babu, Niranjan. *Vastu.* Twin Lakes, Wisconsin: Lotus Press, 1999.

Braha, James T. *Ancient Hindu Astrology for the Modern Western Astrologer.* N. Miami, Fl.: Hermetician Press, 1986.

Charak. K.S. *Elements of Vedic Astrology.* New Delhi, India: Systems Vision, 1996.

Charak. K.S. *Essentials of Medical Astrology.* New Delhi, India: Systems Vision, 1996.

Charak, K.S. *Yogas in Vedic Astrology.* New Delhi, India: Systems Vision, 1996

Frawley, David. *Ayurvedic Healing: A Comprehensive Guide.* Salt Lake City, Utah: Passage Press, 1990.

Frawley, David and Lad, Vasant. *The Yoga of Herbs: An Ayurvedic Guide to Herbal Medicine.* Santa Fe, NM: Lotus Press, 1986.

Frawley, David. *Yoga and Ayurveda: Self-Healing and Self-Realization.*Twin Lakes,Wisconsin: Lotus Press, 1999.

Harness, Dr. Dennis. *The Nakshatras: The Lunar Mansions of Vedic Astrology.* Twin Lakes, Wisconsin: Lotus Press, 1999.

Mihira, Varaha. *Brihat Jataka.* New Delhi: India: Munshiram Manoharlal, 1979.

Mihira, Varaha. *Brihat Samhita.* Delhi, India: Motilal Banarsidass, 1986.

Parasara, Maharshi. *Brihat Parasara Hora Sastra,* Vol.I and II (R. Santhanam trans.). New Delhi, India: Ranjan Publications, 1984.

Raman, B.V. *A Manual of Hindu Astrology.* Bangalore, India: IBH Prakashana, 1979

Raman, B.V. *Graha and Bhava Balas.* Bangalore, India: IBH Prakashana, 1979.

Raman, B.V. *Three Hundred Important Combinations.* Bangalore, India: IBH Prakashana, 1979.

Varma, K. *Saravali* (R.Santhanam trans.). New Delhi, India: Ranjan Publications, 1983.

Yukteswar, Sri Swami. *The Holy Science.* Los Angeles, CA: Self-Realization Fellowship, 1984.

3– RESOURCES

David Frawley (Vamadeva Shastri)

David Frawley (Vamadeva Shastri) is one of the most respected Vedic teachers (Vedacharyas) in the world today, whose range of study includes Ayurveda, Yoga, Vedanta, Vedic astrology and the ancient Vedas. He is the author of forty published books translated into twenty languages over the last several decades. He has worked with various Vedic and Hindu organizations throughout the world.

Frawley is a rare recipient of the Padma Bhushan Award, the third highest civilian award of the government of India, for his diverse work in the Vedic field. He has a D.Litt. From SVYASA (Swami Vivekananda Yoga Anusandhana Sansthana) the only deemed Yoga university in India, and a second D. Litt. from Avadh University (Ayodhya) in Uttar Pradesh. He was given a National Eminence Award as a Vedacharya from the South Indian Education Society (SIES) in Mumbai.

Frawley is one of the four main advisors of NAMA (National Ayurvedic Medical Association) in the United States, which has honored him as an Ayurvedic doctor. He has been an advisor and Master Educator to the Chopra center since it's founding. He has been a keynote speaker for the ministry of AYUSH India at several conferences. He is an advisor to a number of Ayurvedic schools and organizations worldwide. His books on Ayurveda are among the first published and remain among the most widely used in the field. He has addressed mind and consciousness of in several books on Yoga and Vedanta as well.

@drdavidfrawley Facebook - @davidfrawleyved, Twitter

American Institute of Vedic Studies

Frawley is the director of the American Institute of Vedic Studies (www.vedanet.com, @americanvedic Facebook), which is an on-line educational center for Vedic Studies for students throughout the world. His wife Yogini Shambhavi joins him for teaching programs and Yoga retreats, as well offering Vedic astrology consultations. The website hosts more than two hundred original articles by Frawley on Vedic studies and a variety of resources, including regular new postings.

The institute offers four on-line courses

1) Ayurvedic Healing foundation course in Ayurveda – Ayurvedic view of body and mind, constitution, disease and treatment, emphasizing herbal and life-style therapies, since 1988.

2) Yoga, Ayurveda, Mantra and Meditation foundation course – including Ayurveda and Raja Yoga, *Yoga Sutras* and Sanskrit mantras, Vedanta and consciousness, since 2004.

3) Integral Vedic Counseling foundation course – sharing educational and communication skills and Vedic life guidance relative to all Vedic fields, since 2017.

4) Ayurvedic Astrology foundation course in Vedic astrology – fundamentals of Vedic astrology from birth charts to Muhurta, with special emphasis on the astrology of healing through Ayurveda, since 1985.

Index

David Frawley Titles

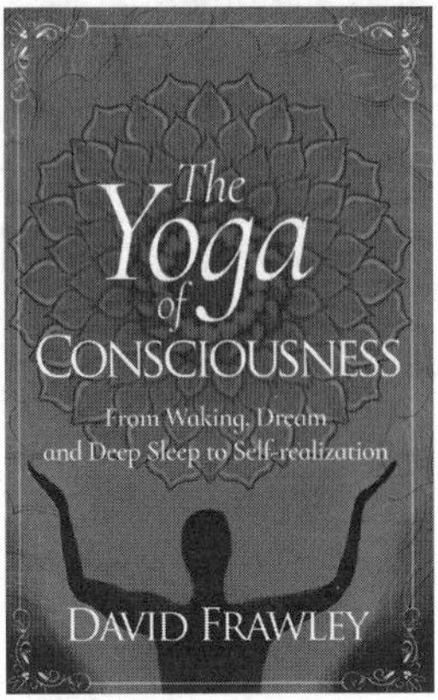

The Yoga of Consciousness

From Waking, Dream and Deep Sleep to Self-realization

David Frawley

272 pp os • $17.95 • ISBN: 978-1-6086-9238-5

The Yoga of Consciousness is an experiential exploration of the wonders of Consciousness and its daily unfoldment in a comprehensive and systematic manner. In it Vamadeva unfolds the essence of Yoga and Vedanta echoing great Vedic sages like Vishvamitra and Parashara, with their worship of the eternally wakeful cosmic fire within us, and Advaitic gurus like Adi Shankara and Ramana Maharshi who take us directly to the Self that transcends birth and death.

The book asks many profound questions but shows how we can discover the answers by simply observing our own daily movement in consciousness from waking to sleep with an inner opening to the reality of light behind the senses. The Yoga of Consciousness shows us the universal reality of Yoga as the unity and oneness behind all the brilliant diversity and endless expansion of all that we see.

"In this brilliant book David Frawley (Vamadeva Shastri) explains with elegance how reality differs in daily states of consciousness and how the true purpose of Yoga is to discover your true liberated timeless immortal Self and change your identity from your provisional personality to your universal essence."
– **Deepak Chopra MD**, Author of *Metahuman*

"The Yoga of Consciousness addresses the question of consciousness directly. Vamadeva skillfully shows that consciousness is not the same as the contents of the mind, but is rather the light of awareness that shines on all things."
– **Prof. Subhash Kak**, Author of *The Circle of Memory and Arrival and Exile*

"Vamadeva Shastri, himself a yogi and teacher of the highest order, embodies in this volume the wisdom of India's ancient tradition of Self-realization, as expounded in the Upanishads."
– **Prof. Makarand R. Paranjape**, Director, Indian Institute of Advanced Study

---

Herbs and other natural health products and information are often available at natural food stores or metaphysical bookstores. If you cannot find what you need locally, you can contact one of the following sources of supply.

Sources of Supply:

The following companies have an extensive selection of useful products and a long track-record of fulfillment. They have natural body care, aromatherapy, flower essences, crystals and tumbled stones, homeopathy, herbal products, vitamins and supplements, videos, books, candles, incense and bulk herbs, teas, massage tools and products and numerous alternative health items across a wide range of categories.

WHOLESALE:

Wholesale suppliers sell to stores and practitioners, not to individual consumers buying for their own personal use. Individual consumers should contact the RETAIL supplier listed below. Wholesale accounts should contact with business name, resale number or practitioner license in order to obtain a wholesale catalog and set up an account.

Lotus Light Enterprises, Inc.
PO Box 1008
Silver Lake, WI 53170 USA
262 889 8501 (phone)
262 889 8591 (fax)
800 548 3824 (toll free order line)
Website: www.lotuslight.com
email: lotuslight@lotuspress.com

RETAIL:

Retail suppliers provide products by mail order direct to consumers for their personal use. Stores or practitioners should contact the wholesale supplier listed above.

Internatural
PO Box 489
Twin Lakes, WI 53181 USA
800 643 4221 (toll free order line)
262 889 8581 office phone
EMAIL: internatural@internatural.com
WEB SITE: www.internatural.com

Web site includes an extensive annotated catalog of more than 14,000 items that can be ordered “on line” for your convenience 24 hours a day, 7 days a week.